스파르타 新 TOEIC 실전 LC 1000제 Vol. 2

레벨별 학습법	4
PART 1 고득점 전략	6
PART 2 고득점 전략	8
PART 3 고득점 전략	10
PART 4 고득점 전략	12

실전 모의고사

■ TEST 01	14
■ TEST 02	28
■ TEST 03	42
■ TEST 04	56
■ TEST 05	70
■ TEST 06	84
■ TEST 07	98
■ TEST 08	112
■ TEST 09	126
■ TEST 10	140

정답 및 스크립트

■ ANSWER KEYS	156~158
■ 1회 정답 & 스크립트	159
■ 2회 정답 & 스크립트	166
■ 3회 정답 & 스크립트	173
■ 4회 정답 & 스크립트	180
■ 5회 정답 & 스크립트	187
■ 6회 정답 & 스크립트	194
■ 7회 정답 & 스크립트	201
■ 8회 정답 & 스크립트	208
■ 9회 정답 & 스크립트	215
■ 10회 정답 & 스크립트	222
■ OMR 답안지	231
■ 점수 환산표	240

초판 1쇄 발행 2017년 6월 4일
초판 2쇄 발행 2018년 1월 8일

저 자   이윤우, 남수연, 허창환, 김수현
펴낸이   박성호
펴낸곳   잉글리쉬앤 (주)

총 괄   이용선
편집 기획 박고우니
원고 교정 윤호재
디자인   이경희

주소 서울 특별시 관악구 쑥고개로 67-1
대표전화 (02) 878-1945
출판등록 2002년 3월 3일 제 320-2002-00045호

ISBN 978-89-6715-100-3 13740

저작권자 2018 잉글리쉬앤(주)
이 책은 잉글리쉬앤(주)에 의해 출간되었으므로
저자와 출판사의 서면에 의한 허락 없이 글과 그림의 인용, 복제, 발췌를 금합니다.

* 해설 및 음원은 온라인에서 다운로드 가능합니다. (http://books.english.co.kr)
* 가격은 표지에 있습니다. 잘못된 책은 바꾸어 드립니다.
     www.english.co.kr

신토익 소개

2016년 5월 29일 첫 시행 新토익

이렇게 바뀌었다!

구성	Part	구 토익		신 토익		시간	배점
		내용	문항 수	내용	문항 수		
듣기 (LC)	1	사진 묘사	10	사진 묘사	6	45분	495점
	2	질의 응답	30	질의 응답	25		
	3	짧은 대화	30	짧은 대화	39		
	4	담화문	30	담화문	30		
읽기 (RC)	5	단문 공란 채우기 (문법/어휘)	40	단문 공란 채우기 (문법/어휘)	30	75분	495점
	6	장문 공란 채우기	12	장문 공란 채우기	16		
	7	독해 — 단일 지문	28	독해 — 단일 지문	29		
		독해 — 이중 지문	20	독해 — 복수 지문	25		
TOTAL		7 Parts	200문항	7 Parts	200문항	120분	990점

✓ 주요 변경 내용

- **Listening Comprehension**
  - Part 1, 2 문항 수 감소 (Part 1: 10문항 → 6문항 / Part 2: 30문항 → 25문항) Part 3 문항 수 증가 (30문항 → 39문항)
  - 일부 대화문에서 말의 길이가 짧아지고 대화를 주고받는 횟수 증가
  - 일부 대화문에는 3명의 화자 등장 NEW
  - 일부 대화문에 Elisions (생략형: going to → gonna 등) 등장
  - 대화문 또는 설명문과 시각 정보(도표, 그래픽 등) 연계해서 푸는 유형 출제 NEW
  - 대화문 또는 설명문에서 맥락상 화자의 의도를 묻는 유형 출제 NEW

- **Reading Comprehension**
  - Part 5 문항 수 감소 (Part 5: 40문항 → 30문항)
  - Part 6, 7 문항 수 증가 (Part 6: 12문항 → 16문항 / Part 7: 48문항 → 54문항)
  - 지문 흐름의 이해도를 묻는 유형 출제 NEW
    - 지문 중간에 들어갈 맥락에 맞는 문장 찾기
    - 주어진 문장이 지문의 어느 위치에 들어갈지 찾기
  - 다수가 참여하는 문자 메시지, 메신저 대화, 온라인 채팅 대화문 출제 NEW
  - 3개의 연계 지문에 대한 이해도를 묻는 유형 출제 NEW
  - 문맥상 주어진 단어들에 대한 이해도를 묻는 유형 출제

레벨별 학습법

토익은 특별한 스킬과 체력을 요하는 수영, 골프 같은 스포츠와 같다. 체력과 기술이 부족한 상태에서 무작정 문제만 푸는 것은 힘든 것은 물론이고, 노력한만큼의 효과가 나타나지 않는다. **자신의 레벨과 약점을 확인하고 '가장 빠르고 효율적으로' 목적지에 다다를 수 있도록 훈련하자.** 〈스파르타 신토익 LC 1000제 Vol. 2〉는 400점 이상의 토익 고득점을 목표로, 495점 만점을 달성하기 위한 LC 집중 학습 교재이다. 본인의 레벨을 확인하고 가장 알맞은 집중 훈련 방법을 찾도록 하자. 본 교재의 모의고사 또는 파트별 집중 문제집으로 사용함으로써 실전 감각과 고난도 문제에 대한 자신감을 얻을 수 있을 것이다.

토익 초보자의 고민
토익은 냅나는데 어떻게 공부해야 할지 막막하나.
최대한 빠르게 고득점을 얻고 싶다!

LEVEL 1 토익 왕초보 (LC 330점 이상 목표)

▶ **무엇이 문제인가?**
 토익은 소문으로만 듣고 아는 것이 전혀 없다.
 도대체 무엇을 어떻게 공부해야 남들이 말하는 것처럼 빨리 고득점을 얻을 수 있을지 궁금하다.
 토익뿐만 아니라 영어에 대한 자신감도 떨어진 상황이라 더 불안하다.

▶ **학습 전략**
 토익 파트별 유형 정리 ➡ 질문 유형별 구조 파악하기/ 유형별 정답 표현 암기하기
 기초 청취 훈련 ➡ 스크립트 없이 영어 듣기 훈련/ 안 들리는 발음 듣기 훈련

▶ **본서 이용 방법**
 초보는 토익 유형에 대한 이해와 자주 출제되는 유형의 문제를 안정감 있게 풀 수 있는 능력이 가장 중요하다. 〈스파르타 신토익 700/800〉 교재를 통해 유형 분류와 기초 청취 부분을 학습하고 본 교재에 도전하자. 단기간 학습 플랜을 계획하고 있다면 〈스파르타 실전 1000제 Vol. 1, 2〉를 병행하는 것도 가능하다. 시험 2주 전부터 〈스파르타 LC 1000제 Vol. 1, 2〉의 문제를 Half Test 형태로 풀면서 실전 시험 대비 훈련을 하자.

LEVEL 2 토익을 시작해 봤다 (LC 380점 이상 목표)

▶ **무엇이 문제인가?**
 간헐적인 공부로 이것저것 건드린 것은 많은데 머리 속에서 토익이란 시험과 유형이 정립되지 않았다.
 토익의 7개 파트 중에서 무엇을 우선적으로 집중 학습할지 고민 중이다.

▶ **학습 전략**
 토익 파트별 유형 정리 & 유형별 문제 풀이 ➡ 배운 유형을 실전 문제를 통해 찾아내고 정답을 맞히는 훈련을 한다.
 기초 청취(문장 구조별) 훈련 ➡ 단순히 안 들리는 어휘나 발음이 아닌, 문장 구조상에서의 안 들리는 구문을 정리한다.
 (수동태, 완료형, 관계사절 등의 구조를 녹음으로 들을 수 있도록 한다.)

▶ **본서 이용 방법**
 토익 초보는 유형에 대한 정리가 가장 시급하지만, 이제 시험장에서 실력을 발휘할 수 있도록 실전 문제 형태도 같이 병행해야 한다. 〈스파르타 신토익 800 LC〉 교재를 통해 심화 유형 분류를 완성하고, 〈스파르타 신토익 LC 1000제 Vol. 1, 2〉의 문제를 Half Test 형태로 풀면서 실전 시험 대비 훈련을 하자.

토익 중상급자의 고민
토익 공부를 좀 했으나 점수가 정체된다.
어떻게 하면 실수를 줄이고 집중력이 높일 수 있는지 알고 싶다.
토익 공부 EXIT PLAN을 알고 싶다!

LEVEL 3 토익 본격적으로 공부할 준비가 되었다 (LC 430점 이상 목표)

▶ **무엇이 문제인가?**
토익에 대해 들어본 것도 많고 좀 알지만, 막상 문제를 풀면 생각보다 많이 틀린다.
다른 사람들에 비해 점수 향상 속도가 느린 것 같아서 불안하다.

▶ **학습 전략**
계속적인 정리와 이해만 가지고는 효율적으로 문제를 풀 수 없다. 이해는 그만, 문제를 풀어서 맞히자!
실전 형태에서 정답을 맞힐 수 있도록, 다수의 문제를 한꺼번에 푸는 훈련이 필요하다.
자신이 어떤 문제에 약하고 강한지를 분류하고, 오답 노트를 통해 취약 파트를 보완하자.

▶ **본서 이용 방법**
고득점 목표를 위해 만들어진 〈스파르타 LC 1000제 Vol. 1, 2〉의 문제를 한 번에 100문제씩 풀면서 집중력을 키운다. 틀린 문제의 복습은 반복해서 문제 풀기: ① 문제 풀기, ② 다시 풀기, ③ 틀린 문제 다시 풀기의 형태로 해석/해설을 보기 전까지 충분히 문제 풀기를 통해 훈련한다. 전체 복습이 아닌 많이 틀린 문제만 뽑아서 집중적으로 풀고, 구문 해석과 청취 공부를 통해 한 유형씩 차례대로 완벽하게 마스터한다.

LEVEL 4 토익 LC 만점 목표 (LC 495점 만점 목표)

▶ **무엇이 문제인가?**
토익에 쏟아부은 시간이 얼마인데 왜 아직 안 될까 고민한다.
어려운 건 없는 것 같은데, 해도 해도 실수가 줄지 않아 고민이다.
아는 것은 많은데도 현장 시험에서 실력을 보여주지 못하는 본인의 집중력에 실망할 때가 있다.

▶ **학습 전략**
고난도 문제가 등장해도 당황하지 않고 실수를 줄일 수 있는 전략을 짠다.
많은 문제를 풀어도 집중력이 떨어지지 않도록 훈련한다.
어려운 문제를 접해 보고 실전에서 당황하지 않고 풀 수 있도록 훈련한다.

▶ **본서 이용 방법**
LC 만점을 위해서는 기출 레벨 문제를 반복해서 푸는 것으로는 충분하지 않다. 난이도 높은 문제를 풀어서 어떤 문제가 나오더라도 집중할 수 있도록 하는 것이 필요하다. 난이도 높은 문제는 ① 빠른 속도, ② 난해한 동의 표현으로 나올 수 있다.

PART 1 고득점 전략

스파르타 고득점 Point! : 보이는 것이 다가 아니다!

- 동사와, 동사 시제를 마스터 한다.
- 지우기를 완성시켜 언제나 Best Answer를 고르자.

사진을 보고, 그 사진을 영어로 가장 잘 묘사한 표현을 고르는 것이 PART 1이다. 그러나 실전 토익에서는 그림을 잘 묘사한 것을 섣불리 고르려고 하다가는 오히려 실수하기 쉽다. 난이도가 점점 올라갈수록 사진에서 잘 보이는 어휘는 오답에 포함되는 경우가 많고, 사진을 보고 추측하기 힘든 표현이 정답이 되기 때문이다. 지우기 훈련을 통해서 특정 어휘가 마음에 들어도 틀린 부분이 있으면 지우고, 특별히 마음에 드는 어휘가 없으면 남는 선택지 중에서 Best Answer 고르는 훈련을 하자.

(낮은 레벨)
They are painting the wall. (O)
그들은 벽에 페인트칠을 하고 있다.

(고난도 레벨)
The walls are being painted. (O)
벽이 페인트칠 되어지고 있다.
They are using tools to paint the wall. (O)
그들은 도구를 이용해 벽에 페인트칠을 하고 있다.
There are paintings on the wall. (X)
벽에 그림들이 있다.

▶ 동사를 마스터 하자! 행동/상태 동사 암기 & 능동/수동태, 진행/완료형 시제 청취력
  능동형: 현재형(동사현재형), 진행형(be+ing형), 완료형(have+p.p.형)
  수동형: 현재형(be+p.p.형), 수동태 진행형(be+being+p.p.형), 수동태 완료(have been+p.p.형)
  ➡ 틀린 문제의 시제를 완벽하게 이해하고 사진과 매칭한다.

▶ 문장 구조를 이해하고 틀린 부분을 "골라내는" 훈련을 한다.
  '주어+동사+목적어+부사구' 형태의 문장을 들으면서 틀린 부분이 있으면 전체 문장을 오답 처리를 하고, 틀린 부분이 없거나 또는 해석이 안 되고 그림이 이해되지 않는 경우에는 지우지 않고 둔다. 오답 처리를 하지 않은 선택지 중에서 가장 좋은 것을 정답으로 골라낸다.
  ➡ 어떤 부분에서 틀렸는지 골라내는 훈련을 한다.

빠른 고득점 획득을 위한 스파르타 전략

스파르타 만점 Point! : 보이는 것이 다가 아니다!

- 고난도 풍경 별 어휘를 암기하자.
- 고난도 지우기 문제를 풀어 얼마나 정답이 "치사" 할 수 있는지 익혀 두자.

시험 현장에서 어려운 문제를 실수하지 않고 풀기 위해서는 평소에 그와 같은 레벨 또는 그보다 높은 레벨의 문제를 많이 풀어서 고난도 문제가 나와도 당황하지 말아야 한다. PART 1 사진에서는 인물 사진이나 자주 접할 수 있는 일상생활 관련 사진 이외에 '특정 표현'이 등장하는 소위 고난도 유형의 사진들이 있다. 주로 공사 현장이나 선착장 등의 야외 풍경 사진으로, 자주 접해 보지 못한 표현들이 등장하므로 당황하지 않고 답을 고를 수 있도록 훈련하자.

Mountains overlook the lake. (O)
산들이 물을 내려다 보고 있다. (물가에 산이 있다)

Trees are reflected on the water. (O)
나무들이 물에 반사되고 있다.

A boat is secured at a dock. (O)
배가 선착장에 고정되어 있다.

▶ 고난도 풍경 사진 (풍경) – 출제 빈도는 낮지만 꾸준한 최고 난이도 문제
  공사장: 외바퀴 손수레를 밀다(pushing a wheelbarrow), 흙을 파고 있다(digging the soil/dirt/earth)
  선착장: 선착장에 배가 대져 있다(be tied/docked/anchored), 물 위를 항해한다(be sailing/floating)
  길/계단/다리 묘사: 길이 쭉 뻗다, 휘어지다, 연결된다(The path extends/leads to/curves/runs)
  ➡ 풍경 관련 어휘를 통해서 사진에서 잘 보이지 않는 정답 표현을 익힌다.

▶ 고난도 사진 – 사진에서 잘 보이지 않는 구석, 천정, 바닥 등을 정답으로 만든 문제
  하늘 묘사: 하늘에 구름(clouds in the sky), 연기가 하늘로 올라간다(smoke rising in the air)
  바닥 묘사: 그림자를 드리우다(casting shadows), 길 위의 자동차 타이어 자국(tracks left on the ground)
  안 보이는 소품 묘사: 벽에 콘센트가 꽂혀 있다(power cord has been plugged in)
  ➡ 사진에 안 보이는 부분으로 정답을 묘사하는 문제를 풀어, 실전에서 함정에 빠지지 않도록 훈련하자.

PART 2 고득점 전략

스파르타 고득점 Point! : 질문 듣기 & 지우기를 훈련하라!

- 의문문 앞에 3~4단어를 듣고 유형을 파악하자.
- "오답 지우기"를 완성시켜 언제나 Best Answer를 고르자.

청취력의 의존도가 높지만, 청취력만 가지고는 고득점을 받기 힘든 것이 PART 2이다. 난이도가 낮은 문제에서는 질문을 듣고, 내가 생각한 문장이 정답으로 등장하는 경우가 꽤 많다. 하지만, 점점 올라갈수록 추측하기 힘든 표현이 정답이 된다. 이런 경우에는 오히려 전형적인 오답을 통해서 정답을 고르는 것이 안전하다. 질문과 대답 세트를 많이 암기해두는 것을 기초로 해서, (A), (B), (C) 정답지에서 오답을 지우기 훈련을 통해서 특정 어휘가 마음에 들어도 틀린 부분이 있으면 지우고, 특별히 마음에 드는 어휘가 없으면 남는 선택지 중에서 Best Answer를 고르는 훈련을 하자.

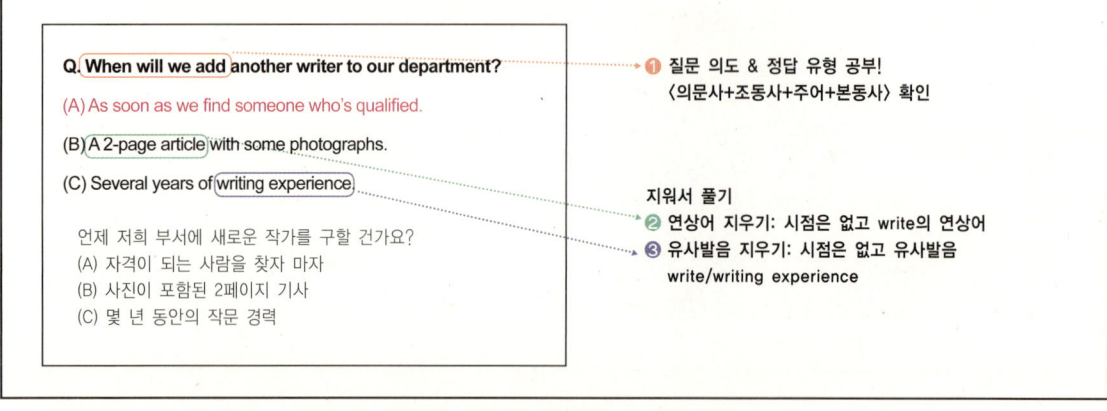

▶ 질문 파악과 정답 유형의 80% 이상을 좌우하는 첫 3~4단어를 마스터하라!

무엇보다도 질문을 듣고 해석하고 정답을 파악할 수 있으면 유리하다. 첫 3~4단어로 의문문 유형/시제/주어를 한번에 파악할 수 있도록 훈련하자. 토익 빈출 정답 표현으로 먼저 정답부터 암기한다.
의문사 의문문의 유형별 정답: 의문사 Who/Where/When/How/Why/Which/What 각각 파악
Yes/No 의문문의 유형별 정답: 선택/권유청유형/긍정/부정/부가/간접/평서문을 각각 파악

— 주로 앞쪽 문제(7~25번)에서는 정답 유형으로, 뒤쪽 문제(26~31번)에서는 지우기 유형이 자주 출제된다. 틀린 문제는 오답 노트를 작성해서 정답 유형, 오답 유형을 파악해 두자.

▶ 정답만큼 중요한 전형적인 오답 유형을 익히자.

유사 발음이 등장하거나 연상어 등장 오답들은 토익에 익숙하지 않은 학생들이 오답 지우기로 가장 많이 사용하는 전략이다. 하지만 맹목적인 오답 처리는 만점 전략과 맞지 않는다. 유사 발음이 하나도 등장하지 않은 문제 세트나, 선택지 3개 모두 유사 발음이 등장하는 문제도 있기 때문이다. 발음이 익숙하거나 연상되는 언어로 고르지 않는 것이 좀 더 안정적인 고득점 전략이다. 오답 유형을 틈틈이 정리해 두면 자주 등장하는 함정도 파악알 수 있다.

— 유사 발음/연상어의 전형적인 오답 형태의 어휘/표현으로 오답을 지우고 정답을 남기는 훈련을 하자.

빠른 고득점 획득을 위한 스파르타 전략

스파르타 만점 Point! : 매번 실수하는 "약점"을 없애라!

- Yes/No 의문문의 최고 인기스타인 "평서문"을 정복하자.
- Yes/No 의문문에 Yes/No가 빠진 상태로 대답하는 유형을 훈련하자.

PART 2는 LC 전체에서 쉬운 문제와 어려운 문제의 난이도 폭이 제일 넓은 파트이다. 기본적으로 70%의 정답을 맞히는 것이 가능하다. 그 다음부터는 본인의 약점을 본격적으로 파악하고 보완하는 것이 필요하다. 최근에 출제 빈도가 꾸준히 늘고 있는 것은 평서문으로, 맨 앞만 듣고 해석이 안 되는 경우가 많고, 다양한 반응(response)이 정답이 되어 고난도 유형으로 뽑힌다. 〈스파르타 신토익 LC 1000제 Vol. 2〉는 평서문은 물론 고득점자가 약점으로 꼽는 Yes/No 없는 Yes/No 의문문 유형에 특별히 집중했다. 본인의 약점을 파악한 후 보완할 수 있도록 하자.

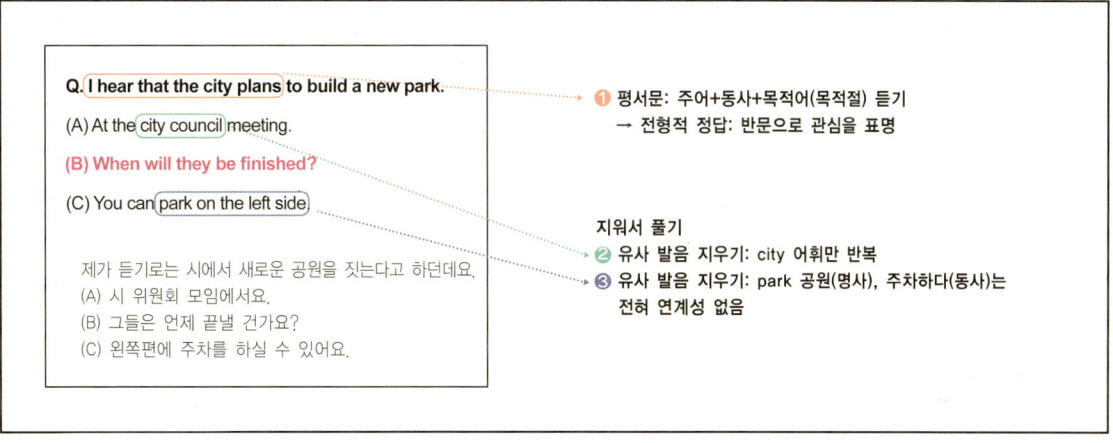

▶ 최대 약점인 "평서문"에 세부 지식으로 반문, 조건을 제시하는 "전형적인 반응"을 익히자.
평서문도 유형별 정리가 가능하다. ① 문제점, ② 좋은 소식, ③ 나쁜 소식, ④ 의견, ⑤ FACT 전달 등이다. 다른 유형과 마찬가지로, 각각의 평서문 유형에 세부지식을 요청하는 전형적인 유형을 익히도록 하자.
ex) 9시에 회의한다 – 어디서/누가/무슨 준비물을 해야 하나 등의 전형적이 형태의 반응이다.
➡ 평서문도 유형별로 정답/오답을 정리하면 쉽게 넘어갈 수 있는 산이다.

▶ Yes/No 없이 대답하는 고난도 정답
모든 시험에서 고득점은 유형 분류가 기본적으로 전제되어야 한다. 대부분의 학생들이 Yes/No 의문문의 유형 분류를 제대로 하지 않고 해석으로만 풀려다 보니 조금만 난이도가 올라가면 당황하게 된다. Yes/No 의문문에 양쪽으로 〈Yes + 긍정 내용〉〈No + 부정 내용〉으로 대답하는 훈련을 하면 Yes/No가 빠진 것도 정답을 맞히는 것이 가능하다.
ex) 내일 만날까? – (안 돼.) 마이애미에 출장가는데. 결국 〈No + 바쁘다〉의 변형으로 볼 수 있다.
➡ Yes/No 의문문의 고난도 정답은 전형적인 유형의 변형이다. 오답 노트로 극복하자.

PART 3 고득점 전략

스파르타 고득점 Point! : 읽은 만큼 들린다! 완벽하게 준비하자!

- 녹음 전에 문제를 파악하고 기억하자!
- 新토익 문제 유형도 "미리 파악"하여 준비한다.

2016년 신토익 변경 이후에 LC에서 가장 문항 수가 많고(39문제) 난이도가 높은 것이 PART 3이다. 하지만 신토익에서 어렵게 출제된다기보다는 여전히 문제를 미리 읽고 파악한 후에 2~3사람의 긴 대화가 집중하기 힘들게 하는 것뿐이다. 정확하게 문제를 읽고 파악해 두면 본문의 흐름은 물론, 정답 예측까지 가능한 것이 PART 3~4이다. PART 3의 경우, 다수의 등장인물이 정신없이 대화하는 것 같지만, 본문을 다 듣고 summary하는 것이 아니라 각각의 문제에서 원하는 것만을 '정확하게 집어내는 것'이 목표라는 것을 잊지 말자.

Company	Location
Gourmet W	Newton
Sky View	Summerville
Tao Ling Food	Medford
Jessica's Cafe	Boston

68. What event is the company sponsoring?
(A) A race

69. What is the man concerned about?
(C) A limited budget

70. Look at the Graphic. Which company will the speakers choose?
(A) Gourmet W
(B) Sky View
(C) Tao Ling Food
(D) Jessica's Cafe

Questions 68 through 70 refer to the following conversation and a list.

M: Heather, I'm excited about the race our company is sponsoring. A lot of people will be running in it. So it'll be great publicity.
W: That reminds me. Have you looked over this list of catering firms we are considering to hire for the vent?
M: I can look at it now. Hmm – Skyview has the best options, but we need a company that's a little less expensive. Our budget is being reduced since last year's race.
W: Good point. Let's go for the one that is right here in Medford. They have a good reputation and their prices are reasonable.

M: 헤더, 우리 회사가 이번에 후원하고 있는 경주에 대해서 굉장히 기대돼요. 많은 사람들이 참가를 할거고 아주 좋은 홍보가 될 거예요.
W: 그러니 생각나네요. 그 행사에 사용할 출장 요리업체 목록 봤어요?
M: 지금 보면 돼죠. 스카이뷰가 선택 폭이 좋은데 조금 싼 업체가 필요해요. 우리 예산이 작년 경주 이후 줄었거든요.
W: 맞아요. 여기 메드포드 지역에 있는 곳으로 하죠. 그곳은 평판도 좋고 가격도 합리적이에요.

▶ 문제 3개를 읽고 기억하는 것은 기본이다. GQ/SQ 각각의 유형을 파악해 두고 준비한다.
정확하게 문제를 읽고 유형을 분류하고 "지문에서 어떻게 정답 단서를 줄까"를 예측하면서 듣는다.
신유형의 표 관련 문제도 "문제&표"를 읽고 표의 어떤 부분을 녹음으로 들려줄지 예측한다.
➡ 지문에서 정답 단서를 포착해서 듣고, 문제 읽기를 훈련해서 정답을 맞힌다.

빠른 고득점 획득을 위한 스파르타 전략

스파르타 만점 Point! : 매번 실수하는 "약점"을 없애라!

- 독해형 문제의 긴 정답지 (A), (B), (C), (D)를 읽고 빠르게 요점을 파악할 수 있도록 훈련하자.
- 들은 단어를 "넓은 의미"의 동의 표현으로 바꾸어 고른다.

문제를 미리 읽고 파악한 후, 들으면서 동시에 풀어야 하는 파트에서는 다양하게 난이도를 조절할 수 있다. PART 3에서 문제를 어렵게 만들려면 ① 눈으로 읽는 부분인 문제 부분을 길고 난해하게 만들거나, ② 문제도 읽고 준비를 했는데도 불구하고 마치 정답이 없는 것과 같은 트릭으로 본문에서 나온 어휘로 동의 표현으로 바꾸어서 고르게 하는 경우이다. 특히, 초보는 읽는 속도가 느려 ①에서 많이 틀리고, 고득점자들은 ②의 동의 표현에서 고민한다. 특히, ②의 경우에 다 듣고 알아들었는데 고를 정답이 없는 경우가 생기는 것이다. 고난도 문제를 맞히기 위해서는 조금은 "어렵게" 본문과 타협해서 동의 표현을 고르는 훈련이 필요하다.

---

70. Why does the woman direct the man to the company's website?

(A) To make an online payment
(B) To get directions to the store
(C) To view available design options
(D) To revise an existing policy

W: If you visit our company website, you'll be able to search through the designs we do offer.

W: 당신의 저희 회사의 웹사이트를 방문하시면, 저희가 제공하는 디자인의 찾아보실 수 있을 겁니다.

▶ 독해형 문제의 유형을 파악하고 훈련한다.
 ① 언급형 (what is mentioned/said about the ~?)
 ② 화자의 의도 파악 문제 (What does the woman mean when she says, " "~?)
 ③ 그 이외의 의문사 Why/What을 사용해서 목적/이유를 묻는 문제 (What made the speaker do ~?)
긴 문장을 빨리 읽고 파악하지 못한다면 LC는 물론 PART 6, 7에서도 고득점을 받기 힘들다. 〈스파르타 신토익 실전 1000제 Vol. 2〉에 나온 긴 선택지를 처음 읽을 때 문장 구조의 주어/동사를 마킹하면서 빠르게 문제를 읽고 풀자. 오답노트 만들 때 해석이 안 되는 구문을 따로 익히는 훈련을 하자.
 ➡ 긴 (A),(B),(C),(D)의 정답지들의 각각의 주요 포인트가 무엇인지를 파악하는 훈련을 하자.

▶ 주어진 보기 중에 Best Answer인 동의 표현(Paraphrasing) 고르는 훈련을 한다.
문제를 미리 읽고 본문에서 어떤 성우가 말할 것인지 위치를 파악했는데도 정답을 고르지 못했다는 것은 본문에 나온 어휘가 그대로 선택지에 나오지 않았기 때문이다. LC의 경우, 빈출 동의 표현을 암기하는 것만으로는 부족하다. 최상위의 동의 표현은 단순 동의 표현이 아니라, 주어진 정답지 중 가장 좋은 것을 고르는 Best Answer이기 때문이다. 녹음을 듣고, 주어진 보기 중에서 가장 좋은 선택지를 고르는 것에 익숙해지자.
 ➡ 자주 등장하는 동의 표현을 암기하고, 주어진 것 보기에 가장 좋은 선택지를 고르는 훈련을 하자.

PART 4 고득점 전략

스파르타 고득점 Point! : 읽은 만큼 들린다! 완벽하게 준비하자!

- 녹음 전에 문제를 파악하고 기억하자!
- TOPIC 별 유형/어휘를 익혀서 "정답" 부분을 좀 더 쉽게 맞힌다.

2016년 신토익 변경 이후에 PART 3~4에 신유형으로 시각자료 및 화자 의도 유형이 새롭게 포함되었다. 하지만 복수의 등장인물이 정신없이 대화하는 PART 3에 비해, PART 4는 1명의 화자(speaker)가 주어진 주제에 대해 일정한 방향으로 발표를 이끌어 나간다. 회화의 연장선에 있는 PART 3와 달리, PART 4는 사람들 앞에서의 발표(speech)로 문어체적인 딱딱한 면이 있기에 소위 기습 공격 같은 문제는 자주 등장하지 않는다. 다소 생소한 문어체 표현의 벽만 넘으면 오히려 PART 3보다 정답을 맞히는 것이 쉽다.

Program	
Presenter	Time
Dr. Randolph	9:30 a.m.
Ms. Nelson	11:00 a.m.
Break	12:00~1:30 p.m.
Workshops	2:00 p.m.

98. What is the purpose of this announcement?
(C) To provide a schedule overview

99. Look at the graphic. Which program has the incorrect information?
(A) Dr. Randolph's
(B) Ms. Nelson's
(C) Lunch break
(D) Workshops

100. Where can the listeners find information on local restaurants?
(C) In the conference program

Thank you for coming to the opening day of public speaking seminar. As you can see in your program, we have an exciting day ready for you today. But before we start, I have a brief announcement about the schedule. Dr. Steve Randolph' speech on image training will be at 10 o'clock instead of 9:30 due to some technical difficulties in the meeting room B. But, I'm sure his speech will worth the wait. There will be a break for lunch at 12:00 noon as scheduled. For your convenience, we've provided a list of local restaurants on the back page of the program, or you can visit the downstairs cafeteria. In the afternoon, we will break into groups and you can either take intensive workshops around 2 o'clock, or visit the exhibition halls. I hope you enjoy the best of what we have prepared for you.

연설 기술 세미나의 첫 날에 와주셔서 감사합니다. 여러분의 프로그램을 보시면 저희가 여러분을 위해서 재미있는 하루를 준비해 놓은 것을 아실 겁니다. 하지만 저희가 시작하기 전에 일정표에 대해서 간단히 안내드릴 것이 있습니다. 9시반에 이미지 트레이닝에 대한 스티브 랜돌프 박사의 연설이 기술적인 문제로 30분 지연되어 9시반이 아닌 10시에 시작하겠습니다. 그 분의 발표는 기다릴 값어치가 있을 겁니다. 일정대로 12시에는 점심 시간이 있을 예정이고요. 여러분의 편의를 위해서 프로그램 뒤편에 근처의 식당목록을 드렸습니다. 또한, 간단한 식사를 위해서는 아래층의 구내 식당을 이용하실 수 있습니다. 오후에는 그룹으로 나누어서 심화 워크숍을 들으시거나 전시홀을 방문하실 수 있습니다. 저희가 여러분을 위해 준비한 것들을 최대한 즐기시기 바랍니다.

▶ 문제 3개를 읽고 기억하는 것은 기본이다. 문제 3개와 표를 통해서 TOPIC 별 추측이 가능하다.

문제를 정확히 읽고 유형을 분류한 후 "지문에서 어떻게 정답 단서를 줄까"를 예측하며 듣는다. 특히 PART 4는 TOPIC별로 같은 문제/표현이 정답이 되는 경우가 많다. 신유형의 시각자료 문제도 "문제&표"를 읽고 시각자료의 어떤 부분을 녹음으로 들려줄지 예측한다.

— 지문에서 정답 단서를 포착할 수 있도록 문제 읽기를 훈련해서 정답을 맞힌다.

빠른 고득점 획득을 위한 스파르타 전략

스파르타 만점 Point! : 어려운 주제(Topic)를 마스터하라!

- 90번대 이후로 출제되는 고난이도 주제(TOPIC)를 훈련하라.
- 독해형 문제의 긴 정답지 (A), (B), (C), (D)를 읽고 빠르게 요점을 파악할 수 있도록 훈련하자.

문제를 미리 읽고 파악하고, 들으면서 동시에 풀어야 하는 파트이다. 물론 간단히 녹음을 빠르게 할 수도 있겠지만, PART 3에서 문제를 어렵게 만들려면 ① 눈으로 읽는 부분인 문제 부분을 길고 난해하게 만들거나, ② 문제도 읽고 준비를 했는데도 불구하고 마치 정답이 없는 것과 같은 트릭으로 본문에서 나온 어휘로 동의 표현으로 바꾸어 고르게 하는 경우이다. 특히, 초보는 읽는 속도가 느려서 ①에서 많이 틀리고, 고득점자들은 ②의 동의 표현에서 고민한다. 특히, ②의 경우에 다 듣고 알아들었는데 고를 정답이 없는 경우가 생기는 것이다. 고난도 문제를 맞히기 위해서는 조금은 "어렵게" 본문과 타협해서 동의 표현을 고르는 훈련이 필요하다.

---

98. Where do the speakers most likely work?

(A) A food processing plant

(B) A financial services corporation

(C) A corporate law firm

(D) A video production company

I have a few words to say about our meeting with the representatives from Wong's Foods next week. Let's remember that Wong's Foods is our video production's biggest client. It is critical that we get the contract.

다음 주에 있을 웡푸드 사 직원들과의 회의에 대해 몇마디 드리고 싶습니다. 웡푸드는 우리 비디오 생산의 가장 큰 고객이라는 것을 다시 한번 알려 드리고 싶습니다. 우리가 계약을 따는 것은 정말 중요합니다.

▶ 뉴스 관련 주제는 자주 등장하는 Project를 이해하자.

① Business News: 기업체의 CEO가 준 정보를 기업 인수/합병/신상품/공장신설 등의 중요한 결정에 대한 내용을 기자(reporter)나 방송국의 아나운서(announcer)가 전달한다.

② Local News: 시장(mayor)과 시 위원회(city council)가 지역 공동체의 활성화를 위해서 다양한 건설/문화 Project를 제안하고 승인하는 내용이 등장한다.

어휘나 표현이 딱딱하고 까다롭지만 PART 6나 7에서도 고난도 문제로 출제될 수 있는 내용으로 고득점으로 가기 위해 반드시 익혀야 될 내용이다.

➡ 지역 공동체(local community)와 한 사업체의 비즈니스 활동 관련 주제를 마스터하자.

▶ 업무 배정(project assignment)은 고객사(client)와 하청/공급업체(agency/supplier) 관계를 이해하자.

① Staff Meeting: 특정 기업체의 특정 부서의 특정인에게 일(Project)를 배정하는 내용에 익숙해지자. 특히 다양한 업체의 부서별 업무의 특징을 파악하면 정답을 맞히는 데 도움이 될 것이다.

주제는 계약(Contract)일 수 있으나 계약을 하는 쌍방(both parties)의 상관 관계를 이해하는 것이 추론 문제 등에서 도움이 될 것이다. 이 주제도 PART 6와 7에 자주 등장하는 내용이다.

➡ 특정 업체(business)의 업무(Contract-Project-Task)를 이해할 수 있도록 비즈니스 상식을 키우자.

Test

파트별 점수 분석(맞은 숫자)

PART 1	
PART 2	
PART 3	
PART 4	
총 맞은 갯수	

정답 및 스크립트: 159p

01

LISTENING TEST

In the Listening test, you will be asked to demonstrate how well you understand spoken English. The entire Listening test will last approximately 45 minutes. There are four parts, and directions are given for each part. You must mark your answers on the separate answer sheet.
Do not write your answers in your test book.

PART 1

Directions: For each question in this part, you will hear four statements about a picture in your test book. When you hear the statements, you must select the one statement that best describes what you see in the picture. Then find the number of the question on your answer sheet and mark your answer. The statements will not be printed in your test book and will be spoken only one time.

Sample Answer
Ⓐ ● Ⓒ Ⓓ

Statement (B), "They're shaking hands," is the best description of the picture, so you should select answer (B) and mark it on your answer sheet.

1.

2.

Go on to the next page

3.

4.

5.

6.

Go on to the next page

PART 2

Directions: You will hear a question or statement and three responses spoken in English. They will not be printed in your test book and will be spoken only one time. Select the best response to the question or statement and mark the letter (A), (B), or (C) on your answer sheet.

7. Mark your answer on your answer sheet.
8. Mark your answer on your answer sheet.
9. Mark your answer on your answer sheet.
10. Mark your answer on your answer sheet.
11. Mark your answer on your answer sheet.
12. Mark your answer on your answer sheet.
13. Mark your answer on your answer sheet.
14. Mark your answer on your answer sheet.
15. Mark your answer on your answer sheet.
16. Mark your answer on your answer sheet.
17. Mark your answer on your answer sheet.
18. Mark your answer on your answer sheet.
19. Mark your answer on your answer sheet.
20. Mark your answer on your answer sheet.
21. Mark your answer on your answer sheet.
22. Mark your answer on your answer sheet.
23. Mark your answer on your answer sheet.
24. Mark your answer on your answer sheet.
25. Mark your answer on your answer sheet.
26. Mark your answer on your answer sheet.
27. Mark your answer on your answer sheet.
28. Mark your answer on your answer sheet.
29. Mark your answer on your answer sheet.
30. Mark your answer on your answer sheet.
31. Mark your answer on your answer sheet.

PART 3

Directions: You will hear some conversations between two or more people. You will be asked to answer three questions about what the speakers say in each conversation. Select the best response to each question and mark the letter (A), (B), (C), or (D) on your answer sheet. The conversations will not be printed in your test book and will be spoken only one time.

32. What mode of transportation will the speakers use?
    (A) Aircraft
    (B) Car
    (C) Boat
    (D) Train

33. What time do the speakers plan to travel?
    (A) At 5:00 A.M.
    (B) At 9:00 A.M.
    (C) At 11:30 A.M.
    (D) At 12:00 P.M.

34. What will the woman probably do next?
    (A) Attend a meeting
    (B) Have lunch
    (C) Travel to Detroit
    (D) Book tickets

35. What is the main topic of the conversation?
    (A) An upcoming corporate merger
    (B) A round of layoffs
    (C) The promotion of a coworker
    (D) Plans for summer vacation

36. When will the discussed event happen?
    (A) Immediately
    (B) In a week
    (C) In three weeks
    (D) In the New Year

37. What is the timing of the event dependent upon?
    (A) Someone's retirement
    (B) The opening of a location
    (C) The redecoration of an office
    (D) The completion of training

38. Why is the woman calling?
    (A) To request a refund
    (B) To request a service visit
    (C) To ask for directions to the store
    (D) To get help with a product

39. What did the woman have trouble with?
    (A) Activating the lighting display
    (B) Deciding what ingredients to add
    (C) Assembling the product
    (D) Setting the timer

40. What did the woman say she had already done?
    (A) Spoken to a service technician
    (B) Looked over the manual
    (C) Turned the product off and on
    (D) Exchanged the product

41. What is the main topic of the conversation?
    (A) Arranging a date
    (B) Seeing a doctor
    (C) Signing up for a training
    (D) Finishing an assignment

42. What is the due date?
    (A) Friday
    (B) Monday
    (C) Tuesday
    (D) Thursday

43. What will the woman probably do next?
    (A) Send an e-mail
    (B) Finish an assignment
    (C) Visit a director
    (D) Go to a movie

Go on to the next page

44. What job does Jinny most likely do?
    (A) Factory worker
    (B) Dental assistant
    (C) Doctor's receptionist
    (D) Personal trainer

45. What day can the man come in?
    (A) Friday
    (B) Monday
    (C) Tuesday
    (D) Wednesday

46. What does the woman ask the man to do?
    (A) Call another branch of the business
    (B) Call to advise them of any changes
    (C) Consult a specialist
    (D) Pay a deposit in advance

47. What is the man asking about?
    (A) Why the CEO wants to see him
    (B) Where to buy cleaning supplies
    (C) The date and time of a meeting
    (D) The status of a utility bill

48. What department is the man the head of?
    (A) Marketing
    (B) Maintenance
    (C) Accounting
    (D) Public relations

49. What idea does the woman have?
    (A) Having a meeting with the CEO
    (B) Reorganizing the department
    (C) Reducing air conditioning and heating
    (D) Finding cheaper suppliers for cleaning supplies

50. What event will happen the day after tomorrow?
    (A) A training seminar
    (B) A management meeting
    (C) A cooking lesson
    (D) A meal with employees

51. Where will the event most likely happen?
    (A) At a Chinese restaurant
    (B) At a Mongolian buffet
    (C) At the company cafeteria
    (D) In the manager's home

52. What does the man mean when he says, "When I was there last, we were packed into one that should have had about six fewer people in it"?
    (A) The food was not good.
    (B) Some of the staff didn't show up.
    (C) The room was too small.
    (D) The wait staff was not polite.

53. What is the main topic of the conversation?
    (A) A retirement party
    (B) A printing order
    (C) An employee training seminar
    (D) The promotion of a colleague

54. What is the company in the process of doing?
    (A) Signing a contract
    (B) Hiring new employees
    (C) Relocating its offices
    (D) Changing its phone number

55. What will the man probably do next?
    (A) Order lunch
    (B) Contact a company
    (C) Go home for the day
    (D) Arrange a meeting

56. What is the main topic of the conversation?
    (A) A new staff member
    (B) A rescheduled meeting
    (C) An office relocation
    (D) A new training program

57. What does the man mean when he says, "He'll probably want to try out a few of the ideas that he has been working on"?
    (A) Company travel will be reduced.
    (B) New office furniture will be ordered.
    (C) New ideas will be implemented.
    (D) Staff numbers will be reduced.

58. What has Mr. Aimes recently done?
    (A) Completed his MBA
    (B) Fired a poorly performing employee
    (C) Canceled a sales seminar
    (D) Trained a new secretary

59. Where does the woman most likely work?
    (A) At a doctor's office
    (B) At a post office
    (C) At a ski resort
    (D) At a health club

60. How much extra does the receipt confirmation cost?
    (A) $0.00
    (B) $5.00
    (C) $10.75
    (D) $15.65

61. What does the woman ask the man to do?
    (A) Attend a seminar
    (B) Submit a report
    (C) Deliver a letter
    (D) Complete a form

Company	Location
Supreme Design	New York
Modern Art	Philadelphia
Hoo Design	Miami
Great View Art	San Francisco

62. What type of event is the company sponsoring?
    (A) A musical event
    (B) An auction
    (C) A theater performance
    (D) A sporting event

63. What is the man concerned about?
    (A) A lack of volunteers
    (B) A customer complaint
    (C) A limited budget
    (D) A delayed concert

64. Look at the graphic. Which company do the speakers choose?
    (A) Great View Art
    (B) Hoo Design
    (C) Supreme Design
    (D) Modern Art

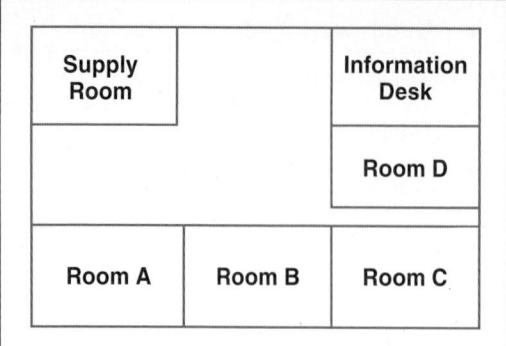
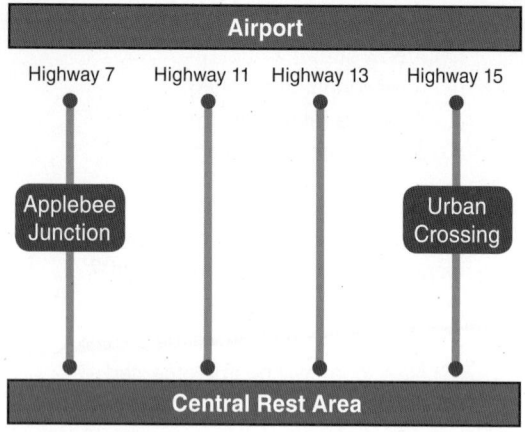

65. According to the man, what will the woman be doing today?

    (A) Shopping for some office supplies
    (B) Reporting a renovation plan
    (C) Taking public transportation
    (D) Preparing a press release

66. Look at the graphic. Which office has been assigned to the man?

    (A) Room A
    (B) Room B
    (C) Room C
    (D) Room D

67. What does the woman say will take place next week?

    (A) A new product launch
    (B) A retirement party
    (C) A conference call
    (D) A staff meeting

68. Where does the conversation take place?

    (A) At an airport
    (B) At a business office
    (C) At a hotel
    (D) At a rest area

69. Look at the graphic. Which route does the man suggest the woman take?

    (A) Highway 7
    (B) Highway 11
    (C) Highway 13
    (D) Highway 15

70. Why is the woman going to Seoul?

    (A) To attend a meeting
    (B) To visit a relative
    (C) To interview for a job
    (D) To buy a car

PART 4

Directions: You will hear some talks given by a single speaker. You will be asked to answer three questions about what the speaker says in each talk. Select the best response to each question and mark the letter (A), (B), (C), or (D) on your answer sheet. The talks will not be printed in your test book and will be spoken only one time.

71. What is the report mainly about?
    (A) Traffic
    (B) Political protests
    (C) The weather
    (D) Transportation costs

72. According to the announcer, what has caused a problem?
    (A) Closed bridges
    (B) Bad weather
    (C) Construction
    (D) A rally

73. What will the listeners probably hear next?
    (A) A music program
    (B) The weather report
    (C) A game show
    (D) The local news

74. What is the advertisement about?
    (A) An exercise program
    (B) A rafting tour
    (C) A holiday sale
    (D) A job opportunity

75. What qualifications should applicants have?
    (A) Previous experience
    (B) Physical fitness
    (C) A pilot's license
    (D) Their own vehicle

76. What are people interested in the job asked to do?
    (A) Come to a job fair
    (B) Contact the company
    (C) Check the Web site
    (D) Complete a test

77. Where does the speaker most likely work?
    (A) At a pharmacy
    (B) At a dentist
    (C) At a doctor's office
    (D) At a beauty salon

78. Why is the woman calling?
    (A) To request a payment
    (B) To arrange an appointment
    (C) To cancel a test
    (D) To book a surgery

79. What does the woman mean when she says, "don't forget that the clinic has moved since you were last here"?
    (A) To let the customer know the appointment has been changed
    (B) To remind the customer of the new location of the hospital
    (C) To let the listener know the doctor is not available
    (D) To confirm that the customer must not be late

80. Who most likely is the speaker?
    (A) A flight attendant
    (B) An aviator
    (C) A customs officer
    (D) A businessman

81. Where are the listeners going?
    (A) Tokyo
    (B) Taipei
    (C) Bangkok
    (D) Havana

82. What most likely will happen next?
    (A) Passengers will get off the plane.
    (B) The plane will land.
    (C) Safety procedures will be demonstrated.
    (D) The passengers will receive lunch.

Go on to the next page

83. What is the talk mainly about?
    (A) Events at the conference
    (B) The dinner menu
    (C) Accommodation arrangements
    (D) Rules for the conference

84. What does the man mean when he says, "Welcome to the World Technology Conference"?
    (A) Scientists are attending the conference.
    (B) Musicians are attending the conference.
    (C) Construction workers are attending the conference.
    (D) Fitness coaches are attending the conference.

85. What is the first event of the conference?
    (A) A technology demonstration
    (B) A meal with attendees
    (C) An award presentation
    (D) A roundtable debate

86. What type of work will the interns be doing?
    (A) Laboratory research
    (B) Navigation
    (C) Advertising
    (D) Police work

87. What does the man mean when he says, "I learned the ability to do more than one thing at the same time"?
    (A) He has lab techniques.
    (B) He is good at multitasking.
    (C) He has an ability to keep the records accurately.
    (D) He is available 24-hours a day.

88. How long is the internship program?
    (A) Two weeks
    (B) One month
    (C) Two months
    (D) Three months

89. Who is the intended audience of this talk?
    (A) Potential clients
    (B) Law enforcement officers
    (C) Company employees
    (D) Company shareholders

90. What does the company probably sell?
    (A) Software
    (B) Cars
    (C) Carpet
    (D) Appliances

91. What will Mr. Anderson probably do next?
    (A) Submit a report
    (B) Conduct an interview
    (C) Have dinner
    (D) Award a prize

92. Who most likely is the speaker?
    (A) A bank teller
    (B) A cafeteria employee
    (C) A museum guide
    (D) A marketing manager

93. How long will the tour be?
    (A) 20 minutes
    (B) 45 minutes
    (C) A half hour
    (D) An hour and a half

94. What will the tour members probably do last?
    (A) Go to the airport
    (B) Fill out a form
    (C) Book a tour
    (D) Visit the souvenir shop

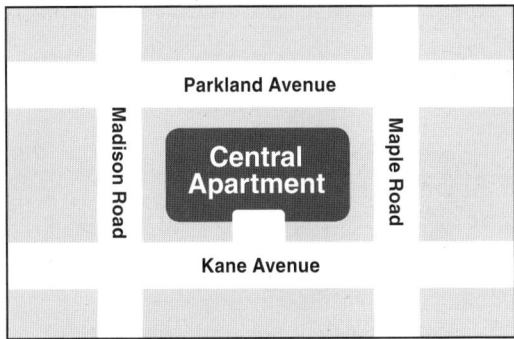

EXPENSE REPORT

DATE	DESCRIPTION	AMOUNT
May 3	Parking	$ 30
May 6	Meal	$ 90
May 8	Car rental	$ 180
May 10	Accommodations	$ 250

95. What will take place on April 15?
    (A) A flea market
    (B) A job fair
    (C) Some road construction
    (D) A sporting event

96. Look at the graphic. Which street will be closed?
    (A) Kane Avenue
    (B) Madison Road
    (C) Maple Road
    (D) Parkland Avenue

97. What does the speaker suggest?
    (A) Heading for the office late
    (B) Making a detour
    (C) Using public transportation
    (D) Considering joining a car pool

98. Why is the speaker calling?
    (A) Some paperwork did not have a signature.
    (B) A reservation has changed.
    (C) A certain receipt was not included.
    (D) The dates of the business trip were wrong.

99. Look at the graphic. Which expense needs to be confirmed?
    (A) Car rental
    (B) Meal
    (C) Parking
    (D) Accommodations

100. What does speaker say he can do?
    (A) Cancel a reservation
    (B) Handle a complaint
    (C) Hire a new employee
    (D) Explain a process

Test

파트별 점수 분석(맞은 숫자)

PART 1	
PART 2	
PART 3	
PART 4	
총 맞은 갯수	

정답 및 스크립트: 166p

02

LISTENING TEST

In the Listening test, you will be asked to demonstrate how well you understand spoken English. The entire Listening test will last approximately 45 minutes. There are four parts, and directions are given for each part. You must mark your answers on the separate answer sheet.
Do not write your answers in your test book.

PART 1

Directions: For each question in this part, you will hear four statements about a picture in your test book. When you hear the statements, you must select the one statement that best describes what you see in the picture. Then find the number of the question on your answer sheet and mark your answer. The statements will not be printed in your test book and will be spoken only one time.

Sample Answer
Ⓐ ● Ⓒ Ⓓ

Statement (B), "They're shaking hands," is the best description of the picture, so you should select answer (B) and mark it on your answer sheet.

1.

2.

3.

4.

5.

6.

PART 2

Directions: You will hear a question or statement and three responses spoken in English. They will not be printed in your test book and will be spoken only one time. Select the best response to the question or statement and mark the letter (A), (B), or (C) on your answer sheet.

7. Mark your answer on your answer sheet.
8. Mark your answer on your answer sheet.
9. Mark your answer on your answer sheet.
10. Mark your answer on your answer sheet.
11. Mark your answer on your answer sheet.
12. Mark your answer on your answer sheet.
13. Mark your answer on your answer sheet.
14. Mark your answer on your answer sheet.
15. Mark your answer on your answer sheet.
16. Mark your answer on your answer sheet.
17. Mark your answer on your answer sheet.
18. Mark your answer on your answer sheet.
19. Mark your answer on your answer sheet.
20. Mark your answer on your answer sheet.
21. Mark your answer on your answer sheet.
22. Mark your answer on your answer sheet.
23. Mark your answer on your answer sheet.
24. Mark your answer on your answer sheet.
25. Mark your answer on your answer sheet.
26. Mark your answer on your answer sheet.
27. Mark your answer on your answer sheet.
28. Mark your answer on your answer sheet.
29. Mark your answer on your answer sheet.
30. Mark your answer on your answer sheet.
31. Mark your answer on your answer sheet.

PART 3

Directions: You will hear some conversations between two or more people. You will be asked to answer three questions about what the speakers say in each conversation. Select the best response to each question and mark the letter (A), (B), (C), or (D) on your answer sheet. The conversations will not be printed in your test book and will be spoken only one time.

32. Why is the man calling?
    (A) To invite the woman to an event
    (B) To book a table
    (C) To order takeout food
    (D) To cancel a reservation

33. What is the problem?
    (A) No tables are available at 8:15.
    (B) The business closes at eight o'clock.
    (C) The restaurant is out of lobster.
    (D) The woman has lost her job.

34. What does the woman suggest?
    (A) Coming another day
    (B) Coming half an hour later
    (C) Trying another location
    (D) Eating at home

35. What does the man need help with?
    (A) A printer
    (B) Internet access
    (C) A filing system
    (D) An answering machine

36. When will the woman most likely return from her meeting?
    (A) The next day
    (B) In an hour
    (C) At 7 P.M.
    (D) On Thursday

37. What will the man probably do to solve the problem?
    (A) Call the IT department
    (B) Consult the manufacturer's Web page
    (C) Buy a new router
    (D) Use the fax machine

38. What are the women looking for?
    (A) An order form
    (B) A filing cabinet
    (C) A measuring tape
    (D) A wardrobe

39. Where most likely are the speakers?
    (A) In a restaurant
    (B) In a church
    (C) In an office storeroom
    (D) On an airplane

40. What does the man offer to do?
    (A) Place an order
    (B) Build something
    (C) Go home early
    (D) Ask his assistant

41. Where did the man expect the woman to be?
    (A) In the conference room
    (B) In San Francisco
    (C) At a training session
    (D) At a job interview

42. Why is the woman at the office?
    (A) She had a meeting there.
    (B) Her conference was canceled.
    (C) Her conference was pushed back.
    (D) She had to pack her bags.

43. Why won't she take a trip next week?
    (A) She has to move to a new office.
    (B) Her schedule will be too busy.
    (C) She has to talk with a client.
    (D) Her office will be renovated.

Go on to the next page

44. What does the woman ask about?
    (A) Directions to the subway
    (B) The duration of a trip
    (C) The cost of a ticket
    (D) The bus schedule

45. Where most likely is the woman?
    (A) In a bakery
    (B) In a museum
    (C) In a cab
    (D) At an airport

46. What will the woman probably do next?
    (A) Arrange a meeting
    (B) Take a taxi
    (C) Collect her change
    (D) Go into the subway station

47. Why is the woman calling?
    (A) She wants a new job.
    (B) She wants to buy a home.
    (C) She wants to arrange a flight.
    (D) She wants to ask for directions.

48. Where does the man most likely work?
    (A) At a software company
    (B) At a moving company
    (C) At a real estate agency
    (D) At an interior decorating company

49. What will the man most likely do next?
    (A) Apply for a job
    (B) Travel to Los Angeles
    (C) Buy a house
    (D) Arrange a meeting time

50. What does the man say he just did?
    (A) Made a telephone call
    (B) Filed a report
    (C) Finished his work
    (D) Canceled an order

51. Why did Mtech call?
    (A) To check on an order
    (B) To cancel a meeting
    (C) To confirm a price
    (D) To hire a new employee

52. What does the man mean when he says, "No problem"?
    (A) He doesn't understand the problem.
    (B) He can't cancel the order.
    (C) He will advise the woman.
    (D) He will help the woman install the material.

53. What does the woman ask the man to do?
    (A) Give her the weekend off
    (B) Suggest some kitchen appliances
    (C) Allow her to work at a tradeshow
    (D) Pay for her hotel costs

54. Why does the woman want to go to Las Vegas?
    (A) She wants to apply for a job.
    (B) She wants to stay at a hotel.
    (C) She wants to enjoy some tradeshows.
    (D) She wants to see her relative.

55. What does the man remind the woman about?
    (A) That she will have to work
    (B) That she must arrive on time
    (C) That she has a meeting this weekend
    (D) That her brother no longer lives in Las Vegas

56. What are the speakers discussing?

    (A) Their favorite actors
    (B) The movie they are watching
    (C) The performance they've just seen
    (D) A rock concert

57. What does the woman mean when she says, "I'm not particularly surprised"?

    (A) She thought it was very sad.
    (B) She thought it was excellent.
    (C) She thought it was too long.
    (D) She didn't like it.

58. What will the speakers most likely do next?

    (A) Hire a babysitter
    (B) Go to a pub
    (C) See a movie
    (D) Go to a musical

59. Why is the woman calling?

    (A) To make a job offer
    (B) To order food
    (C) To cancel a meeting
    (D) To collect an outstanding bill

60. When does the woman want to meet with Ms. Wharton?

    (A) This Monday
    (B) Next Monday
    (C) Next Tuesday
    (D) Over the weekend

61. What does the man say he will do?

    (A) Arrange an interview
    (B) Receive a delivery for Ms. Wharton
    (C) Give Ms. Wharton a message
    (D) Come to the office to meet Ms. Felling

E-1	Lens Malfunction
E-2	No Flash
E-3	Low Battery
E-4	Memory Card Problem

62. Who most likely is the man?

    (A) A mechanic
    (B) A store clerk
    (C) An electrician
    (D) A photo artist

63. Look at the graphic. Which error code is the camera displaying?

    (A) E-1
    (B) E-2
    (C) E-3
    (D) E-4

64. What will the man most likely do next?

    (A) Replace an item
    (B) Purchase a new item
    (C) Read a manual
    (D) Wrap up a camera

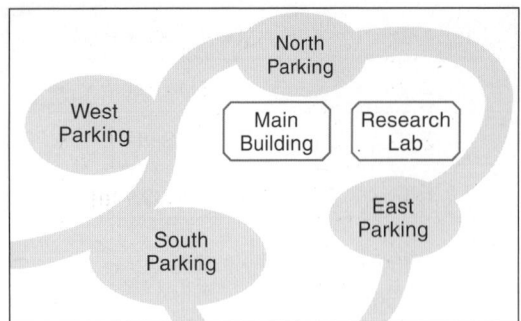

Miracle Office Complex Directory

Office	Location
Kim's Stationery	1F
P&T Restaurant	2F
Miracle Fitness Center	3F
Jane's Clinic	4F

65. Look at the graphic. Which parking area will be closed?

   (A) North
   (B) East
   (C) South
   (D) West

66. What is the woman concerned about?

   (A) Encountering road construction
   (B) Paying parking fees
   (C) Walking a long distance
   (D) Facing heavy traffic

67. What does the man say the board will do?

   (A) Change the company's policy
   (B) Offer complimentary shuttles
   (C) Provide a bonus
   (D) Reimburse employees

68. What is the purpose of the man's visit?

   (A) He is meeting with an accountant.
   (B) He has to pay for parking.
   (C) He will work out.
   (D) He is eating some food.

69. What does the woman say about the parking policy?

   (A) It has a time restriction.
   (B) It isn't available for residents.
   (C) It is for visitors only.
   (D) It is complimentary for visitors.

70. Look at the graphic. Which office name has to be updated on the building directory?

   (A) Kim's Stationery
   (B) P&T Restaurant
   (C) Miracle Fitness Center
   (D) Jane's Clinic

PART 4

Directions: You will hear some talks given by a single speaker. You will be asked to answer three questions about what the speaker says in each talk. Select the best response to each question and mark the letter (A), (B), (C), or (D) on your answer sheet. The talks will not be printed in your test book and will be spoken only one time.

71. Why is the woman calling?
    (A) To buy an appliance
    (B) To cancel a delivery
    (C) To report a problem
    (D) To order food

72. What product is the woman discussing?
    (A) An exercise bike
    (B) A microwave oven
    (C) A stereo system
    (D) A washing machine

73. What does the speaker want the store to do?
    (A) Send spare parts
    (B) Send a service person
    (C) Order a part
    (D) Deliver a replacement

74. What is the purpose of the meeting?
    (A) To announce new management
    (B) To announce a new building project
    (C) To explain a change in policies
    (D) To announce the closure of the facility

75. What type of businesses does Angela Tiller work for?
    (A) A building supply company
    (B) A hospital
    (C) A retirement home
    (D) A delivery service

76. Why did Ms. Tiller's predecessor leave?
    (A) He was transferred.
    (B) He went into retirement.
    (C) He had a personal matter.
    (D) He was dismissed.

77. What is the purpose of the talk?
    (A) To order new equipment
    (B) To announce layoffs
    (C) To discuss the sales results
    (D) To discuss tax returns

78. According to the speaker, what positive results were there?
    (A) Overseas sales increased.
    (B) Domestic sales have hit a target.
    (C) Expenses were reduced.
    (D) The sales force was increased.

79. What course of action does the speaker announce?
    (A) Restrictions on corporate travel
    (B) Taking over another company
    (C) Hiring additional employees
    (D) A series of planning meetings

80. What is the speaker calling about?
    (A) Car rental
    (B) Emergency arrangements
    (C) Airline tickets
    (D) A package delivery

81. What information does the speaker require?
    (A) A shipping address
    (B) A telephone number
    (C) A family member's name
    (D) A list of contents

82. How does the speaker request that Mr. Wilson contact him?
    (A) By online chat
    (B) By mail
    (C) By telephone
    (D) By e-mail

Go on to the next page

83. Where would this talk most likely be heard?
  (A) On the radio
  (B) In a supermarket
  (C) At a construction site
  (D) In a hospital

84. What field does Sandra Beard work in?
  (A) Geology
  (B) Chemistry
  (C) Environmental science
  (D) Medicine

85. What did Sandra Beard do recently?
  (A) Started a company
  (B) Returned from Africa
  (C) Wrote a book
  (D) Invented a product

---

86. Who is Mr. Harrison?
  (A) A professional athlete
  (B) A journalist
  (C) A magazine editor
  (D) A photographer

87. What does the caller want to discuss with Mr. Harrison?
  (A) Political issues
  (B) Sporting events
  (C) Current affairs
  (D) Writing assignments

88. What should Mr. Harrison do if Ms. Phelps does not answer the phone?
  (A) Press 3
  (B) Leave a message
  (C) Call back later
  (D) Send a letter

---

89. Who is Mr. Pratha?
  (A) The CEO of the company
  (B) A shipping manager
  (C) A clerical worker
  (D) One of the executives of the company

90. What does the speaker say about Mr. Pratha?
  (A) He is being offered a promotion.
  (B) He was with the company for 25 years.
  (C) He recently joined the company.
  (D) He has not been very reliable.

91. What does the man mean when he says, "Here is Mr. Pratha to say a few words"?
  (A) Mr. Pratha will install a new word processor software.
  (B) Mr. Pratha will type on a keyboard.
  (C) Mr. Pratha will make a speech at the ceremony.
  (D) Mr. Pratha will talk to guests one-on-one.

---

92. Who most likely is the speaker?
  (A) A human resources director
  (B) A computer programmer
  (C) A safety worker
  (D) A salesperson

93. What is the announcement about?
  (A) A problem with the plumbing
  (B) A fire drill
  (C) The elevators being serviced
  (D) A staff meeting

94. What does the man mean when he says, "I will take attendance"?
  (A) The activity is mandatory.
  (B) The activity was postponed.
  (C) The activity was canceled.
  (D) The activity will go smoothly.

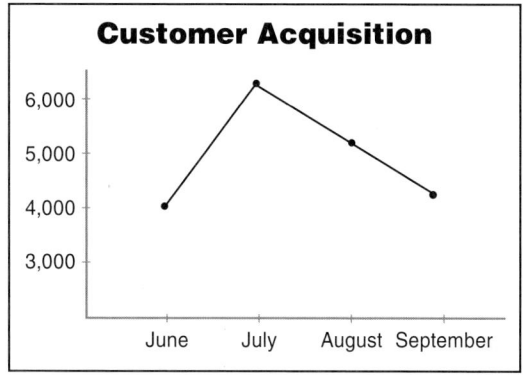

Thursday Schedule

9:00	
10:00	Staff meeting
11:00	
12:00	
13:00	Lunch with a client
14:00	
15:00	Conference call
16:00	

95. Where most likely does the speaker work?
(A) At an insurance company
(B) At a home appliance company
(C) At a supermarket
(D) At a design company

96. Look at the graphic. When was the promotional event held?
(A) In June
(B) In July
(C) In August
(D) In September

97. According to the speaker, what is the company going to do to improve their Web site?
(A) Hold an emergency meetingm
(B) Launch a new product
(C) Conduct a promotional event
(D) Employ some experts

98. Where most likely does the speaker work?
(A) At a shipping company
(B) At an accounting firm
(C) At an event planning agency
(D) At a law firm

99. What would the speaker like to discuss with the listener?
(A) A recruiting process
(B) A staff layoff
(C) A project budget
(D) A client claim

100. Look at the graphic. What time does the speaker want to meet?
(A) At 9:00
(B) At 11:00
(C) At 12:00
(D) At 14:00

Test

파트별 점수 분석(맞은 숫자)

PART 1	
PART 2	
PART 3	
PART 4	
총 맞은 갯수	

정답 및 스크립트: 173p

03

LISTENING TEST

In the Listening test, you will be asked to demonstrate how well you understand spoken English. The entire Listening test will last approximately 45 minutes. There are four parts, and directions are given for each part. You must mark your answers on the separate answer sheet.
Do not write your answers in your test book.

PART 1

Directions: For each question in this part, you will hear four statements about a picture in your test book. When you hear the statements, you must select the one statement that best describes what you see in the picture. Then find the number of the question on your answer sheet and mark your answer. The statements will not be printed in your test book and will be spoken only one time.

Sample Answer
Ⓐ ● Ⓒ Ⓓ

Statement (B), "They're shaking hands," is the best description of the picture, so you should select answer (B) and mark it on your answer sheet.

1.

2.

3.

4.

5.

6.

Go on to the next page

PART 2

Directions: You will hear a question or statement and three responses spoken in English. They will not be printed in your test book and will be spoken only one time. Select the best response to the question or statement and mark the letter (A), (B), or (C) on your answer sheet.

7. Mark your answer on your answer sheet.
8. Mark your answer on your answer sheet.
9. Mark your answer on your answer sheet.
10. Mark your answer on your answer sheet.
11. Mark your answer on your answer sheet.
12. Mark your answer on your answer sheet.
13. Mark your answer on your answer sheet.
14. Mark your answer on your answer sheet.
15. Mark your answer on your answer sheet.
16. Mark your answer on your answer sheet.
17. Mark your answer on your answer sheet.
18. Mark your answer on your answer sheet.
19. Mark your answer on your answer sheet.
20. Mark your answer on your answer sheet.
21. Mark your answer on your answer sheet.
22. Mark your answer on your answer sheet.
23. Mark your answer on your answer sheet.
24. Mark your answer on your answer sheet.
25. Mark your answer on your answer sheet.
26. Mark your answer on your answer sheet.
27. Mark your answer on your answer sheet.
28. Mark your answer on your answer sheet.
29. Mark your answer on your answer sheet.
30. Mark your answer on your answer sheet.
31. Mark your answer on your answer sheet.

PART 3

Directions: You will hear some conversations between two or more people. You will be asked to answer three questions about what the speakers say in each conversation. Select the best response to each question and mark the letter (A), (B), (C), or (D) on your answer sheet. The conversations will not be printed in your test book and will be spoken only one time.

32. Why is the man talking to the woman?
    (A) To deliver a package
    (B) To see a doctor
    (C) To reserve a spot at a conference
    (D) To make an appointment for tomorrow

33. Why does the man decide not to see Dr. Paulson the next morning?
    (A) He will be at the conference with Dr. Chung.
    (B) He needs prompt assistance.
    (C) He has a meeting.
    (D) He will be out of town.

34. What will the man most likely do?
    (A) Come back tomorrow morning
    (B) Visit a nearby pharmacy
    (C) Meet with a different physician
    (D) Call Dr. Paulson on the phone

35. Why does the woman want to see Ms. Maeda?
    (A) To ask about a court date
    (B) To sign a contract
    (C) To give her some documents
    (D) To tell her she is leaving the country

36. Where is Ms. Maeda?
    (A) Overseas
    (B) At home
    (C) At a legal conference
    (D) In her office

37. What will the man do next?
    (A) Write a note
    (B) Call Ms. Maeda
    (C) Go home
    (D) Deliver a message

38. What is the woman working on?
    (A) Next year's budget
    (B) A set of presentation slides
    (C) A meeting agenda
    (D) A speech

39. What does the woman promise to do?
    (A) Reassign some work to Cathy
    (B) Make a copy of the agenda
    (C) Update the man on her work progress
    (D) Meet the man at the board meeting

40. What does the man ask the woman to do?
    (A) Include names on the agenda
    (B) Rehearse for a speech
    (C) Send the agenda out before speaking to Cathy
    (D) Let her revise the agenda

41. What does Professor Van Saint teach?
    (A) Spanish
    (B) Business marketing
    (C) French
    (D) Accounting

42. Why is the class canceled?
    (A) Bad weather
    (B) Marriage of the professor's relative
    (C) Sickness of the professor
    (D) Public holiday

43. How long was the class supposed to be?
    (A) 60 minutes
    (B) 90 minutes
    (C) 30 minutes
    (D) 2 hours

Go on to the next page

44. Where does the conversation take place?

    (A) At a museum
    (B) At a department store
    (C) At a library
    (D) At a bookstore

45. What does the man imply when he says, "Oh, I think I know that one"?

    (A) He knows what she is talking about.
    (B) The store has only one copy remaining.
    (C) The man knows the woman well.
    (D) The man will show the woman a review.

46. What will the woman most likely do?

    (A) Go to another store
    (B) Buy two copies
    (C) Ask the man to call her husband
    (D) Purchase a gift

47. What are the speakers discussing?

    (A) A trip to Korea
    (B) A language course
    (C) Lecture schedules
    (D) A management meeting

48. When will the classes start?

    (A) The middle of next month
    (B) Tomorrow
    (C) Next week
    (D) On Tuesday

49. What is mentioned about the hotel?

    (A) It is located in Korea.
    (B) Its marketing has focused on Korea recently.
    (C) It has only three employees.
    (D) It has been accommodating many foreign guests.

50. Where most likely do the speakers work?

    (A) At a restaurant
    (B) At a limo service
    (C) At a hotel
    (D) At a wedding hall

51. Why is Micron Technologies calling?

    (A) To book a wedding
    (B) To reserve rooms for next week
    (C) To ask about a car service
    (D) To complain about poor service

52. What will the man probably do next?

    (A) Contact a car company
    (B) Call Micron Technologies back
    (C) Reschedule a wedding
    (D) Clean a hotel room

53. What type of business do the speakers probably work in?

    (A) A restaurant
    (B) A hotel
    (C) A newspaper
    (D) A travel agency

54. According to the woman, what did the critic say?

    (A) He is friends with the chef.
    (B) The menu was innovative.
    (C) The service was fantastic.
    (D) The food was ordinary.

55. What does one of the men say he will do?

    (A) Close down the business
    (B) Write something on the wall
    (C) Think of new menu items
    (D) Post the article

56. Where does the conversation probably take place?
    (A) At a university
    (B) At a large hospital
    (C) At a clinic
    (D) At an exam center

57. What does the man propose that the woman do?
    (A) Come back tomorrow
    (B) Go to a different institution
    (C) Decide which tests she wants
    (D) Take medicine regularly

58. What will the man probably do next?
    (A) Prepare a document
    (B) See another patient
    (C) Call the general hospital
    (D) Conduct a specialized test

59. What does the man mention about the snowstorm?
    (A) It covered the bakery in snow.
    (B) The bakery is not doing very well.
    (C) The price of strawberries nearly doubled.
    (D) The price of strawberry pies has gone up.

60. What does the woman imply?
    (A) They may need to close down the bakery.
    (B) They should apply cost-cutting measures.
    (C) The price of strawberries is going to continue to rise.
    (D) They have already started losing customers.

61. What does the man say he will do tonight?
    (A) Call a few customers
    (B) Cut down on the number of ingredients
    (C) Buy more strawberries
    (D) Review financial records

62. What are the speakers trying to do?
    (A) Organize a group lunch
    (B) Choose between soda and juice
    (C) Prepare for a presentation
    (D) Reserve a meeting room

63. What does the woman imply when she says, "I'm way ahead of you"?
    (A) She already took care of it.
    (B) She is in front of the man.
    (C) She is almost done.
    (D) She will win the race.

64. What will the woman do next?
    (A) Distribute copies of the presentation
    (B) Order snacks and drinks
    (C) Give a presentation
    (D) Help the man with the projector

Program	
Performer	Time
Henry	1:00 ~ 1:30
Melissa	1:40 ~ 2:10
Martha	2:20 ~ 2:50
Michael	3:00 ~ 3:30

Type	Office Furniture Type	Price
A	Standard office chair	$100
B	Standard office desk with drawers	$575
C	Large, executive-style desk with drawers	$720
D	Large, president-style office chair	$350

65. Look at the graphic. Who will be performing right before Michael?

(A) Henry
(B) Melissa
(C) Martha
(D) Nobody

66. What kind of performance will Martha do?

(A) Dancing
(B) Singing
(C) Musical instrument
(D) Monologue

67. Why did the program change?

(A) The show has been postponed.
(B) Martha still needs to practice her piece.
(C) Melissa is sick.
(D) Martha will go over the allotted time.

68. What does the department head want?

(A) A stapler
(B) A desk
(C) A new job
(D) A comfortable chair

69. What did the man last order from the catalog?

(A) Staples
(B) Printer paper
(C) An office desk
(D) Staplers

70. Look at the graphic. What item will the woman probably order?

(A) A
(B) B
(C) C
(D) D

PART 4

Directions: You will hear some talks given by a single speaker. You will be asked to answer three questions about what the speaker says in each talk. Select the best response to each question and mark the letter (A), (B), (C), or (D) on your answer sheet. The talks will not be printed in your test book and will be spoken only one time.

71. Where is the announcement being made?
    (A) At a stadium
    (B) At a restaurant
    (C) At a university library
    (D) At a museum

72. What does the speaker ask the listeners to do?
    (A) Be careful when touching the sculptures
    (B) Not eat but feel free to drink anywhere
    (C) Be at the appointed place on time
    (D) Go directly home after viewing the exhibits

73. When must the listeners leave the building?
    (A) 12:00 P.M.
    (B) 3:00 P.M.
    (C) 4:00 P.M.
    (D) 8:00 P.M.

74. Where is the announcement being made?
    (A) On a local bus
    (B) At a monorail station
    (C) At a hotel
    (D) On a monorail train

75. Why was the announcement made?
    (A) The train will stop and wait.
    (B) The train will head back.
    (C) The train will continue on to the hotel.
    (D) The train needs to be repaired.

76. According to the speaker, what can listeners do?
    (A) Wait two hours on the train
    (B) Walk back to the monorail station
    (C) Help the workers repair the track
    (D) Take a bus or taxi to the hotel

77. Who is James Cotton?
    (A) A pastor
    (B) A cotton farmer
    (C) A therapist
    (D) A magazine editor

78. What happened to James Cotton last month?
    (A) He won an award.
    (B) He was featured in a magazine.
    (C) He opened the Cottonwood Clinic.
    (D) He was out of town.

79. How can patients get a discount?
    (A) By calling next Monday
    (B) By presenting a coupon
    (C) By bringing a copy of a book
    (D) By making an appointment this week

80. Where can this morning's recital be heard?
    (A) In the auditorium
    (B) On the radio
    (C) In Japan
    (D) At Carnegie Hall

81. What does the speaker say about Dimitry Olanov?
    (A) He lives in Russia.
    (B) He does not perform outside Canada.
    (C) He does not play a musical instrument.
    (D) He won only one competition.

82. What will Dimitry Olanov most likely do this morning?
    (A) Talk about his childhood
    (B) Travel to Canada
    (C) Discuss his love for Vivaldi
    (D) Play a musical instrument

Go on to the next page

83. Who most likely are the listeners?

    (A) Clients
    (B) Consultants
    (C) Salespeople
    (D) Children

84. Why does the speaker say, "we could not have achieved this level of success without each and every one of you"?

    (A) She wants to achieve success.
    (B) She has a new project for the team.
    (C) She wants to praise the team members.
    (D) She is ready for a vacation.

85. What will the listeners do in October?

    (A) Go on vacation
    (B) Finish up the project
    (C) Lower costs
    (D) Start on a new project

86. What is the speaker mainly talking about?

    (A) A subway station
    (B) A boutique law firm
    (C) An office relocation
    (D) A prestigious building

87. What is the merit of the change?

    (A) Smaller space
    (B) More publicity
    (C) Increased rent
    (D) Parking

88. What does the speaker say about the Conway Center?

    (A) It is on top of a train station.
    (B) It is next to a shopping mall.
    (C) It is the tallest building in the city.
    (D) It is on the other side of town.

89. What is the report mainly about?

    (A) A new construction project
    (B) A business merger
    (C) An innovative software product
    (D) Social media platforms

90. What can be inferred about GenuTech's future plans?

    (A) It will focus more on online marketing.
    (B) It will seek to merge with Veriline.
    (C) It will market only in the United States.
    (D) It will hire someone new as its first CEO.

91. What does the speaker suggest about the reason behind GenuTech's formation?

    (A) To increase sales revenues
    (B) To deal with a market competitor
    (C) To streamline costs
    (D) To come up with global marketing strategies

Time	Music
0:00	BGM 1
2:12	BGM 2
5:25	BGM 3
5:50	BGM 4
6:41	BGM 3
7:01	BGM 1

92. Why does the speaker say, "I need to make one change, though"?

    (A) He wants to revise the chart.
    (B) He has to change his background.
    (C) He needs change for the vending machine.
    (D) He wants to make a new song.

93. What does the speaker expect the listener to do?

    (A) Pay him $100
    (B) Compose background music
    (C) Complete the task by Thursday
    (D) Help him shoot a video

94. Look at the graphic. What can you tell about the speaker's request?

    (A) BGM 4 should be the opening music.
    (B) BGM 2 comes after BGM 4.
    (C) BGM 2 should be played in two spots.
    (D) Background music should be inserted 5 times.

	Monday	Tuesday
8:00 A.M.~10:00 A.M.	Italian Cuisine	Singing in Italian
12:00 P.M.~2:00 P.M.	Italian 101	Italian Opera
2:00 P.M.~4:00 P.M.	Italian Opera	Italian 301
3:30 P.M.~5:30 P.M.	Italian 201	Italian 101
7:00 P.M.~9:00 P.M.	Singing in Italian	Italian Cuisine

	Saturday, April 1	Sunday, April 2	Monday, April 3
Hawaii to Seattle	10:00 P.M.	4:00 P.M.	9:00 A.M.
Hawaii to Los Angeles	10:00 A.M.	11:00 A.M.	5:00 P.M.
Hawaii to Atlanta	3:30 P.M.	3:30 P.M.	3:30 P.M.

95. Who are the listeners?
    (A) Italian teachers
    (B) Foreigners
    (C) Students
    (D) Employees

96. What is mentioned about the classes?
    (A) New students can take up to two classes.
    (B) Students may take Italian 201 and Italian 301 simultaneously.
    (C) The first day of classes is on Saturday.
    (D) No more than ten students are allowed in one class.

97. Look at the graphic. Which of the following combinations is possible for a new student?
    (A) Italian 101 (Mon), Singing in Italian (Mon), and Italian Cuisine (Tues)
    (B) Italian 101 (Mon) and Italian 301 (Tues)
    (C) Italian 101 (Mon) and Italian 201 (Tues)
    (D) Italian Cuisine (Mon) and Italian 101 (Tues)

98. Why did Megan make a phone call?
    (A) To say she is going to be leaving early
    (B) To say she has lost some luggage
    (C) To report that her flight schedule got delayed
    (D) To say she will be traveling next to Boston

99. What does Megan say about her schedule?
    (A) She was originally scheduled to leave today.
    (B) She is transferring in Hawaii.
    (C) Her final destination is Seattle.
    (D) She can depart from Hawaii tomorrow if she wants to.

100. Look at the graphic. Which day will Megan go home?
    (A) Saturday
    (B) Sunday
    (C) Monday
    (D) Tuesday

Test

파트별 점수 분석(맞은 숫자)

PART 1	
PART 2	
PART 3	
PART 4	
총 맞은 갯수	

정답 및 스크립트: 180p

04

LISTENING TEST

In the Listening test, you will be asked to demonstrate how well you understand spoken English. The entire Listening test will last approximately 45 minutes. There are four parts, and directions are given for each part. You must mark your answers on the separate answer sheet.
Do not write your answers in your test book.

PART 1

Directions: For each question in this part, you will hear four statements about a picture in your test book. When you hear the statements, you must select the one statement that best describes what you see in the picture. Then find the number of the question on your answer sheet and mark your answer. The statements will not be printed in your test book and will be spoken only one time.

Sample Answer
Ⓐ ● Ⓒ Ⓓ

Statement (B), "They're shaking hands," is the best description of the picture, so you should select answer (B) and mark it on your answer sheet.

1.

2.

3.

4.

5.

6.

PART 2

Directions: You will hear a question or statement and three responses spoken in English. They will not be printed in your test book and will be spoken only one time. Select the best response to the question or statement and mark the letter (A), (B), or (C) on your answer sheet.

7. Mark your answer on your answer sheet.
8. Mark your answer on your answer sheet.
9. Mark your answer on your answer sheet.
10. Mark your answer on your answer sheet.
11. Mark your answer on your answer sheet.
12. Mark your answer on your answer sheet.
13. Mark your answer on your answer sheet.
14. Mark your answer on your answer sheet.
15. Mark your answer on your answer sheet.
16. Mark your answer on your answer sheet.
17. Mark your answer on your answer sheet.
18. Mark your answer on your answer sheet.
19. Mark your answer on your answer sheet.
20. Mark your answer on your answer sheet.
21. Mark your answer on your answer sheet.
22. Mark your answer on your answer sheet.
23. Mark your answer on your answer sheet.
24. Mark your answer on your answer sheet.
25. Mark your answer on your answer sheet.
26. Mark your answer on your answer sheet.
27. Mark your answer on your answer sheet.
28. Mark your answer on your answer sheet.
29. Mark your answer on your answer sheet.
30. Mark your answer on your answer sheet.
31. Mark your answer on your answer sheet.

PART 3

Directions: You will hear some conversations between two or more people. You will be asked to answer three questions about what the speakers say in each conversation. Select the best response to each question and mark the letter (A), (B), (C), or (D) on your answer sheet. The conversations will not be printed in your test book and will be spoken only one time.

32. Why did the woman call the man?
    (A) To get help fixing a problem
    (B) To replace a device with a new one
    (C) To send him an urgent document
    (D) To connect the monitor properly

33. According to the woman, what did she do in the morning?
    (A) Turned on her computer
    (B) Came in earlier than usual
    (C) Tried connecting her monitor again
    (D) Printed the weekly report from her computer

34. What will the man probably do next?
    (A) Submit the report for Stella
    (B) Meet Stella in her office
    (C) Bring his computer to the 2nd floor
    (D) Try plugging the computer into another outlet

35. Why does the woman ask the man for help?
    (A) A coworker is not feeling well.
    (B) She is very sick.
    (C) She is out of town this afternoon.
    (D) She will take some time off.

36. What does the man need?
    (A) A key to a truck
    (B) A telephone number
    (C) A director's contact information
    (D) Directions to a store

37. What does the woman remind the man to do?
    (A) Get a signature
    (B) Notify his manager
    (C) Become a member
    (D) Sign the contract

38. Why will the man visit the woman's house?
    (A) To verify her name and address
    (B) To reschedule an appointment
    (C) To improve the network speed
    (D) To sell a telecommunication device

39. Why does the man ask the woman's name?
    (A) He is trying to be polite.
    (B) Some information is not accurate.
    (C) He'll write her a letter afterwards.
    (D) He wants to record the woman's voice.

40. What time does the woman want the upgrade to be finished by?
    (A) By 2:00 P.M.
    (B) By 2:20 P.M.
    (C) By 2:30 P.M.
    (D) By 3:00 P.M.

41. Where are the speakers working?
    (A) At an advertising agency
    (B) At a law firm
    (C) At an architectural company
    (D) At a design school

42. What does the woman mean when she says, "I really can't say"?
    (A) She is not allowed to reveal certain information.
    (B) She should cancel the appointment.
    (C) She cannot make a commitment yet.
    (D) She has to revise some mistakes.

43. What does the man propose?
    (A) Making an itinerary
    (B) Preparing a negotiation
    (C) Delaying a meeting
    (D) Reviewing the project together

Go on to the next page

44. What problem are the speakers mainly discussing?
    (A) They must launch a Web site in a hurry.
    (B) There are not as many participants as they expected.
    (C) They have make a change in a plan.
    (D) The president won't be able to deliver a speech.

45. Why does the man say, "it was worth a try"?
    (A) He is comforting the woman.
    (B) He doesn't want to take the risk.
    (C) He knew that Mr. Dice would turn them down.
    (D) He regrets he had to meet the speaker in person.

46. What does the woman say she will do?
    (A) Send text messages
    (B) Update a Web page
    (C) Contact the president
    (D) Convince Mr. Dice to attend the event

47. Who most likely is the woman?
    (A) A pharmacist
    (B) An optician
    (C) A receptionist
    (D) An appraiser

48. When is the man supposed to come?
    (A) Wednesday morning
    (B) Wednesday evening
    (C) Thursday morning
    (D) Thursday evening

49. What is suggested about the clinic?
    (A) Dr. Jenkins is the only doctor working there.
    (B) This is the first time Mr. Ortega has contacted it.
    (C) It is open from 10 A.M. to 8 P.M. on weekends.
    (D) It keeps some patients' medical records.

50. Who most likely are Chris and Nancy?
    (A) Apartment managers
    (B) Interior designers
    (C) Realtors
    (D) Potential buyers

51. What are Chris and Nancy concerned about?
    (A) The placement of smoke detectors
    (B) The size of a property
    (C) The expense of renovation
    (D) The range of interior design companies

52. What is mentioned about the owner?
    (A) She owns several stores.
    (B) She'll start a new business.
    (C) She can recommend qualified workers.
    (D) She wants to change the interior.

53. What is the woman unable to do?
    (A) Log on to her computer
    (B) Organize a workshop
    (C) Print a document
    (D) Create a password

54. According to the man, what happened yesterday?
    (A) The power went out.
    (B) Some servers were changed.
    (C) Some equipment was broken.
    (D) Computers were installed.

55. What does the man say he will do?
    (A) Restart a computer
    (B) Install new software
    (C) Call a coworker
    (D) Put in a help request

56. What are the speakers mainly talking about?
    (A) The cost of living
    (B) Overseas branches
    (C) An online business
    (D) A proposed budget

57. What does the man say about the Rome expenses?
    (A) They have been underestimated.
    (B) They are the same as last year's.
    (C) The quotes look good.
    (D) The living costs were not in the budget.

58. What does the woman say she will do?
    (A) Spend less money
    (B) Estimate a price
    (C) Use last year's records
    (D) Update some information

59. Why is the woman calling the man?
    (A) To report an equipment malfunction
    (B) To check a device
    (C) To request personal information
    (D) To set up a meeting

60. What does the woman imply when she says, "I'm interviewing someone here in 10 minutes"?
    (A) She needs help urgently.
    (B) She does not want to be interrupted.
    (C) She is not satisfied with an assignment.
    (D) She will not attend another meeting.

61. What does the woman say is unique about the interview?
    (A) It will be recorded.
    (B) It will be filmed.
    (C) It will be conducted face-to-face.
    (D) It will last for more than an hour.

Departure	Gate	Time	Status
Melbourne	A8	15:30	Delayed
Sydney	B14	15:45	On time
Perth	A9	16:00	Canceled
Brisbane	C10	17:00	On time

62. Where is the conversation taking place?
    (A) At a bus terminal
    (B) At an airport
    (C) At a business conference
    (D) At a train station

63. Why isn't the man staying for the entire conference?
    (A) He has a scheduling conflict.
    (B) He is about to go on holiday.
    (C) He has a presentation.
    (D) He could not find a later flight.

64. Look at the graphic. What city are the speakers going to?
    (A) Melbourne
    (B) Sydney
    (C) Perth
    (D) Brisbane

	stairs		restroom
Room 301 (Sales department)	Room 302		Room 303
stairs			
		elevators	
Room 304	copy room	Room 305	staff lounge

From	Subject
Brian Swann	Budget Report
Yianni Ellenikiotis	Conference Agenda
Helen Yang	ATTACHED: Quarterly Sales figures
Brittany Seymour	DELAYED: Management workshop

65. Look at the graphic. Which room are the speakers moving into on Monday?
    (A) Room 302
    (B) Room 303
    (C) Room 304
    (D) Room 305

66. According to the woman, what would her colleagues say about their new room?
    (A) They're glad to take the biggest room.
    (B) They are pleased to be situated near the stairs.
    (C) They're not happy to be located near the staff lounge.
    (D) They enjoy the advantages of sound proof insulation.

67. Why does the man have to leave early today?
    (A) He has to meet a client at two o'clock.
    (B) He has an appointment in the afternoon.
    (C) He has to pack up his belongings in advance.
    (D) He has to pick up something in the staff lounge.

68. Why is the man unable to access his e-mail?
    (A) He's using an incorrect password.
    (B) His Internet connection isn't available.
    (C) He forgot to update some software.
    (D) His computer is malfunctioning.

69. Look at the graphic. Who sent the e-mail the speakers are referring to?
    (A) Brian Swann
    (B) Yianni Ellenikiotis
    (C) Helen Yang
    (D) Brittany Seymour

70. What does the man ask the woman to do?
    (A) Call the technician
    (B) Present the quarterly sales figures
    (C) Print out a document
    (D) Arrange a meeting this afternoon

PART 4

Directions: You will hear some talks given by a single speaker. You will be asked to answer three questions about what the speaker says in each talk. Select the best response to each question and mark the letter (A), (B), (C), or (D) on your answer sheet. The talks will not be printed in your test book and will be spoken only one time.

71. What is the purpose of the talk?
    (A) To ask for donations
    (B) To publicize the museum
    (C) To discuss modern art
    (D) To introduce an exhibit

72. What will the speaker distribute?
    (A) Entrance tickets
    (B) A brochure
    (C) A map of the museum
    (D) An audio player

73. According to the speaker, what will begin at two o'clock?
    (A) An auction
    (B) A concert
    (C) A talk
    (D) A reception

74. Why did the speaker leave a message?
    (A) To talk about a problem with an order
    (B) To find out when to make a delivery
    (C) To get more information about furniture
    (D) To ask for help choosing a new chair

75. When does the speaker say he can deliver similar chairs?
    (A) In 4 weeks
    (B) Tomorrow
    (C) This evening
    (D) In two days

76. What does the speaker say he will do today?
    (A) Work at the store all day long
    (B) Record some messages
    (C) Send the package
    (D) Deliver items

77. How long has the business been operating?
    (A) For twelve years
    (B) For two decades
    (C) For a decade
    (D) For fifteen years

78. What type of business is being advertised?
    (A) An airline
    (B) A bus company
    (C) A travel agency
    (D) A bookstore

79. What special offer is the business making now?
    (A) Free calling cards
    (B) Reduced rates on certain flights
    (C) Package tours to Asia and other countries in Europe
    (D) Free accommodation in Venice and Florence

80. What does the speaker say will happen at the end of the month?
    (A) A new City Hall will be built.
    (B) Traffic congestion will take place.
    (C) Construction on new bus lanes will commence.
    (D) A hotel association will select a new president.

81. Who is Tom Kenny?
    (A) A local politician
    (B) A news reporter
    (C) A bus driver
    (D) A city spokesperson

82. What will listeners probably hear next?
    (A) A sports game
    (B) A local news report
    (C) A sponsor's message
    (D) A weather forecast

Go on to the next page

83. What type of business does the speaker work for?
    (A) A recruiting agency
    (B) A computer retailer
    (C) An office equipment manufacturer
    (D) An education center

84. Why does the speaker say, "the copier is in room 305"?
    (A) He was asked if a copier is available.
    (B) The attendees will learn how to make copies today.
    (C) The teaching assistants need to copy the roll book.
    (D) Some people should go to another room to prepare some document.

85. What does the speaker ask the listeners to do?
    (A) Sign the contract
    (B) Introduce themselves
    (C) Team up with their colleagues
    (D) Submit their applications in advance

86. What does the speaker mainly talk about?
    (A) Building a welfare center
    (B) Drawing more volunteers
    (C) Organizing a fundraising event
    (D) Becoming a teacher

87. What problem does the welfare center have?
    (A) There are not many schools in the area.
    (B) It cannot afford free meals for the beneficiaries.
    (C) The center hasn't launched any education programs yet.
    (D) They don't have enough money for a plan.

88. What are the listeners asked to do?
    (A) Contact the schools in the area
    (B) Look for a suitable contractor
    (C) Attract more young teens
    (D) Ask for their parents' support

89. What is the speaker doing for Ms. Shirley?
    (A) Finding a place to live
    (B) Reserving a hotel room
    (C) Buying an office building
    (D) Renovating an interior design

90. What does the speaker imply when she says, "But it's not a problem"?
    (A) She wants to recommend a moving company.
    (B) She asks for a specific reason.
    (C) She feels disappointed.
    (D) She thinks that she can resolve the issue.

91. What does the speaker ask Ms. Shirley to do?
    (A) Arrange an appointment
    (B) Sign the contract
    (C) Choose the color of the wallpaper
    (D) Update contact information

92. Why is the speaker calling?
    (A) To schedule a meeting
    (B) To confirm the listeners' presence at a conference
    (C) To arrange suitable travel date
    (D) To reschedule a conference call

93. What did Mr. Reece's secretary tell Mr. Stanton?
    (A) His availability is uncertain.
    (B) His interest is negligible.
    (C) His attendance is mandatory.
    (D) His schedule is canceled.

94. What does the speaker say he will do?
    (A) Mail the proposed agenda
    (B) Arrange a flight
    (C) Send information electronically
    (D) Check the time difference

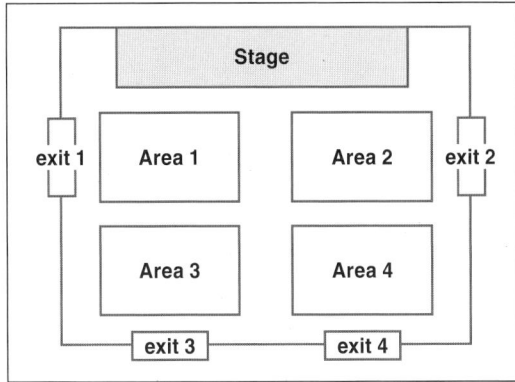

Survey Results	
Design	40%
Color Scheme	25%
Durability	15%
Material	20%

95. Who most likely are the listeners?
(A) Photographers
(B) Performers
(C) Ushers
(D) Audience members

96. Look at the graphic. What section does the speaker want the listeners to sit in?
(A) Area 1
(B) Area 2
(C) Area 3
(D) Area 4

97. What are listeners asked to do when the show ends?
(A) Have some refreshments
(B) Sign autographs
(C) Revise a magazine
(D) Attend a photo shoot

98. According to the speaker, why did the company conduct the survey?
(A) To satisfy consumers
(B) To release the running shoes
(C) To cut operating expenses
(D) To correct a questionnaire

99. Look at the graphic. Which survey result does the speaker want to address now?
(A) Design
(B) Color Scheme
(C) Durability
(D) Material

100. What does the speaker ask the listeners to do?
(A) Conduct safety inspections
(B) Give some feedback
(C) Mention some potential employees
(D) Contact the product development team

Test

파트별 점수 분석(맞은 숫자)

PART 1	
PART 2	
PART 3	
PART 4	
총 맞은 갯수	

정답 및 스크립트: 187p

05

LISTENING TEST

In the Listening test, you will be asked to demonstrate how well you understand spoken English. The entire Listening test will last approximately 45 minutes. There are four parts, and directions are given for each part. You must mark your answers on the separate answer sheet.
Do not write your answers in your test book.

PART 1

Directions: For each question in this part, you will hear four statements about a picture in your test book. When you hear the statements, you must select the one statement that best describes what you see in the picture. Then find the number of the question on your answer sheet and mark your answer. The statements will not be printed in your test book and will be spoken only one time.

Sample Answer
Ⓐ ● Ⓒ Ⓓ

Statement (B), "They're shaking hands," is the best description of the picture, so you should select answer (B) and mark it on your answer sheet.

1.

2.

3.

4.

5.

6.

PART 2

Directions: You will hear a question or statement and three responses spoken in English. They will not be printed in your test book and will be spoken only one time. Select the best response to the question or statement and mark the letter (A), (B), or (C) on your answer sheet.

7. Mark your answer on your answer sheet.
8. Mark your answer on your answer sheet.
9. Mark your answer on your answer sheet.
10. Mark your answer on your answer sheet.
11. Mark your answer on your answer sheet.
12. Mark your answer on your answer sheet.
13. Mark your answer on your answer sheet.
14. Mark your answer on your answer sheet.
15. Mark your answer on your answer sheet.
16. Mark your answer on your answer sheet.
17. Mark your answer on your answer sheet.
18. Mark your answer on your answer sheet.
19. Mark your answer on your answer sheet.
20. Mark your answer on your answer sheet.
21. Mark your answer on your answer sheet.
22. Mark your answer on your answer sheet.
23. Mark your answer on your answer sheet.
24. Mark your answer on your answer sheet.
25. Mark your answer on your answer sheet.
26. Mark your answer on your answer sheet.
27. Mark your answer on your answer sheet.
28. Mark your answer on your answer sheet.
29. Mark your answer on your answer sheet.
30. Mark your answer on your answer sheet.
31. Mark your answer on your answer sheet.

PART 3

Directions: You will hear some conversations between two or more people. You will be asked to answer three questions about what the speakers say in each conversation. Select the best response to each question and mark the letter (A), (B), (C), or (D) on your answer sheet. The conversations will not be printed in your test book and will be spoken only one time.

32. Why does the man choose to shop at the store?
    (A) It is conveniently located.
    (B) The staff is very kind.
    (C) He saw an online advertisement.
    (D) One of his colleagues recommended the store.

33. What does the woman ask about?
    (A) An identification card
    (B) A receipt
    (C) A discount coupon
    (D) An advertisement flyer

34. Why does the man say he will go home?
    (A) He wants to come with his parents.
    (B) He has to answer the phone.
    (C) He left something behind.
    (D) He doesn't want to buy this product.

35. Where is the conversation most likely taking place?
    (A) At a coffee shop
    (B) At an office
    (C) At a clothing factory
    (D) At a dry cleaner's

36. What is the woman doing on Friday?
    (A) Meeting a client
    (B) Interviewing for a job
    (C) Going on a vacation
    (D) Visiting relatives

37. What does the man offer to do?
    (A) Exchange a defective product
    (B) Cancel a reservation
    (C) Offer an express service
    (D) Place a special order

38. Why will the man visit the woman's office?
    (A) To set up appliances
    (B) To make a repair
    (C) To deliver a speech
    (D) To get a refund

39. What does the woman say she will do?
    (A) Cancel an appointment
    (B) Meet with a client
    (C) Talk to a security officer
    (D) Provide a receipt

40. What does the woman ask the man to leave with the security guard?
    (A) An estimate
    (B) A manual
    (C) An invoice
    (D) An agreement

41. What is the woman shopping for?
    (A) Stationery
    (B) Wrapping paper
    (C) Children's book
    (D) Paint

42. What does Christopher say about the items?
    (A) They're sold out.
    (B) They're offered at a discounted price.
    (C) They've already been delivered.
    (D) They're on a different floor.

43. What additional service does Christopher mention?
    (A) Express delivery
    (B) Free packaging
    (C) A free estimate
    (D) On-site repair

Go on to the next page

44. What are the speakers organizing?

    (A) A job interview
    (B) A music concert
    (C) A conference
    (D) A wedding party

45. What problem does the woman mention?

    (A) An event has been delayed.
    (B) A flight was canceled.
    (C) Hotels are all booked up.
    (D) A speaker has canceled.

46. What most likely will the man do next?

    (A) Send an invitation card
    (B) Make a phone call
    (C) Make a reservation
    (D) Prepare a meeting

47. Where do the speakers most likely work?

    (A) At a fitness center
    (B) At a police station
    (C) At a department store
    (D) At a heavy equipment facility

48. What does the man imply when he says, "I can't do it alone"?

    (A) He is asking for a pay increase.
    (B) He wants to know the exact number of members.
    (C) He thinks that a task is impossible.
    (D) He is satisfied with his current position.

49. What does the woman offer to do?

    (A) Change the schedule
    (B) Move the equipment
    (C) Clean up the facility
    (D) Recruit more members

50. What are the speakers discussing?

    (A) Selecting new computer system
    (B) Checking maintenance information
    (C) Starting a business
    (D) Finishing a report

51. Why was the man unable to complete a task?

    (A) Sales revenue has decreased.
    (B) A system was not working properly.
    (C) A colleague was out of town.
    (D) A meeting was canceled.

52. What does the woman say she will do?

    (A) Prepare for a meeting
    (B) Change a reservation
    (C) Contact the maintenance department
    (D) Email a report

53. What does the man say he will do next month?

    (A) Participate in a medical forum
    (B) Go away on business
    (C) Move to a different city
    (D) Finish a medical course

54. According to the conversation, what did Jennifer do in the morning?

    (A) She rescheduled an appointment.
    (B) She prescribed some medicine.
    (C) She printed some documents.
    (D) She treated a patient.

55. What does Jennifer ask the man to do?

    (A) Make a payment
    (B) Wait for a while
    (C) Sign a form
    (D) Call a doctor's office

56. Why is the man calling?
    (A) He wants to buy another product.
    (B) His order has not yet been delivered.
    (C) He needs to know the store's Web site address.
    (D) He was charged twice for a purchase.

57. What does the woman explain about?
    (A) A technical issue
    (B) A renovation project
    (C) An inventory shortage
    (D) A credit card expiration date

58. What does the woman ask the man to do?
    (A) Return a product
    (B) Respond to a survey
    (C) Visit a Web site
    (D) Keep a receipt

59. Where most likely is the woman?
    (A) At a building entrance
    (B) In a meeting room
    (C) At an airport
    (D) In an elevator

60. What does the man ask for?
    (A) A department name
    (B) An employee number
    (C) A password
    (D) A telephone number

61. Why does the man say, "It's against the company policy"?
    (A) To postpone a meeting
    (B) To refuse a request
    (C) To ask for a help
    (D) To make up for a mistake

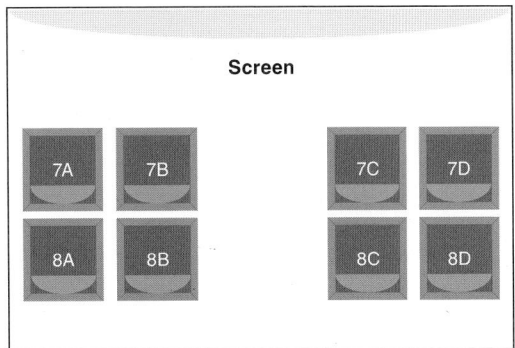

62. What is the purpose of the conversation?
    (A) To explain refund regulations
    (B) To introduce a new film
    (C) To offer a special discount
    (D) To resolve a problem

63. Look at the graphic. What seat was the woman originally assigned to?
    (A) 7A
    (B) 7B
    (C) 8A
    (D) 8B

64. What does the woman ask the man to do?
    (A) Check the time when the movie starts
    (B) Choose another movie
    (C) Request a discount coupon
    (D) Change the seat

Go on to the next page

Schedule	
Stage 1	Redesign lobby
Stage 2	Install furniture, flooring, lighting
Stage 3	Revamp fitness center
Stage 4	Paint outside

65. What most likely is the man's profession?

    (A) Engineer
    (B) Construction manager
    (C) Real estate agent
    (D) Salesperson

66. Look at the graphic. What stage of the renovation will begin next week?

    (A) Stage 1
    (B) Stage 2
    (C) Stage 3
    (D) Stage 4

67. What does the woman ask the man to send?

    (A) An estimated price
    (B) Some photos
    (C) A schedule
    (D) A hotel address

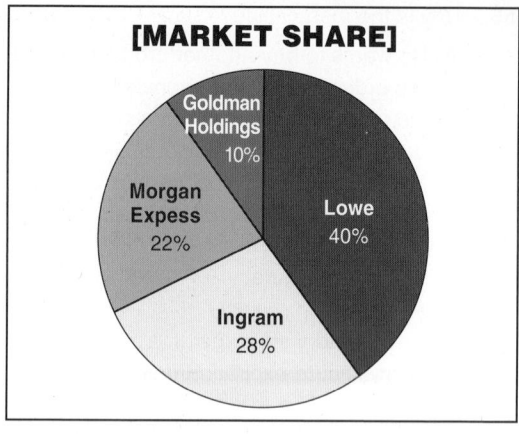

68. What are the speakers mainly discussing?

    (A) An annual plan
    (B) Unemployment rates
    (C) A business acquisition
    (D) A budget report

69. Look at the graphic. Where do the speakers work?

    (A) Lowe
    (B) Ingram
    (C) Morgan Express
    (D) Goldman Holdings

70. Why does the man say he is not convinced?

    (A) He didn't read the report.
    (B) Some information is inaccurate.
    (C) The man is not good at analyzing data.
    (D) A company's profits have reduced recently.

PART 4

Directions: You will hear some talks given by a single speaker. You will be asked to answer three questions about what the speaker says in each talk. Select the best response to each question and mark the letter (A), (B), (C), or (D) on your answer sheet. The talks will not be printed in your test book and will be spoken only one time.

71. What service is being advertised?
    (A) Home delivery
    (B) A recycling program
    (C) Product repair
    (D) An education course

72. How can listeners get a discount?
    (A) By making a donation
    (B) By taking a class
    (C) By purchasing a certain item
    (D) By recommending a company

73. What does the speaker say is available on a Web site?
    (A) A product line
    (B) Information on a company
    (C) A promotional video
    (D) A list of locations

74. Where is the announcement probably being made?
    (A) At an airport
    (B) At a bus station
    (C) At a taxi stand
    (D) At a ticket office

75. What does the speaker ask listeners to do?
    (A) Meet with a representative
    (B) Cancel a ticket
    (C) Visit the company's Web site
    (D) Book a hotel

76. According to the speaker, what will be offered?
    (A) A free dinner
    (B) Free refreshments
    (C) An itinerary
    (D) Maps

77. What is the purpose of the message?
    (A) To set up a meeting
    (B) To receive an order
    (C) To get an approval
    (D) To make a contract

78. What does the speaker imply when she says, "we have only three months left before the opening of the new branch"?
    (A) She should find a place to conduct an interview.
    (B) She wants the listener to visit a branch.
    (C) A branch office should be opened soon.
    (D) A decision should be made as soon as possible.

79. What most likely will the speaker do next?
    (A) Make a list of candidates
    (B) Email some documents
    (C) Call a branch office
    (D) Fill out an application

80. Where does the speaker work?
    (A) At a museum
    (B) At a hotel
    (C) At a store
    (D) At a coffee shop

81. What will the listeners be doing today?
    (A) Making a flyer
    (B) Going on a tour
    (C) Distributing leaflets
    (D) Taking pictures

82. What has the speaker done for the listeners?
    (A) Made a reservation for a restaurant
    (B) Ordered gifts
    (C) Provided complimentary tickets
    (D) Circled places on a map

Go on to the next page

83. What kind of business does the speaker work for?
    (A) An advertising agency
    (B) A furniture store
    (C) A library
    (D) A financial institution

84. What is the speaker announcing?
    (A) An award winner
    (B) A resignation
    (C) A promotion
    (D) A retirement

85. What does the speaker say about Emmy Kunis's work?
    (A) It made an agency increase in its value.
    (B) It led to changes in a company's regulations.
    (C) It took advantage of the latest technology.
    (D) It helped its client boost profits.

86. What is the main topic of the meeting?
    (A) A new department
    (B) A user manual
    (C) Survey results
    (D) Product defects

87. What feature of the product does the speaker mention?
    (A) An energy-saving function
    (B) A digital display
    (C) Its durability
    (D) A removable rack

88. What does the speaker imply when she says, "So the related department is now editing this"?
    (A) The manual can only be viewed online.
    (B) The manual is available in multiple languages.
    (C) The manual should be shortened.
    (D) Customers should read it thoroughly.

89. What is the talk mainly about?
    (A) Attracting foreign companies
    (B) Opening an art gallery
    (C) Building a park
    (D) Solving traffic congestion

90. What problem does the speaker mention?
    (A) A delayed schedule
    (B) A transportation system
    (C) Lack of funds
    (D) A manpower shortage

91. What are the listeners asked to do?
    (A) Hold a meeting
    (B) Carry out a survey
    (C) Come up with a list of local businesses
    (D) Purchase items

92. What type of business does the speaker work for?
    (A) A law firm
    (B) A hospital
    (C) An employment agency
    (D) A manufacturer

93. What does the speaker imply when he says, "this process could take some time"?
    (A) He wants the listeners to be patient.
    (B) He points out that the office is very busy.
    (C) He says that the scheduled date could be canceled.
    (D) He suggests that the listeners be ready anytime.

94. What does the speaker ask the listeners to do?
    (A) Submit their application
    (B) Receive a letter of recommendation
    (C) Make a copy of their identification
    (D) Fill out some documents

- Order form -

Item	Quantity
Chocolate bar	100
Milk in bottles	200
Cups	300
Cereal flakes	250

95. Look at the graphic. Which quantity of the order form will be changed?

    (A) 100
    (B) 200
    (C) 300
    (D) 250

96. What is the speaker doing next week?

    (A) She is going on a vacation.
    (B) She is moving to a different country.
    (C) She is remodeling her house.
    (D) She is changing her job.

97. What does the speaker say about John?

    (A) He will be dealing with some accounts.
    (B) He will cancel an order.
    (C) He will print some documents.
    (D) He will introduce a new product.

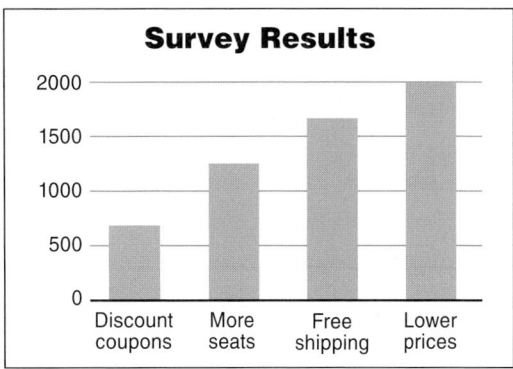

98. Where does the talk take place?

    (A) At a bookstore
    (B) At a factory
    (C) At a hotel
    (D) At the airport

99. Look at the graphic. Which suggestions will the company begin to work on?

    (A) Discount coupons
    (B) More seats
    (C) Free shipping
    (D) Lower prices

100. What will the people receive for completing the survey?

    (A) A complimentary book
    (B) A discount coupon
    (C) Refreshments
    (D) A store gift card

Test

파트별 점수 분석(맞은 숫자)

PART 1	
PART 2	
PART 3	
PART 4	
총 맞은 갯수	

정답 및 스크립트: 194p

06

LISTENING TEST

In the Listening test, you will be asked to demonstrate how well you understand spoken English. The entire Listening test will last approximately 45 minutes. There are four parts, and directions are given for each part. You must mark your answers on the separate answer sheet.
Do not write your answers in your test book.

PART 1

Directions: For each question in this part, you will hear four statements about a picture in your test book. When you hear the statements, you must select the one statement that best describes what you see in the picture. Then find the number of the question on your answer sheet and mark your answer. The statements will not be printed in your test book and will be spoken only one time.

Sample Answer
Ⓐ ● Ⓒ Ⓓ

Statement (B), "They're shaking hands," is the best description of the picture, so you should select answer (B) and mark it on your answer sheet.

1.

2.

3.

4.

5.

6.

Go on to the next page

PART 2

Directions: You will hear a question or statement and three responses spoken in English. They will not be printed in your test book and will be spoken only one time. Select the best response to the question or statement and mark the letter (A), (B), or (C) on your answer sheet.

7. Mark your answer on your answer sheet.
8. Mark your answer on your answer sheet.
9. Mark your answer on your answer sheet.
10. Mark your answer on your answer sheet.
11. Mark your answer on your answer sheet.
12. Mark your answer on your answer sheet.
13. Mark your answer on your answer sheet.
14. Mark your answer on your answer sheet.
15. Mark your answer on your answer sheet.
16. Mark your answer on your answer sheet.
17. Mark your answer on your answer sheet.
18. Mark your answer on your answer sheet.
19. Mark your answer on your answer sheet.
20. Mark your answer on your answer sheet.
21. Mark your answer on your answer sheet.
22. Mark your answer on your answer sheet.
23. Mark your answer on your answer sheet.
24. Mark your answer on your answer sheet.
25. Mark your answer on your answer sheet.
26. Mark your answer on your answer sheet.
27. Mark your answer on your answer sheet.
28. Mark your answer on your answer sheet.
29. Mark your answer on your answer sheet.
30. Mark your answer on your answer sheet.
31. Mark your answer on your answer sheet.

PART 3

Directions: You will hear some conversations between two or more people. You will be asked to answer three questions about what the speakers say in each conversation. Select the best response to each question and mark the letter (A), (B), (C), or (D) on your answer sheet. The conversations will not be printed in your test book and will be spoken only one time.

32. Why is the woman at the shop?
    (A) To buy a mobile phone
    (B) To ask about a device
    (C) To sell a computer
    (D) To charge a battery

33. What is the problem with the computer?
    (A) It turns off by itself.
    (B) It ran out of battery.
    (C) It is not connected to the Internet.
    (D) It was not fully charged.

34. What will the man probably do next?
    (A) Give a full refund
    (B) Replace the battery
    (C) Update the device
    (D) Report the problem to the manufacturer

35. Why is the man calling?
    (A) To ask about a membership card
    (B) To sign up for an exhibition
    (C) To check a ticket reservation
    (D) To inquire about a delivery service

36. What will happen next month?
    (A) A museum exhibition
    (B) A book signing
    (C) An international music festival
    (D) A pottery-making demonstration

37. What additional information does the woman ask for?
    (A) A price estimate
    (B) An e-mail address
    (C) The sizes of some items
    (D) The man's seating number

38. Why is the man calling the woman?
    (A) To return her résumé
    (B) To notify her of an interview
    (C) To ask her to visit him again
    (D) To give details about the job opening

39. Why is the woman unavailable tomorrow?
    (A) She will be traveling.
    (B) She will be working.
    (C) She will be giving a presentation.
    (D) She will be finishing an assignment.

40. What does the man ask the woman to do?
    (A) Submit a résumé
    (B) Write an article
    (C) Read an employee handbook
    (D) Write a novel

41. What are the speakers mainly discussing?
    (A) The details of a booklet
    (B) Bad weather
    (C) Driving to the airport
    (D) Revising a document

42. What is suggested by the speakers?
    (A) The woman revised the marketing report.
    (B) The rain has finally stopped.
    (C) The man has finished the report.
    (D) There will be a meeting at three o'clock.

43. What will the woman probably do next?
    (A) See an executive at the airport
    (B) Correct errors in a paper
    (C) Tell the man an e-mail address
    (D) Book a flight

Go on to the next page

44. What type of event are the speakers attending?

   (A) A professional conference
   (B) An employee orientation
   (C) A book signing
   (D) A staff meeting

45. Why does the man say, "Let's just sit in this row"?

   (A) He thinks they have no choice.
   (B) He wants to encourage the woman to work harder.
   (C) He is disappointed in the presentation.
   (D) He thinks his team is more competent than other teams.

46. What does the man say about the seats?

   (A) They are all occupied.
   (B) They are available near the entrance.
   (C) They are not enough for everyone.
   (D) They are broken.

47. Why will the woman probably be late?

   (A) She is buying a present on the way.
   (B) She is held up by a traffic jam.
   (C) She had a computer malfunction.
   (D) She needs to give a message to Elizabeth.

48. What does the woman recommend?

   (A) Taking a taxi instead
   (B) Going to her office
   (C) Calling her again later
   (D) Getting a message from Elizabeth

49. What does the man imply when he says, "They are for the last part of the event"?

   (A) Jessica doesn't need to prepare the congratulatory message.
   (B) Jessica doesn't need to be at the event from the beginning.
   (C) Jessica doesn't need to tell him the password to her computer.
   (D) Jessica doesn't need to meet Elizabeth at the ceremony.

50. What is suggested about the book?

   (A) It is a used book.
   (B) It is expensive.
   (C) It has a defect.
   (D) It was on sale.

51. What does the man ask the woman to do?

   (A) Switch the item
   (B) Make a copy
   (C) Buy a book
   (D) Give a discount

52. What does the woman ask for?

   (A) A credit card number
   (B) Proof of purchase
   (C) A billing address
   (D) An exchange

53. What has the man recently done?

   (A) Relocated to a new place
   (B) Sent a package
   (C) Had a medical check-up
   (D) Seen a doctor

54. What problem does the woman mention?

   (A) An appointment was delayed.
   (B) A payment was not received.
   (C) An address is incorrect.
   (D) A document has not been signed.

55. What does the woman say she will do?

   (A) Sign the contract
   (B) Update the contact information
   (C) Email a document
   (D) Send something by express mail

56. Where do the women most likely work?

(A) At an electronics store
(B) At a movie production company
(C) At a TV station
(D) At a movie theater

57. What job requirement do the speakers discuss?

(A) Being professionally certified
(B) Using the proper equipment
(C) Having camera operation skills
(D) Handling some urgent tasks

58. What will the man do next?

(A) Show his work sample
(B) Make a video
(C) Meet a director
(D) Buy a laptop

---

59. What will happen next month?

(A) A dedication
(B) A holiday party
(C) A company outing
(D) A retirement celebration

60. What is the man considering?

(A) Whether to use a catering company
(B) Where to hold an event
(C) When to begin the company function
(D) Who should be invited

61. What does the woman imply when she says, "That's a good point"?

(A) She agrees with the man's opinion.
(B) She wants to bring some food.
(C) She'll send an e-mail.
(D) She suggests ordering some food.

Admission Price per Person	
Children under 12	$8
Group of 10 or more	$12
Member	$15
Non-member	$20

62. What type of event are the speakers discussing?

(A) A theater performance
(B) A museum exhibition
(C) A new movie
(D) A live music concert

63. Look at the graphic. What ticket price will the speakers probably pay?

(A) $16
(B) $24
(C) $30
(D) $40

64. What does the woman say she will do?

(A) Leave work early
(B) Purchase the tickets
(C) Pay with a credit card
(D) Visit the theater

Go on to the next page

Parramatta Park	
April 5	Ashifield Consulting
April 12	Burwood Church
April 19	SummerMax Advertising
April 26	Amax Accounting

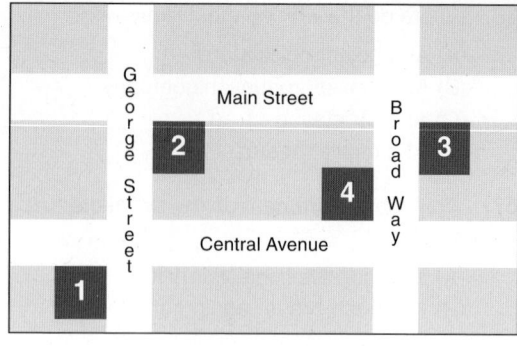

65. Why is the woman calling?
    (A) To cancel the event
    (B) To change the location
    (C) To change the date
    (D) To give an invitation

66. According to the woman, what will her company do in May?
    (A) Relocate to a different city
    (B) Expand a budget
    (C) Enlarge a work area
    (D) Hire additional workers

67. Look at the graphic. When will the woman use the park?
    (A) April 5
    (B) April 12
    (C) April 19
    (D) April 26

68. What do the speakers want to do?
    (A) Plan a party for customers
    (B) Celebrate a company's anniversary
    (C) Express their gratitude
    (D) Send out invitations

69. What does the man suggest doing?
    (A) Making a presentation
    (B) Purchasing a present
    (C) Writing a report
    (D) Giving an award

70. Look at the graphic. Where is the gift shop located?
    (A) 1
    (B) 2
    (C) 3
    (D) 4

PART 4

Directions: You will hear some talks given by a single speaker. You will be asked to answer three questions about what the speaker says in each talk. Select the best response to each question and mark the letter (A), (B), (C), or (D) on your answer sheet. The talks will not be printed in your test book and will be spoken only one time.

71. Where does the speaker work?
    (A) At an electronics store
    (B) At a hardware store
    (C) At a car repair shop
    (D) At a cleaning service

72. What does the speaker say he has done?
    (A) Scheduled an appointment
    (B) Completed a repair
    (C) Replaced a light
    (D) Ordered a part

73. What does the speaker offer?
    (A) A rental car service
    (B) An extended warranty
    (C) A free inspection
    (D) An express delivery

74. What is the speaker mainly discussing?
    (A) A change to project timelines
    (B) Plans to use teleconferencing
    (C) Some expected job opportunities
    (D) Camera installation

75. According to the speaker, what will happen next week?
    (A) Employees will learn new procedures.
    (B) Salespeople will meet with clients.
    (C) Designers will create video materials.
    (D) Technicians will replace old computers.

76. What does the speaker ask the listeners to do?
    (A) Distribute handouts
    (B) Compile sales data
    (C) Set up the equipment
    (D) Refer to the instructions

77. Where is the tour most likely taking place?
    (A) At a nature center
    (B) In a parking area
    (C) At a flower shop
    (D) At an outdoor market

78. Where will the group have lunch?
    (A) At a mountain cabin
    (B) At a waterfall
    (C) At the summit
    (D) In a parking lot

79. What are the listeners asked to do?
    (A) Throw away trash when they return
    (B) Refrain from picking flowers on the trail
    (C) Not interrupt while the speaker is talking
    (D) Take a group photo after the hike

80. Who is this advertisement for?
    (A) Traffic police
    (B) Driving instructors
    (C) Auto mechanics
    (D) New drivers

81. What is being advertised?
    (A) A discount on driving instruction
    (B) A sale on used cars
    (C) Automobile insurance
    (D) A job opening for driving instructors

82. How can the listeners sign up for a service?
    (A) By visiting an office
    (B) By sending for a brochure
    (C) By visiting a Web site
    (D) By making a phone call

Go on to the next page

83. What kind of business does the speaker work for?
    (A) A repair center
    (B) A home appliance company
    (C) A market research firm
    (D) A cleaning company

84. What is the most popular feature of the current model?
    (A) Waterproof motor
    (B) Self-cleaning
    (C) Detachable parts
    (D) High power consumption

85. What does the speaker imply when she says, "strengthen the strengths and make up for the weaknesses"?
    (A) She believes the new model has to be more expensive.
    (B) She doesn't want to give up the advantages of the previous model.
    (C) She regrets the Brown 150 model was designed too poorly.
    (D) She doesn't agree with the customers about their complaints.

86. Why is the speaker calling?
    (A) To receive a message
    (B) To apologize to a customer
    (C) To order some items
    (D) To inquire about a product

87. What problem does the speaker mention?
    (A) Some items are faulty.
    (B) A machine is broken.
    (C) A shipment is late.
    (D) Some items are out of stock.

88. Why does the speaker say, "We can just handle everything"?
    (A) To make up for a mistake
    (B) To purchase the item
    (C) To provide a sample
    (D) To give a special gift

89. What type of business is being discussed?
    (A) A fabric manufacturer
    (B) An ice cream factory
    (C) A local business
    (D) A cooking school

90. What can be inferred about the company?
    (A) It has never operated in this city before.
    (B) Its headquarters moved to another city.
    (C) It is celebrating its 10th anniversary.
    (D) It is expanding a building.

91. What will some customers receive before noon?
    (A) A free sample
    (B) Some coupons
    (C) A promotional brochure
    (D) Complimentary recipes

92. What kind of work needs to be done?
    (A) Electrical maintenance
    (B) Computer system upgrades
    (C) Software installation
    (D) Floor cleaning

93. When will the work begin?
    (A) Tonight
    (B) Tomorrow
    (C) This weekend
    (D) Next week

94. What are some listeners asked to do?
    (A) Hire the technicians
    (B) Use personal electronics
    (C) Attend the meeting in the conference room
    (D) Remove important documents from the computer

Order Form

Item	Item code	Quantity
Ink cartridge	FC505	1
Colored pencils, Set (12 colors)	PW74	3
Stapler	HK250	2
Paper cups	DC303	150

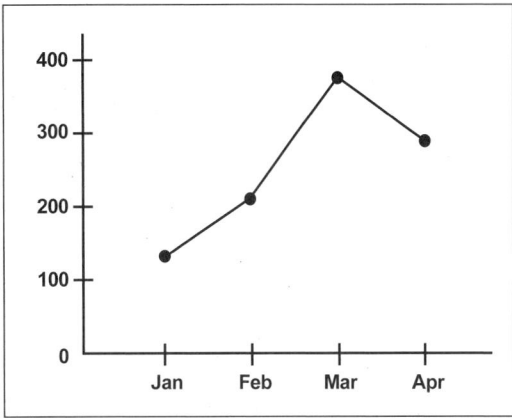

95. Look at the graphic. Which item does the speaker want to be checked?
    (A) FC505
    (B) PW74
    (C) HK250
    (D) DC303

96. What is suggested about Tim Falcon?
    (A) He has ordered from this store before.
    (B) He has a new printer in his office.
    (C) He works for a printing company.
    (D) He works until 9:30.

97. Why would Tim Falcon call back?
    (A) To check the working hours
    (B) To order more stationery
    (C) To receive a new printer
    (D) To confirm an item code

98. Where most likely does the speaker work?
    (A) At an advertising agency
    (B) At a beauty parlor
    (C) At a cosmetics store
    (D) At a supermarket

99. Look at the graphic. When was the discount event held?
    (A) In January
    (B) In February
    (C) In March
    (D) In April

100. What does the business plan to do next quarter?
    (A) Offer a free dyeing event
    (B) Open a new branch
    (C) Use eco-friendly items
    (D) Upgrade a Web site

Test

파트별 점수 분석(맞은 숫자)

PART 1	
PART 2	
PART 3	
PART 4	
총 맞은 갯수	

정답 및 스크립트: 201p

07

LISTENING TEST

In the Listening test, you will be asked to demonstrate how well you understand spoken English. The entire Listening test will last approximately 45 minutes. There are four parts, and directions are given for each part. You must mark your answers on the separate answer sheet.
Do not write your answers in your test book.

PART 1

Directions: For each question in this part, you will hear four statements about a picture in your test book. When you hear the statements, you must select the one statement that best describes what you see in the picture. Then find the number of the question on your answer sheet and mark your answer. The statements will not be printed in your test book and will be spoken only one time.

Sample Answer
Ⓐ ● Ⓒ Ⓓ

Statement (B), "They're shaking hands," is the best description of the picture, so you should select answer (B) and mark it on your answer sheet.

1.

2.

3.

4.

5.

6.

PART 2

Directions: You will hear a question or statement and three responses spoken in English. They will not be printed in your test book and will be spoken only one time. Select the best response to the question or statement and mark the letter (A), (B), or (C) on your answer sheet.

7. Mark your answer on your answer sheet.
8. Mark your answer on your answer sheet.
9. Mark your answer on your answer sheet.
10. Mark your answer on your answer sheet.
11. Mark your answer on your answer sheet.
12. Mark your answer on your answer sheet.
13. Mark your answer on your answer sheet.
14. Mark your answer on your answer sheet.
15. Mark your answer on your answer sheet.
16. Mark your answer on your answer sheet.
17. Mark your answer on your answer sheet.
18. Mark your answer on your answer sheet.
19. Mark your answer on your answer sheet.
20. Mark your answer on your answer sheet.
21. Mark your answer on your answer sheet.
22. Mark your answer on your answer sheet.
23. Mark your answer on your answer sheet.
24. Mark your answer on your answer sheet.
25. Mark your answer on your answer sheet.
26. Mark your answer on your answer sheet.
27. Mark your answer on your answer sheet.
28. Mark your answer on your answer sheet.
29. Mark your answer on your answer sheet.
30. Mark your answer on your answer sheet.
31. Mark your answer on your answer sheet.

PART 3

Directions: You will hear some conversations between two or more people. You will be asked to answer three questions about what the speakers say in each conversation. Select the best response to each question and mark the letter (A), (B), (C), or (D) on your answer sheet. The conversations will not be printed in your test book and will be spoken only one time.

32. Where most likely does the woman work?
    (A) At a library
    (B) At a stadium
    (C) At a performance hall
    (D) At a music shop

33. What is the purpose of the man's call?
    (A) To ask for a refund
    (B) To cancel a reservation
    (C) To sign up for a class
    (D) To inquire about tickets

34. What will the man probably do next?
    (A) Verify a seating chart
    (B) Check his calendar
    (C) Talk with his friends
    (D) Buy tickets online

35. Who most likely is the woman?
    (A) A staff trainer in a local company
    (B) A radio producer
    (C) A maintenance engineer
    (D) A TV reporter

36. What items would probably be serviced by Good Hands?
    (A) Toys
    (B) Bicycles
    (C) Photocopiers
    (D) Vehicles

37. According to the man, how does Good Hands differ from its competitors?
    (A) It provides extended guarantees.
    (B) It has a lot of state-of-the-art equipment.
    (C) It provides faster on-site service than its competitors.
    (D) It has very skilled employees.

38. What does the woman ask the man to do?
    (A) Accept a package
    (B) Attend a morning meeting
    (C) Take a phone call
    (D) Enter some data

39. What information does the man request?
    (A) A time
    (B) A contact number
    (C) An address
    (D) A price

40. What does the woman say she will do?
    (A) Postpone a meeting
    (B) Redirect her phone
    (C) Check her schedule
    (D) Cancel an appointment

41. What type of business does the woman most likely work for?
    (A) A used car dealer
    (B) A repair shop
    (C) A car rental agency
    (D) A paid parking lot

42. What is the man concerned about?
    (A) Being charged for a repair
    (B) Doing some paperwork
    (C) Attending an important meeting
    (D) Driving to Oregon from his company

43. For how long is the man renting the car?
    (A) One day
    (B) Two days
    (C) Three days
    (D) Four days

Go on to the next page

44. Why is the woman moving out?

    (A) Her rental agreement has expired.
    (B) She has found a less expensive house.
    (C) Her husband decided to relocate.
    (D) She wants a bigger house.

45. What does the woman offer to do?

    (A) Move out as soon as possible
    (B) Help look for a new tenant
    (C) Contact a moving company
    (D) Pay the rent fee for two months

46. According to the man, why would the woman be willing to help him?

    (A) To find a new house in Atlanta
    (B) To get a new job
    (C) To save the excessive rental fee
    (D) To renovate her house within 4 weeks

47. What impressed the women about the man?

    (A) His appearance
    (B) His managing skills
    (C) His previous career
    (D) His upcoming performances

48. According to the man, why did he apply to this company?

    (A) He wants to earn more money.
    (B) He is eager to try overnight shoots.
    (C) He wants to lead his own team.
    (D) He wants to work for a bigger company.

49. What does the new job require of the man?

    (A) Excellent presentation skills
    (B) Experience in health matters
    (C) The willingness to work overtime
    (D) Frequent overseas performances

50. What does the man like about the updated Web site?

    (A) The clear images
    (B) The faster response time
    (C) The easier usability
    (D) The detailed floor guide

51. What does the man imply when he says, "It didn't work for me"?

    (A) He did not work yesterday.
    (B) He already tried pressing the F5 key.
    (C) He wants to consult with Jim.
    (D) He had the same issue before the update.

52. What does the woman recommend?

    (A) Installing some new software
    (B) Checking for computer viruses
    (C) Restarting his desktop computer
    (D) Including an image with his report

53. Where most likely does the man work?

    (A) At a laboratory
    (B) At a farm
    (C) At a fried chicken restaurant
    (D) At a government agency

54. What has the man recently done?

    (A) Called to confirm the management number
    (B) Moved to a new location
    (C) Sold a number of eggs
    (D) Bred a lot of poultry

55. What does the woman say she is unable to do?

    (A) Vaccinate the animals
    (B) Offer a discount
    (C) Provide financial support
    (D) Verify the information of the farm

56. Where does the man most likely work?
 (A) At a food store
 (B) At a car repair shop
 (C) At a cold storage facility
 (D) At a delivery service

57. What does the man imply when he says, "I was expecting you"?
 (A) He is ready to take the order.
 (B) They already know each other.
 (C) He knew Ms. Williams would come.
 (D) He will deliver the items to Ms. Williams' house himself.

58. What is the woman most likely to do next?
 (A) Go home
 (B) Provide her telephone number
 (C) Pick up the items at the warehouse
 (D) Ask for a door-to-door delivery

---

59. What is the purpose of the contest?
 (A) To create a themed campaign
 (B) To reduce expenditure
 (C) To increase the customer base
 (D) To recruit additional employees

60. Why is the woman unsure about participating?
 (A) She is going on vacation.
 (B) She will be changing jobs.
 (C) She does not have any related experience.
 (D) She has a deadline for work.

61. What will the winner receive?
 (A) A plaque
 (B) A hotel voucher
 (C) A trip abroad
 (D) A cash bonus

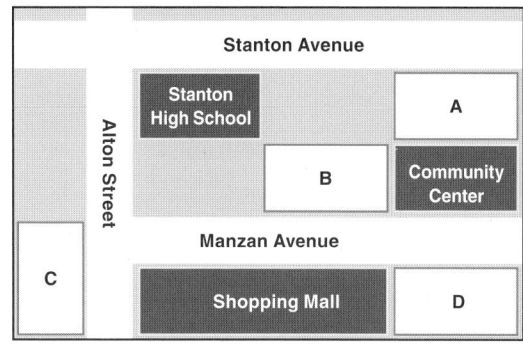

62. What are the speakers mainly talking about?
 (A) The woman's new apartment
 (B) Joining a sports club
 (C) Driving a long distance
 (D) A newly arrived student

63. What is the woman concerned about?
 (A) The cost of joining a gym
 (B) The amount of spare time she has
 (C) The location of the new office
 (D) The distance she would travel

64. Look at the graphic. Where is the Hillsberry Building?
 (A) A
 (B) B
 (C) C
 (D) D

Attachment: Pictures Checklist			
Branch Name	Phone No.	Manager	Taken at
Alpha Center	7590-4761	Martin Clause	Nighttime
Glanstown	(N/A)	Laura Bright	Daytime
McMillan	7550-8761	(N/A)	Daytime
Unicorn Building	7575-4561	Aaron Smith	Daytime

Floor Guide:

4F	Cafeteria
3F	Auditorium
2F	Counseling Office
1F	Administration Office
B1	Parking lot

65. What most likely is the man's job?
    (A) Branch manager
    (B) Office interior designer
    (C) Photographer
    (D) Web site developer

66. What does the woman ask the man to help with?
    (A) Assigning a manager
    (B) Photocopying some images
    (C) Getting some photographs
    (D) Installing a telephone

67. Look at the graphic. Which site's photograph is not suitable to be posted on the Web site?
    (A) Alpha Center branch
    (B) Glanstown branch
    (C) McMillan branch
    (D) Unicorn Building branch

68. What document will be issued to the man?
    (A) An application form
    (B) A work permit
    (C) A membership card
    (D) A recommendation letter

69. Look at the graphic. Where should the man go to meet the woman on Tuesday?
    (A) 1st floor
    (B) 2nd floor
    (C) 3rd floor
    (D) 4th floor

70. What does the woman ask the man to do?
    (A) Submit an application as soon as possible
    (B) Mail extra copies of his certificates
    (C) Attend a training session
    (D) Give her his autograph

PART 4

Directions: You will hear some talks given by a single speaker. You will be asked to answer three questions about what the speaker says in each talk. Select the best response to each question and mark the letter (A), (B), (C), or (D) on your answer sheet. The talks will not be printed in your test book and will be spoken only one time.

71. What type of business is being advertised?
    (A) A cold storage facility
    (B) A catering firm
    (C) A web design service
    (D) A cooking institute

72. According to the advertisement, what does Exo Spices guarantee?
    (A) Unlimited beverages
    (B) Discount vouchers
    (C) A full refund
    (D) Nutritious food

73. What can listeners do online?
    (A) Customize a set menu
    (B) Order samples of some food
    (C) Leave comments
    (D) Track an order

74. What is being rebuilt in Eunice?
    (A) A shopping mall
    (B) A swimming pool
    (C) A playground
    (D) An environmental center

75. Why was the renovation delayed?
    (A) The location was too remote.
    (B) Local residents objected to the renovation.
    (C) Harmful substances were detected.
    (D) Funding was insufficient.

76. According to the speaker, what will take place in July?
    (A) A weekly prize drawing
    (B) An opening ceremony
    (C) A series of lectures
    (D) A charity event

77. What is the purpose of the upcoming event?
    (A) To promote an art class
    (B) To encourage class participation
    (C) To introduce a new lecturer
    (D) To test students' performances

78. What will some students receive?
    (A) Tickets to a musical performance
    (B) Theater discounts
    (C) A complimentary class
    (D) Reduced tuition fees

79. What are the listeners asked to do when entering a class?
    (A) Play the guitar
    (B) Accompany a friend
    (C) Stop by the office
    (D) Apply an ID card

80. Why are the callers unable to speak to a representative immediately?
    (A) More people are calling than usual.
    (B) A hotline system is faulty.
    (C) The shuttles are out of service.
    (D) The Internet connection is unavailable.

81. Why would callers press 4 on their phones?
    (A) To check the shuttle schedules
    (B) To get advice on road travel
    (C) To check the weather forecast
    (D) To locate a nearby shelter

82. What does the speaker mention about the Web site?
    (A) It is updated every day.
    (B) It is currently inaccessible.
    (C) You need to log on to check the contents.
    (D) It provides the current weather status.

Go on to the next page

83. Who most likely are the listeners?
    (A) Fashion designers
    (B) Corporate executives
    (C) Factory workers
    (D) Salespeople

84. What will happen this spring?
    (A) A womenswear collection will be discontinued.
    (B) A new client list will be introduced.
    (C) A new range will be launched.
    (D) A new outlet will be opened.

85. What will the listeners do next?
    (A) Visit their clients
    (B) View sample items
    (C) Report their sales strategies
    (D) Attend a regular meeting

86. What type of business does the speaker work for?
    (A) An advertising company
    (B) A photography studio
    (C) A clothing company
    (D) A travel agency

87. What should the listener submit to join the contest?
    (A) A series of photographs
    (B) A sketch
    (C) A video clip
    (D) A travel essay

88. What will the winner receive?
    (A) Cash
    (B) Coupons
    (C) Flight tickets
    (D) Camping equipment

89. Who most likely is the speaker?
    (A) A stadium vendor
    (B) A sports announcer
    (C) A football player
    (D) A match referee

90. What prize is being offered?
    (A) Dinner with an athlete
    (B) Tickets for the final
    (C) A two-week trip
    (D) Autographed football shirts

91. What does the man imply when he says, "It couldn't be simpler"?
    (A) Everyone can send the message free of charge.
    (B) The rules for soccer are not complicated.
    (C) It is easy to join the event.
    (D) All the names of the players need to be memorized.

92. What is being announced?
    (A) A meeting schedule
    (B) An increase in salaries
    (C) A new working arrangement
    (D) An overtime project

93. Why is a change being made?
    (A) To attract new employees
    (B) To create to a survey
    (C) To improve working practices
    (D) To reward hard-working employees

94. What does the woman imply when she says, "there would be no difficulty in that"?
    (A) It is impossible to comply with the change.
    (B) The survey was conducted without any trouble.
    (C) The change will cause some confusion.
    (D) A shorter lunch break is not a big deal.

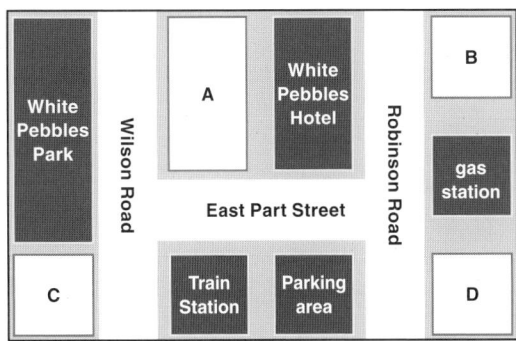

Renovation Schedule	
Noise Inspection	May 24 (Mon.)
Painting the walls	May 25 (Tue.)
Painting the ceilings	May 26 (Wed.)
Replacing the windows	May 27 (Thu.)

95. Why does the speaker recommend the property?

   (A) It is in a flood-prone area.
   (B) The landlord wants to sell it cheap.
   (C) The building is in a good condition.
   (D) There is a subway station nearby.

96. What disadvantage does the speaker mention?

   (A) The deposit is too high.
   (B) The flood risk is high.
   (C) The landlord has another buyer.
   (D) Parking lot is not included.

97. Look at the graphic. Where most likely is the property?

   (A) A
   (B) B
   (C) C
   (D) D

98. What problem is the management responding to?

   (A) Noise from a factory
   (B) A shortage of office supplies
   (C) Renovation expenses
   (D) Broken windows

99. Look at the graphic. When will Mr. Coleman remove the curtains?

   (A) Monday
   (B) Tuesday
   (C) Wednesday
   (D) Thursday

100. What does the speaker encourage listeners to do?

   (A) Clear the blinds
   (B) Wash the curtains
   (C) Change the windows
   (D) Work from home

Test

파트별 점수 분석(맞은 숫자)

PART 1	
PART 2	
PART 3	
PART 4	
총 맞은 갯수	

정답 및 스크립트: 208p

08

LISTENING TEST

In the Listening test, you will be asked to demonstrate how well you understand spoken English. The entire Listening test will last approximately 45 minutes. There are four parts, and directions are given for each part. You must mark your answers on the separate answer sheet.
Do not write your answers in your test book.

PART 1

Directions: For each question in this part, you will hear four statements about a picture in your test book. When you hear the statements, you must select the one statement that best describes what you see in the picture. Then find the number of the question on your answer sheet and mark your answer. The statements will not be printed in your test book and will be spoken only one time.

Sample Answer
Ⓐ ● Ⓒ Ⓓ

Statement (B), "They're shaking hands," is the best description of the picture, so you should select answer (B) and mark it on your answer sheet.

1.

2.

3.

4.

5.

6.

PART 2

Directions: You will hear a question or statement and three responses spoken in English. They will not be printed in your test book and will be spoken only one time. Select the best response to the question or statement and mark the letter (A), (B), or (C) on your answer sheet.

7. Mark your answer on your answer sheet.
8. Mark your answer on your answer sheet.
9. Mark your answer on your answer sheet.
10. Mark your answer on your answer sheet.
11. Mark your answer on your answer sheet.
12. Mark your answer on your answer sheet.
13. Mark your answer on your answer sheet.
14. Mark your answer on your answer sheet.
15. Mark your answer on your answer sheet.
16. Mark your answer on your answer sheet.
17. Mark your answer on your answer sheet.
18. Mark your answer on your answer sheet.
19. Mark your answer on your answer sheet.
20. Mark your answer on your answer sheet.
21. Mark your answer on your answer sheet.
22. Mark your answer on your answer sheet.
23. Mark your answer on your answer sheet.
24. Mark your answer on your answer sheet.
25. Mark your answer on your answer sheet.
26. Mark your answer on your answer sheet.
27. Mark your answer on your answer sheet.
28. Mark your answer on your answer sheet.
29. Mark your answer on your answer sheet.
30. Mark your answer on your answer sheet.
31. Mark your answer on your answer sheet.

PART 3

Directions: You will hear some conversations between two or more people. You will be asked to answer three questions about what the speakers say in each conversation. Select the best response to each question and mark the letter (A), (B), (C), or (D) on your answer sheet. The conversations will not be printed in your test book and will be spoken only one time.

32. What is the woman concerned about?
    (A) A family matter
    (B) A newspaper page
    (C) A travel itinerary
    (D) A group presentation

33. What does the woman ask the man to do?
    (A) Take some pictures
    (B) Revise an article
    (C) Buy some food
    (D) Work overtime

34. What does the woman say she will do?
    (A) Read a proposal
    (B) Mail a package
    (C) Arrange for some food
    (D) Create an advertisement

35. Who is Patrick Spencer?
    (A) A computer engineer
    (B) A DVD seller
    (C) A health trainer
    (D) An ad executive

36. What did Patrick Spencer advise the woman to do?
    (A) Sit up straight in her chair
    (B) Work on her computer
    (C) Lean against a wall
    (D) Upgrade her computer

37. What does the woman offer to do?
    (A) Share some information with her colleagues
    (B) Assist in preparing a demonstration
    (C) Buy the man a computer
    (D) Make a list of interested employees

38. What are the clients worried about?
    (A) The color of the paint
    (B) The cost of the work
    (C) The deadline for the project
    (D) The material of the wallpaper

39. What does the man imply when he says, "I would like to allay their worries"?
    (A) He wants to satisfy the clients.
    (B) He needs more time to finish the project.
    (C) He's going to ask for a budget increase.
    (D) He doesn't want to work for Starwood.

40. What does the man suggest?
    (A) Finding a different hotel
    (B) Consulting with the supplier
    (C) Ignoring the customer's expectations
    (D) Postponing the meeting

41. What is the conversation mainly about?
    (A) Getting a general checkup
    (B) Designing a book
    (C) Publishing an article
    (D) Giving a talk

42. What are the speakers worried about?
    (A) The length of a text
    (B) The difficulty of an article
    (C) The access to an online forum
    (D) The deadline for publishing

43. What does the man offer to do?
    (A) Participate in the research
    (B) Carry a different article
    (C) Provide a list of words
    (D) Vaccinate the patients

Go on to the next page

44. What are the speakers discussing?
    (A) A renovation project
    (B) A job interview
    (C) A road development
    (D) A work schedule

45. What is the woman impressed by?
    (A) The improved environment of the office
    (B) How quickly the job was performed
    (C) The professionalism of the workers
    (D) How little the construction cost

46. What does the man say he will suggest?
    (A) Rescheduling some appointments
    (B) Moving to a new building
    (C) Calling the maintenance office
    (D) Employing the same company again

47. What was the purpose of the man's trip?
    (A) To look at the new factory sites
    (B) To source new suppliers
    (C) To sell goods abroad
    (D) To arrange interviews

48. What does the man say about the company in Copenhagen?
    (A) It has many manufacturing plants.
    (B) It is favorably located.
    (C) It welcomes business from abroad.
    (D) It is close to an airport.

49. What does the woman remind the man to do?
    (A) Ask for an extended vacation
    (B) Report the loss of his luggage
    (C) Submit his report
    (D) Update his current client details

50. What department does the man work in?
    (A) Maintenance
    (B) Customer service
    (C) Reception
    (D) Human resources

51. What does the woman ask about?
    (A) The start date of a job
    (B) The qualifications for a job
    (C) The name of the human resources manager
    (D) The location of the training session

52. What does the woman say she will probably do?
    (A) Hand over her present duties to her colleague
    (B) Teach the man how to do his job properly
    (C) Move to a new location
    (D) Submit a job application

53. Who most likely is the man?
    (A) An administrative assistant
    (B) A sales representative
    (C) An interior designer
    (D) A maintenance employee

54. What problem does the woman mention?
    (A) A project is not complete.
    (B) An office is locked.
    (C) Some electric equipment is defective.
    (D) Some materials are not available.

55. According to the woman, what is scheduled to take place in the afternoon?
    (A) A safety check
    (B) A meeting
    (C) A job interview
    (D) A power outage

56. What problem is the woman talking about?
    (A) She cannot meet her manager today.
    (B) She cannot find any problem with her mobile phone.
    (C) She cannot contact her clients from the office.
    (D) She cannot fix the defective cables.

57. What does the woman imply when she says, "That's no good to me"?
    (A) She has to leave early today.
    (B) She can't wait for the cables to be repaired.
    (C) She will visit the clients in person.
    (D) She doesn't want to use a three-way call.

58. What will the woman probably do next?
    (A) Check the telephone downstairs
    (B) Contact the telephone company again
    (C) Make a speech at the conference
    (D) List some time-sensitive issues

59. What type of company is Amberhues?
    (A) A travel agency
    (B) A moving company
    (C) A decorating firm
    (D) A hotel

60. Why did the woman choose Amberhues?
    (A) It has been in operation for a long time.
    (B) It is convenient to her office.
    (C) It has a branch in Miami.
    (D) It is the most competitively priced.

61. Why will the work start in July?
    (A) The company has to give approval.
    (B) Furniture cannot be delivered earlier.
    (C) The woman will be away until then.
    (D) The company is busy with other work.

Restaurant Suggestions

Wang's Castle	Chinese	Delicious noodles, Not spicy
Beefy Porky	Barbecue	Outdoor restaurant, Fairly cheap
Indiana's	Steakhouse	Lunchtime discount, Rooms available
Chili Chili	Spicy Ribs	Best for spice lovers, Mexican style

62. According to the woman, what is the purpose of the event?
    (A) To organize an awards ceremony
    (B) To taste some exotic food
    (C) To open a new business
    (D) To celebrate a birthday

63. Look at the graphic. Which place would be most suitable for the event?
    (A) Wang's Castle
    (B) Beefy Porky
    (C) Indiana's
    (D) Chili Chili

64. Why does the woman disagree with the man's idea?
    (A) The restaurant is not big enough.
    (B) They won't be able to get a discount.
    (C) The president doesn't like Japanese food.
    (D) They have no time to book a room.

Pearson Elementary School	**A**	Milton Hotel
B	Tinderbox Restaurant	**C**
Prime Hotel	Gas Station	**D**

Item	Quantity	Subtotal
Speaker	6	$180
Keyboard	2	$50
Mouse	1	$35
Webcam	1	$75
Delivery		$0
Total		$340

65. What most likely is the man's occupation?

    (A) Real estate agent
    (B) Building constructor
    (C) Cooking teacher
    (D) Hotel worker

66. Look at the graphic. Where most likely is the Diana Complex?

    (A) A
    (B) B
    (C) C
    (D) D

67. When does the man say he can visit the Diana Complex?

    (A) This evening
    (B) Later tomorrow
    (C) The day after tomorrow
    (D) The week after

68. Who most likely is the man?

    (A) A storekeeper
    (B) A bank teller
    (C) A delivery man
    (D) A computer repairman

69. What does the woman ask about?

    (A) The delivery time
    (B) The payment options
    (C) The availability of items
    (D) A card approval

70. Look at the graphic. Which information on the list has to be changed now?

    (A) $180
    (B) $50
    (C) $35
    (D) $75

PART 4

Directions: You will hear some talks given by a single speaker. You will be asked to answer three questions about what the speaker says in each talk. Select the best response to each question and mark the letter (A), (B), (C), or (D) on your answer sheet. The talks will not be printed in your test book and will be spoken only one time.

71. What is the announcement mainly about?
    (A) A machine installation
    (B) A company closure
    (C) A safety inspection
    (D) A vehicle check

72. What does the man imply when he says, "Without any doubt, this is good news"?
    (A) He can fix his car by himself now.
    (B) He will gladly do the overtime work.
    (C) They have purchased the machine at a low price.
    (D) The new machine will help them complete the work in less time.

73. What does the speaker ask the listeners to do?
    (A) Attend an opening ceremony
    (B) Welcome a new supervisor
    (C) Work overtime hours
    (D) Review an operations manual

74. Where does the speaker most likely work?
    (A) At a radio station
    (B) At an employment agency
    (C) At a charity organization
    (D) At a publishing house

75. According to the speaker, what will Mr. Elder discuss?
    (A) A community building
    (B) A fundraising event
    (C) A marketing report
    (D) A new plan

76. Why are volunteers needed?
    (A) To advise young people
    (B) To distribute brochures
    (C) To conduct interviews
    (D) To recruit office workers

77. Who is the speaker?
    (A) A government officer
    (B) A head of a certain society
    (C) A police officer
    (D) A lighting expert

78. What permission has the group received?
    (A) Hosting a fundraising event
    (B) Supporting a sports team
    (C) Submitting a bid for funding
    (D) Sponsoring a lighting company

79. Why should listeners contact Megan Bishop?
    (A) To apply to the committee
    (B) To help in preparing the bid
    (C) To purchase some lighting
    (D) To contribute to the newsletter

80. Who is the intended audience for the talk?
    (A) Prospective writers
    (B) A proofreading team
    (C) A book club
    (D) A marketing department

81. According to the speaker, why is the new book unique?
    (A) It is being serialized in the newspaper.
    (B) It is available in e-book format.
    (C) It is the prequel to a series.
    (D) It is written in a different language.

82. What will the speaker most likely do next?
    (A) Review work assignments
    (B) Meet with the editing team
    (C) Distribute copies of a book
    (D) Work out a budget

Go on to the next page

83. What is the announcement mainly about?
    (A) A product recall
    (B) A store relocation
    (C) A store promotion
    (D) A remodeling project

84. What were employees recently trained to do?
    (A) Design a new promotion
    (B) Prepare some cosmetic items
    (C) Offer makeovers
    (D) Inspect some equipment

85. What is the speaker concerned about?
    (A) Finding a new supplier
    (B) Having sufficient seating
    (C) Lowering operating costs
    (D) Providing continuous supplies

86. What item is the speaker calling about?
    (A) An outfit
    (B) A wardrobe
    (C) A television
    (D) An e-mail account

87. Where has the item been advertised?
    (A) In a magazine
    (B) In a local shop
    (C) On a bus window
    (D) On a notice board

88. What does the speaker request?
    (A) Some photographs
    (B) A delivery date
    (C) Pricing information
    (D) The size of the item

89. What does the speaker's company produce?
    (A) Medical appliances
    (B) Office equipment
    (C) Drug supplies
    (D) Audio systems

90. What does the speaker want to arrange?
    (A) An on-site demonstration
    (B) A factory tour
    (C) A payment plan
    (D) A meeting schedule

91. What does the speaker say about the company's products?
    (A) They are highly recommended.
    (B) They are covered by a guarantee.
    (C) They can be replaced every year.
    (D) They are easily transportable.

92. What type of organization did the listener call?
    (A) An artistic group
    (B) A writers' community
    (C) A tutoring program
    (D) A sporting club

93. What does the woman imply when she says, "we are always looking for new people"?
    (A) To inform the listener that they are newly opened
    (B) To find a new place to hold an exhibition
    (C) To reschedule the next event
    (D) To invite more members to the meeting

94. According to the speaker, what is available on the organization's Web site?
    (A) A display of artwork
    (B) A calendar of events
    (C) An application form
    (D) A date for the next meeting

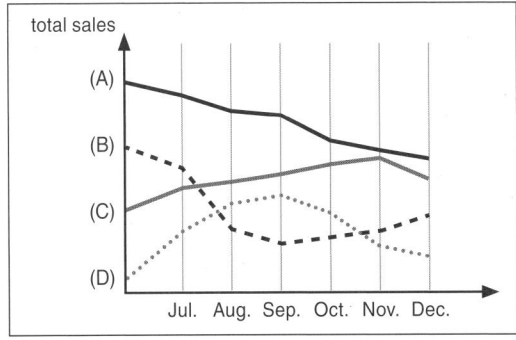

95. What does the speaker want to discuss in this meeting?
    (A) Moving up the release date of the new item
    (B) Criticizing the sales department for the poor performance
    (C) Making a successful marketing plan
    (D) Deciding which products should be discontinued

96. Look at the graphic. Which line indicates the sales results of the computers?
    (A) A
    (B) B
    (C) C
    (D) D

97. What does the speaker say about the new item?
    (A) It will be released in February.
    (B) It won't meet the customers' expectations.
    (C) It is the best-seller as usual.
    (D) It only took 6 months to be developed.

98. What will happen later today?
    (A) Mr. Hunt will leave for Chicago.
    (B) The current marketing plans will be changed.
    (C) A speech will be given by Ms. Bennett.
    (D) A seminar will be postponed to the following week.

99. Look at the graphic. Which information needs to be changed?
    (A) Room 407
    (B) Leah Bennett
    (C) Wed.
    (D) Refreshments provided

100. According to the speaker, why would the listeners contact Julia Watson?
    (A) To report an urgent matter
    (B) To notify her of their availability
    (C) To reschedule a session
    (D) To make inquiries to Mr. Hunt

Test

파트별 점수 분석(맞은 숫자)

PART 1	
PART 2	
PART 3	
PART 4	
총 맞은 갯수	

정답 및 스크립트: 215p

09

LISTENING TEST

In the Listening test, you will be asked to demonstrate how well you understand spoken English. The entire Listening test will last approximately 45 minutes. There are four parts, and directions are given for each part. You must mark your answers on the separate answer sheet.
Do not write your answers in your test book.

PART 1

Directions: For each question in this part, you will hear four statements about a picture in your test book. When you hear the statements, you must select the one statement that best describes what you see in the picture. Then find the number of the question on your answer sheet and mark your answer. The statements will not be printed in your test book and will be spoken only one time.

Sample Answer

Statement (B), "They're shaking hands," is the best description of the picture, so you should select answer (B) and mark it on your answer sheet.

1.

2.

3.

4.

5.

6.

PART 2

Directions: You will hear a question or statement and three responses spoken in English. They will not be printed in your test book and will be spoken only one time. Select the best response to the question or statement and mark the letter (A), (B), or (C) on your answer sheet.

7. Mark your answer on your answer sheet.
8. Mark your answer on your answer sheet.
9. Mark your answer on your answer sheet.
10. Mark your answer on your answer sheet.
11. Mark your answer on your answer sheet.
12. Mark your answer on your answer sheet.
13. Mark your answer on your answer sheet.
14. Mark your answer on your answer sheet.
15. Mark your answer on your answer sheet.
16. Mark your answer on your answer sheet.
17. Mark your answer on your answer sheet.
18. Mark your answer on your answer sheet.
19. Mark your answer on your answer sheet.
20. Mark your answer on your answer sheet.
21. Mark your answer on your answer sheet.
22. Mark your answer on your answer sheet.
23. Mark your answer on your answer sheet.
24. Mark your answer on your answer sheet.
25. Mark your answer on your answer sheet.
26. Mark your answer on your answer sheet.
27. Mark your answer on your answer sheet.
28. Mark your answer on your answer sheet.
29. Mark your answer on your answer sheet.
30. Mark your answer on your answer sheet.
31. Mark your answer on your answer sheet.

PART 3

Directions: You will hear some conversations between two or more people. You will be asked to answer three questions about what the speakers say in each conversation. Select the best response to each question and mark the letter (A), (B), (C), or (D) on your answer sheet. The conversations will not be printed in your test book and will be spoken only one time.

32. What type of event are the speakers planning to attend?
    (A) A trade exhibition
    (B) A sports event
    (C) A budget committee
    (D) An office opening

33. What problem does the man mention?
    (A) A venue is fully booked.
    (B) The cost has increased.
    (C) A company has gone bankrupt.
    (D) An exhibition has been canceled.

34. What does the woman recommend?
    (A) Reducing the size of the display
    (B) Contacting other venues
    (C) Promoting the event on television
    (D) Asking for a discount

35. What kind of product is the woman inquiring about?
    (A) Computer software
    (B) Flooring materials
    (C) Lab equipment
    (D) Hotel pieces

36. What does the man offer to do?
    (A) Stop by the hotel
    (B) Send the woman an order form
    (C) Provide some samples
    (D) Consult a flooring expert

37. What does the woman request?
    (A) An instruction manual
    (B) A use of a product
    (C) An online tutorial
    (D) A tile specialist

38. What problem is mentioned about the airport?
    (A) The check-in line is too long.
    (B) The baggage area is blocked.
    (C) An airplane has been delayed.
    (D) An employee has not arrived.

39. What does the man ask the woman about?
    (A) Payment options
    (B) Business hours
    (C) Round-trip airfares
    (D) Beverage choices

40. What does the woman say she will do?
    (A) Find another airline
    (B) Lend the man some money
    (C) Contact her office
    (D) Use a credit card

41. What does the woman want to do?
    (A) Purchase a product
    (B) Read a product review
    (C) Complain about a device
    (D) Return an item

42. What did the woman read about the Hurricane Power?
    (A) It is inexpensive.
    (B) It is complicated to use.
    (C) It is unreliable.
    (D) It is the most popular model.

43. What does the man suggest the woman do?
    (A) Post messages on a forum
    (B) Browse online
    (C) Contact a sales assistant
    (D) Visit a specific store

Go on to the next page

44. What type of business does the man work for?
    (A) A food supply company
    (B) A post office
    (C) A bookstore
    (D) A courier service

45. What policy does the man mention?
    (A) Delivered goods must be put in the mailbox.
    (B) The invoice must be issued on delivery.
    (C) Damaged items must be returned to the supplier.
    (D) A signature must be provided.

46. What does the woman want to check?
    (A) Her shipping receipt
    (B) Her son's availability
    (C) Her order form
    (D) Her tracking number

47. What was the woman asked to do?
    (A) Drive a coworker to the airport
    (B) Prepare a presentation
    (C) Hire additional workers
    (D) Visit a production facility

48. What does the man imply when he says, "That makes sense"?
    (A) He will pick the woman up at the airport.
    (B) He thinks renting a car is a good idea.
    (C) He knows taking a taxi costs less.
    (D) He can send a taxi for the woman.

49. What does the woman decide to do?
    (A) Leave a meeting early
    (B) Get back to a branch manager
    (C) Use another form of transportation
    (D) Make extra copies of a report

50. What does the woman want to discuss with the man?
    (A) A refund policy
    (B) A travel itinerary
    (C) A checklist sheet
    (D) An insurance claim

51. When does the woman say she submitted the paperwork?
    (A) In June
    (B) Yesterday
    (C) Last week
    (D) Last month

52. According to the man, what may have caused the delay?
    (A) Regular procedure
    (B) Computer errors
    (C) Lost paperwork
    (D) Foreign policy

53. Who does the woman want to take to the Cebuana Lounge?
    (A) Clients
    (B) The management team
    (C) Family members
    (D) Colleagues

54. What does the man want to know about the restaurant?
    (A) Its menu
    (B) Its opening hours
    (C) Its prices
    (D) Its location

55. What does the woman suggest?
    (A) Using her mobile phone
    (B) Booking a table
    (C) Making a phone call
    (D) Checking room availability

56. What is the woman mainly notifying the men of?

    (A) Financial confidentiality
    (B) Recycling guidelines
    (C) Client information
    (D) Presentation schedules

57. What are the men advised to do with confidential documents?

    (A) Keep them in their desk
    (B) Give them to the director
    (C) File them in a locked cabinet
    (D) Keep them in a special container

58. What does Mike imply when he says, "Thanks for the information"?

    (A) He's glad to be informed about the change.
    (B) He's not asked to comply with the regulations.
    (C) He's going to update all the financial documents.
    (D) He's allowed to store all the documents in a cabinet.

---

59. What is the man interested in purchasing?

    (A) A coat
    (B) A hat
    (C) A sweater
    (D) A scarf

60. What is the problem?

    (A) A product is faulty.
    (B) An item is unavailable in a certain color on site.
    (C) Some merchandise has been misplaced.
    (D) Some clothes are too expensive.

61. What does the woman suggest the man do?

    (A) Check on the store's Web site
    (B) Go to a different store
    (C) Return within a week
    (D) Choose another color

Expense Report, 6~9 May

Round-trip ticket	$340
Hotel (2 nights)	$300
Car rental (with insurance)	$120
Meals (2.5 days * 3)	$85

62. What does the woman have to do in the morning?

    (A) Meet with a customer
    (B) Fill out an expense form
    (C) Use her computer
    (D) Organize a training session

63. Look at the graphic. Which item didn't the woman attach a receipt for?

    (A) Round-trip ticket
    (B) Hotel bills
    (C) Car rental
    (D) Meals

64. What does the man say he will do?

    (A) Contact a colleague
    (B) Create a database
    (C) Reschedule his meeting
    (D) Meet the woman in the afternoon

	Admission	Guided Tour
Event Hall A	$60	Not available
Event Hall B	Free	Free. 11:00 A.M., 7:00 P.M.
Event Hall C	$50	Free. 10:00 A.M., 3:00 P.M., 7:00 P.M.
Event Hall D	$20	$10, booklets provided

65. What problem does the man mention?

    (A) A piece of art is missing.
    (B) A staff member is unavailable.
    (C) Some displays are faulty.
    (D) An exhibition is crowded.

66. Look at the graphic. Where is the exhibition the woman wants to see being held?

    (A) Event Hall A
    (B) Event Hall B
    (C) Event Hall C
    (D) Event Hall D

67. What will the woman do next?

    (A) Stay with the man
    (B) Get a free ticket at the box office
    (C) Come back tomorrow
    (D) Go and see another exhibit

Boxing Equipment	Regular price
Boxing Gloves	$54
Protective Gear	$64
Sandbags	$152
Boxing Shoes	$162

68. What is the man calling about?

    (A) Taking sports lessons
    (B) Moving into the Graham Complex
    (C) Purchasing a pair of boxing gloves
    (D) Leaving his office earlier than usual

69. Look at the graphic. How much is the man going to pay for the equipment he needs?

    (A) $44
    (B) $64
    (C) $152
    (D) $162

70. What is suggested about the gym?

    (A) It closes at 6 P.M.
    (B) It's on the first floor.
    (C) It's near the Graham Complex.
    (D) It is far from Mr. Phillips's office.

PART 4

Directions: You will hear some talks given by a single speaker. You will be asked to answer three questions about what the speaker says in each talk. Select the best response to each question and mark the letter (A), (B), (C), or (D) on your answer sheet. The talks will not be printed in your test book and will be spoken only one time.

71. What special event is being held?
    (A) A retirement event
    (B) A training session
    (C) A grand opening ceremony
    (D) A promotion party

72. What is Charles Bailey's profession?
    (A) Computer specialist
    (B) Office manager
    (C) Mechanic
    (D) Factory operative

73. What will most likely happen next?
    (A) Some refreshments will be offered.
    (B) An interview will be conducted.
    (C) A seminar will take place.
    (D) A gift will be presented.

74. What kind of business is the speaker calling?
    (A) A holiday resort
    (B) A medical clinic
    (C) An employment agency
    (D) A pharmaceutical company

75. What does the speaker ask about?
    (A) Vaccination requirements
    (B) Better medication
    (C) A medicine price
    (D) A return to work

76. When does the speaker say she will be available?
    (A) This morning
    (B) This afternoon
    (C) Tomorrow morning
    (D) Tomorrow afternoon

77. What will happen on October 11?
    (A) Lunchtime will be extended.
    (B) Paychecks will be distributed.
    (C) A leaflet will be sent out.
    (D) A demonstration will take place.

78. What does the woman imply when she says, "This also applies to the temporary staff"?
    (A) They are not included in a lunchtime session.
    (B) They are required to fill out a form.
    (C) They will receive less pay.
    (D) They must be in attendance.

79. What are listeners asked to read?
    (A) A customer questionnaire
    (B) A health and safety document
    (C) An instruction flyer
    (D) Dismissal procedures

80. What will happen at the event?
    (A) A sustainable program will be reviewed.
    (B) A magazine will be introduced.
    (C) Awards will be presented.
    (D) New legislation will be announced.

81. What can listeners find on their seats?
    (A) Information about past projects
    (B) Results of a questionnaire
    (C) A membership form
    (D) A list of nominations

82. What is mentioned about *Good Energy Magazine*?
    (A) It is a leading magazine in the environment.
    (B) It is supporting the event.
    (C) It is recruiting new practitioners.
    (D) It is found on the seats.

Go on to the next page

83. Who is the speaker most likely addressing?
    (A) Safety inspectors
    (B) Interior designers
    (C) Factory workers
    (D) Laundry staff

84. What is the main topic of the talk?
    (A) Car painting
    (B) Appliance repairs
    (C) Factory inspections
    (D) Safety procedures

85. Where will listeners find the guidelines?
    (A) Near the chemicals
    (B) In the preservatives
    (C) On a bulletin board
    (D) In front of the paint shop

86. Where is the fitness center located?
    (A) In the vicinity of Danao City
    (B) Near a subway station
    (C) Right next to the city hall
    (D) In front of the community center

87. What class is newly offered?
    (A) Aerobics
    (B) Yoga
    (C) Squash
    (D) Tae-Bo

88. Why would listeners press one?
    (A) To cancel a class
    (B) To arrange a tutorial
    (C) To enroll in a class
    (D) To get directions

89. What has Shiny Clean accomplished over the quarter?
    (A) It launched a new range of products.
    (B) It relocated to Wilmington.
    (C) It increased its share in a specific market.
    (D) It recruited more employees.

90. Who is encouraged to apply for the new position in Wilmington?
    (A) Employees with several years' experience
    (B) Current staff willing to relocate
    (C) Sales managers with an interest in cleaning products
    (D) Those with experience in managing stores

91. What does the man imply when he says, "I have good news for everyone"?
    (A) He's pleased to let everyone know about their success.
    (B) He's willing to move to the headquarters.
    (C) He's glad to have more staff in the new branch.
    (D) He's happy to have a lot of candidates.

92. What kind of service is being advertised?
    (A) Online reservations
    (B) Aerial tours
    (C) Vehicle rental
    (D) Boat rides

93. According to the speaker, what is special about the service?
    (A) It is exclusively a daytime trip.
    (B) It is a brand-new service.
    (C) It takes off once a week.
    (D) It takes place at dusk.

94. What are listeners asked to do?
    (A) Provide a health certificate
    (B) Carry identification
    (C) Reserve a place
    (D) Arrive early

Suppliers list		
Miller's Joy	657-0932	Organic bakery
Herbalist's Delight	458-4273	Artificial flowers, other decorations
Mrs. Millers'	352-1853	Flour, Oil, Spices
Harmony	574-3753	Fruits & Vegetables

95. Who is the speaker?
    (A) A delivery man
    (B) A restaurant manager
    (C) A grocer
    (D) A millworker

96. What does the speaker intend to do?
    (A) Offer an online service
    (B) Alter a menu
    (C) Deliver to local bakeries
    (D) Change his supplier

97. Look at the graphic. Which store is the man most likely calling?
    (A) Miller's Joy
    (B) Herbalist's Delight
    (C) Mrs. Millers'
    (D) Harmony

Healthy Habits

11:00~11:45 P.M., Mon.~Fri.

Weekly Schedule	
Mon.	Child Obesity – A New Threat
Tue.	LIVE Lecture: Eating Habits of Adults
Wed.	Smoking, a Silent Killer
Thu.	LIVE Lecture: Vegetarianism. Is It a MUST?
Fri.	Dietholic

98. According to the speaker, what has Professor Holt recently done?
    (A) Delivered a lecture
    (B) Organized a seminar
    (C) Participated in a university debate
    (D) Published an article

99. Look at the graphic. When does Mr. James say he wants to meet Professor Holt?
    (A) Tuesday
    (B) Wednesday
    (C) Thursday
    (D) Friday

100. What does the speaker ask Professor Holt to do?
    (A) Contribute to a TV program
    (B) Undertake a newspaper interview
    (C) Review some books
    (D) Take a university lecture

Test

파트별 점수 분석(맞은 숫자)

PART 1	
PART 2	
PART 3	
PART 4	
총 맞은 갯수	

정답 및 스크립트: 222p

10

LISTENING TEST

In the Listening test, you will be asked to demonstrate how well you understand spoken English. The entire Listening test will last approximately 45 minutes. There are four parts, and directions are given for each part. You must mark your answers on the separate answer sheet.
Do not write your answers in your test book.

PART 1

Directions: For each question in this part, you will hear four statements about a picture in your test book. When you hear the statements, you must select the one statement that best describes what you see in the picture. Then find the number of the question on your answer sheet and mark your answer. The statements will not be printed in your test book and will be spoken only one time.

Sample Answer
Ⓐ ● Ⓒ Ⓓ

Statement (B), "They're shaking hands," is the best description of the picture, so you should select answer (B) and mark it on your answer sheet.

1.

2.

3.

4.

5.

6.

PART 2

Directions: You will hear a question or statement and three responses spoken in English. They will not be printed in your test book and will be spoken only one time. Select the best response to the question or statement and mark the letter (A), (B), or (C) on your answer sheet.

7. Mark your answer on your answer sheet.

8. Mark your answer on your answer sheet.

9. Mark your answer on your answer sheet.

10. Mark your answer on your answer sheet.

11. Mark your answer on your answer sheet.

12. Mark your answer on your answer sheet.

13. Mark your answer on your answer sheet.

14. Mark your answer on your answer sheet.

15. Mark your answer on your answer sheet.

16. Mark your answer on your answer sheet.

17. Mark your answer on your answer sheet.

18. Mark your answer on your answer sheet.

19. Mark your answer on your answer sheet.

20. Mark your answer on your answer sheet.

21. Mark your answer on your answer sheet.

22. Mark your answer on your answer sheet.

23. Mark your answer on your answer sheet.

24. Mark your answer on your answer sheet.

25. Mark your answer on your answer sheet.

26. Mark your answer on your answer sheet.

27. Mark your answer on your answer sheet.

28. Mark your answer on your answer sheet.

29. Mark your answer on your answer sheet.

30. Mark your answer on your answer sheet.

31. Mark your answer on your answer sheet.

PART 3

Directions: You will hear some conversations between two or more people. You will be asked to answer three questions about what the speakers say in each conversation. Select the best response to each question and mark the letter (A), (B), (C), or (D) on your answer sheet. The conversations will not be printed in your test book and will be spoken only one time.

32. What did the man write about?
    (A) His favorite pets
    (B) Visiting famous museums
    (C) How to make various dishes
    (D) Writing stories on a blog

33. Why is the man delighted?
    (A) He was given a prize for his writings.
    (B) His work will be published.
    (C) His articles earned favorable reviews.
    (D) He was promoted to editor in a publishing company.

34. Why does the woman want to meet with the man?
    (A) To talk about a future project
    (B) To reschedule an appointment
    (C) To receive some samples
    (D) To organize an exhibition

35. What are the speakers discussing?
    (A) A shopping list
    (B) A tourist attraction
    (C) A doctor's prescription
    (D) A canceled appointment

36. Why is the man behind schedule?
    (A) A staff member is out sick.
    (B) A doctor didn't write her a prescription.
    (C) He went out for lunch.
    (D) A pharmacy has been busy.

37. What does the woman say she will do?
    (A) Visit the doctor's office
    (B) Go to a nearby store
    (C) Make a phone call
    (D) Make an appointment

38. Why is the man calling?
    (A) To schedule a meeting
    (B) To complain about a product
    (C) To check a delivery schedule
    (D) To advertise a special promotion

39. What types of products does the man's company sell?
    (A) Home appliances
    (B) Computer
    (C) Office supplies
    (D) Furniture

40. What does the man offer to do for the woman?
    (A) Send a message
    (B) Refund her in full
    (C) Offer free delivery
    (D) Call her office

41. What is the man's complaint?
    (A) His room is dirty.
    (B) His reservation was canceled.
    (C) His air conditioner is broken.
    (D) His room is too small.

42. What does the woman offer to the man?
    (A) A free meal
    (B) A free shuttle bus to the airport
    (C) A room upgrade
    (D) A gift certificate

43. What does the man request?
    (A) Help with his luggage
    (B) A room change
    (C) Free Internet service
    (D) A discount coupon

Go on to the next page

44. Where does the woman work?
    (A) At a travel agency
    (B) At a department store
    (C) At a national museum
    (D) At a health clinic

45. What does the man say he will be doing next month?
    (A) Participating in a conference
    (B) Making a presentation
    (C) Traveling overseas
    (D) Writing a novel

46. What does the man imply when he says, "that's not going to work"?
    (A) He needs a different appointment.
    (B) He does not work on that day.
    (C) He prefers to work on schedule.
    (D) He will go abroad.

47. Why does the woman want to save money?
    (A) To replace a computer
    (B) To purchase a house
    (C) To go on vacation
    (D) To buy a car

48. What does the man recommend?
    (A) Applying for a loan
    (B) Selling a house
    (C) Using an online program
    (D) Cutting down on expenses

49. What is the woman concerned about?
    (A) Web site reliability
    (B) Service costs
    (C) Scheduling conflicts
    (D) A program's expiration date

50. Who most likely is the woman?
    (A) A graphic designer
    (B) An advertising agent
    (C) A store owner
    (D) A writer

51. What is the woman pleased about?
    (A) A final draft of an advertisement
    (B) Recent online reviews
    (C) A store location
    (D) Contact information

52. What does the man offer to do?
    (A) Install a computer program
    (B) Confirm service request
    (C) Print an advertisement
    (D) Enlarge an image

53. What does the woman imply when she says, "I'm really concerned"?
    (A) She is able to do volunteer work.
    (B) She is proud of attending the event.
    (C) She is indifferent about the matter.
    (D) She is worried about the complaints.

54. What is the woman concerned about?
    (A) Making a presentation
    (B) Responding to client complaints
    (C) Translating a different language
    (D) Doing multiple tasks at the same time

55. What does the man say he will do tomorrow?
    (A) Submit some paperwork
    (B) Bring a problem up at a meeting
    (C) Prepare the event
    (D) Conduct a customer survey

56. Where do the interviewers most likely work?
    (A) At a bookstore
    (B) At a kindergarten
    (C) At a publisher
    (D) At a broadcasting company

57. What job requirement do the speakers discuss?
    (A) Possessing the proper license
    (B) Owning the film equipment
    (C) Having related experience
    (D) Being able to work extra hours

58. What does the man agree to do next?
    (A) Show some previous work
    (B) Conduct a survey
    (C) Watch a presentation
    (D) Meet a president

59. What problem does the man mention?
    (A) Business is unusually slow.
    (B) A restaurant received several complaints.
    (C) A restaurant is short-staffed.
    (D) The rent has been gone up.

60. What does the man suggest?
    (A) Offering an outdoor event
    (B) Moving into a different location
    (C) Lowering prices
    (D) Acquiring popular restaurants

61. What does the woman ask the man to do?
    (A) Hire a manager
    (B) Train employees
    (C) Get ready for the holiday season
    (D) Prepare some food samples

62. What industry do the speakers most likely work in?
    (A) Pharmaceutical
    (B) Finance
    (C) Construction
    (D) Entertainment

63. What does the woman say will happen within two years?
    (A) Some research will receive a prize.
    (B) A new product will be introduced.
    (C) A company will hire more employees.
    (D) Another conference will be held.

64. What does the woman imply when she says, "Didn't Martial participate in this project"?
    (A) Some results are not promising.
    (B) A project will be finished soon.
    (C) A slide is missing some information.
    (D) The man must attend the conference.

Office	Location
Prudential Finance	Suite 101
York Foods	Suite 108
UK Express	Suite 111
Morris International	Suite 114

ITEM	PRICE
Computer hard case	$50
Computer bag	$80
Extended warranty	$200
Computer	$1500
Total	**$1830**

65. What is the purpose of the woman's visit?

    (A) To deliver a package
    (B) To have a client meeting
    (C) To go to the pharmacy
    (D) To have a medical appointment

66. What does the man say about parking?

    (A) It is available on the street near the building.
    (B) It is free for visitors with a validated parking ticket.
    (C) It is for tenants in the building.
    (D) It has a time limit.

67. Look at the graphic. Which office name has to be updated on the building directory?

    (A) Prudential Finance
    (B) York Foods
    (C) UK Express
    (D) Morris International

68. Who most likely is the woman?

    (A) A salesperson
    (B) An engineer
    (C) A bank clerk
    (D) A computer programmer

69. What does the man ask about?

    (A) A contract renewal
    (B) A payment method
    (C) Computer accessories
    (D) The price of a computer

70. Look at the graphic. Which amount will be removed from the invoice?

    (A) $50
    (B) $80
    (C) $200
    (D) $1500

PART 4

Directions: You will hear some talks given by a single speaker. You will be asked to answer three questions about what the speaker says in each talk. Select the best response to each question and mark the letter (A), (B), (C), or (D) on your answer sheet. The talks will not be printed in your test book and will be spoken only one time.

71. Where does the speaker work?
    (A) At a radio station
    (B) At a bookstore
    (C) At a university
    (D) At a consulting firm

72. What will Dr. Dooling be discussing?
    (A) Career management
    (B) Publishing books
    (C) Communication skills
    (D) Time management

73. What does the speaker encourage listeners to do?
    (A) Call in with questions
    (B) Register in advance
    (D) Save money
    (D) Buy more books

74. What is the man waiting for?
    (A) His passport to be issued
    (B) His airline ticket to be purchased
    (C) His colleagues to arrive
    (D) His luggage to be returned

75. What is scheduled for Monday?
    (A) A meeting
    (B) A product presentation
    (C) A doctor's appointment
    (D) A press conference

76. Why does the man say, "I know it's a difficult job"?
    (A) To advise the listener to finish the job quickly
    (B) To warn that the job is unnecessary
    (C) To apologize for an inconvenience
    (D) To remind the listener of its risks

77. What is the talk mainly about?
    (A) A wage system
    (B) Security enhancements
    (C) Head office relocation
    (D) A training schedule

78. According to the speaker, what will happen on Tuesday?
    (A) Additional staff will be employed.
    (B) An inspection will be carried out.
    (C) Office supplies will be purchased.
    (D) New procedures will take effect.

79. What must employees do this week?
    (A) Use a different entrance
    (B) Update company's accounts
    (C) Register their fingerprints
    (D) Apply for the program

80. What does the speaker say the company is considering?
    (A) Buying a new product
    (B) Changing the lunch time
    (C) Starting a new business
    (D) Extending business hours

81. What can listeners receive for free tomorrow?
    (A) A laptop
    (B) A T-shirt with a company logo
    (C) Stationery
    (D) Beverages

82. Why should listeners visit Belotti's office?
    (A) To pick up an employee ID card
    (B) To sign up for an employee program
    (C) To donate money
    (D) To submit a form

Go on to the next page

83. Where most likely is this announcement being made?

    (A) At a customer service center
    (B) At a factory
    (C) At a department store
    (D) At an auto repair shop

84. What problem does the speaker mention?

    (A) Some supplies are sold out.
    (B) A manager is sick.
    (C) Inclement weather is expected.
    (D) Some equipment is not working.

85. What will employees be informed about by assembly managers?

    (A) Test results
    (B) Safety regulations
    (C) Work schedule changes
    (D) Hygiene inspection

86. What is the news report about?

    (A) A celebrity's recipe book
    (B) A new seafood restaurant
    (C) Tips for selecting vegetables
    (D) Healthy eating habits

87. What does Dr. Watson recommend that people do?

    (A) Prepare meals at home
    (B) Buy special equipment
    (C) Enroll in a cooking class
    (D) Download recipes online

88. According to the speaker, what can listeners do on a Web site?

    (A) Make a reservation
    (B) Place an order
    (C) Read some survey questions
    (D) Sign up for a subscription

89. Why is the president coming for a visit?

    (A) A project has been completed.
    (B) A facility has been moved.
    (C) A manager will retire.
    (D) A sales record has been accomplished.

90. Why does the speaker say, "this is not a formal visit"?

    (A) To settle a dispute
    (B) To reassure employees
    (C) To apologize for problems
    (D) To check a procedure

91. What event have the listeners been invited to?

    (A) A retirement party
    (B) An opening ceremony
    (C) A welcome reception
    (D) A dinner party

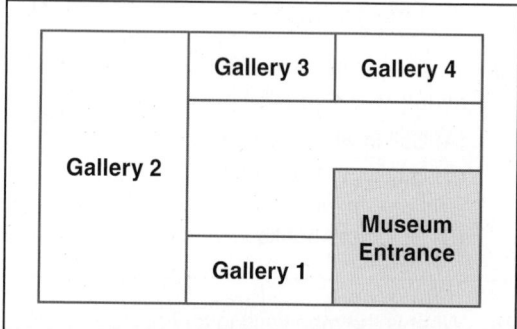

92. What did the listeners see on the tour?

    (A) Sculptures
    (B) Paintings
    (C) Photographs
    (D) Pottery

93. What does the guide recommend listeners do to learn more about the exhibition?

    (A) Visit a Web site
    (B) Attend a program
    (C) Buy a book
    (D) Watch a related movie

94. Look at the graphic. In which room is the exhibition on the works of Chagall?

    (A) Gallery 1
    (B) Gallery 2
    (C) Gallery 3
    (D) Gallery 4

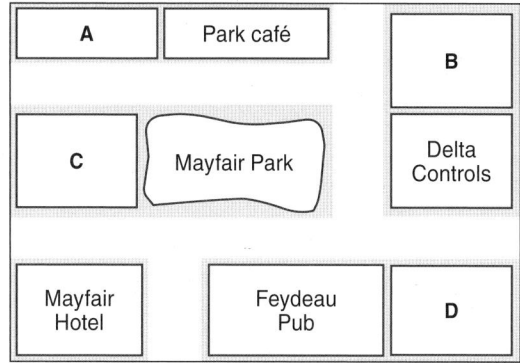
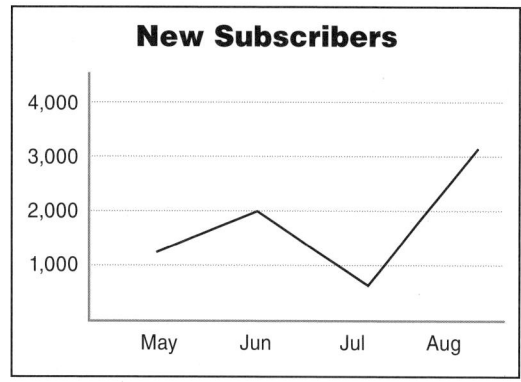

95. Why is the announcement being made?
    (A) To inform listeners about a change in working hours
    (B) To encourage employees to take part in the parade
    (C) To notify listeners of the unavailability of a parking space
    (D) To check the off-site duties for today

96. According to the speaker, what is going to happen in the area today?
    (A) Delta Controls will be closed.
    (B) There will be a big parade all day long.
    (C) Vehicles will be regulated for about 3 hours.
    (D) The streets will get jammed with cars during rush hour.

97. Look at the graphic. Which parking area was recommended by the speaker?
    (A) A
    (B) B
    (C) C
    (D) D

98. Where most likely does the speaker work?
    (A) At an advertising company
    (B) At a magazine publisher
    (C) At a leisure supplies manufacturer
    (D) At a market research institute

99. Look at the graphic. When did the company have its 5th anniversary?
    (A) In May
    (B) In June
    (C) In July
    (D) In August

100. According to the speaker, what does the business plan to do next month?
    (A) Offer a promotional event
    (B) Launch a new product
    (C) Get new advertisers
    (D) Conduct a survey

스파르타
新 TOEIC
실전 LC 1000제

Vol. 2

정답
&
스크립트

ANSWER KEY

TEST 1

1. (D)	21. (A)	41. (D)	61. (D)	81. (C)
2. (B)	22. (C)	42. (B)	62. (A)	82. (C)
3. (B)	23. (B)	43. (C)	63. (C)	83. (A)
4. (A)	24. (B)	44. (C)	64. (C)	84. (A)
5. (D)	25. (C)	45. (C)	65. (C)	85. (B)
6. (B)	26. (A)	46. (B)	66. (C)	86. (A)
7. (A)	27. (C)	47. (A)	67. (D)	87. (B)
8. (C)	28. (C)	48. (B)	68. (D)	88. (C)
9. (A)	29. (C)	49. (C)	69. (D)	89. (C)
10. (C)	30. (B)	50. (D)	70. (B)	90. (A)
11. (C)	31. (A)	51. (A)	71. (A)	91. (D)
12. (A)	32. (A)	52. (C)	72. (D)	92. (C)
13. (C)	33. (B)	53. (B)	73. (B)	93. (C)
14. (B)	34. (D)	54. (D)	74. (D)	94. (D)
15. (C)	35. (C)	55. (B)	75. (B)	95. (D)
16. (C)	36. (C)	56. (A)	76. (B)	96. (A)
17. (B)	37. (A)	57. (C)	77. (C)	97. (B)
18. (C)	38. (D)	58. (A)	78. (B)	98. (C)
19. (B)	39. (D)	59. (B)	79. (B)	99. (D)
20. (A)	40. (B)	60. (A)	80. (B)	100. (D)

TEST 2

1. (D)	21. (A)	41. (C)	61. (C)	81. (A)
2. (A)	22. (C)	42. (C)	62. (B)	82. (C)
3. (D)	23. (C)	43. (B)	63. (D)	83. (A)
4. (B)	24. (A)	44. (B)	64. (A)	84. (D)
5. (B)	25. (B)	45. (C)	65. (B)	85. (B)
6. (C)	26. (A)	46. (D)	66. (C)	86. (B)
7. (A)	27. (C)	47. (B)	67. (B)	87. (D)
8. (A)	28. (C)	48. (C)	68. (A)	88. (A)
9. (A)	29. (B)	49. (D)	69. (D)	89. (D)
10. (C)	30. (C)	50. (A)	70. (C)	90. (B)
11. (B)	31. (A)	51. (A)	71. (C)	91. (C)
12. (B)	32. (B)	52. (C)	72. (D)	92. (C)
13. (C)	33. (A)	53. (C)	73. (B)	93. (B)
14. (A)	34. (B)	54. (D)	74. (A)	94. (A)
15. (C)	35. (B)	55. (A)	75. (C)	95. (B)
16. (C)	36. (B)	56. (C)	76. (C)	96. (C)
17. (A)	37. (A)	57. (D)	77. (C)	97. (D)
18. (A)	38. (B)	58. (B)	78. (A)	98. (A)
19. (B)	39. (C)	59. (A)	79. (D)	99. (A)
20. (A)	40. (A)	60. (C)	80. (D)	100. (B)

TEST 3

1. (A)	21. (A)	41. (C)	61. (D)	81. (A)
2. (B)	22. (A)	42. (B)	62. (C)	82. (D)
3. (D)	23. (A)	43. (A)	63. (A)	83. (B)
4. (C)	24. (C)	44. (D)	64. (B)	84. (C)
5. (A)	25. (A)	45. (D)	65. (B)	85. (A)
6. (A)	26. (B)	46. (D)	66. (C)	86. (C)
7. (C)	27. (A)	47. (B)	67. (D)	87. (B)
8. (B)	28. (B)	48. (C)	68. (B)	88. (A)
9. (A)	29. (B)	49. (D)	69. (D)	89. (B)
10. (A)	30. (C)	50. (C)	70. (C)	90. (A)
11. (B)	31. (B)	51. (B)	71. (D)	91. (B)
12. (C)	32. (B)	52. (A)	72. (C)	92. (A)
13. (B)	33. (B)	53. (A)	73. (C)	93. (C)
14. (A)	34. (C)	54. (B)	74. (D)	94. (D)
15. (C)	35. (C)	55. (D)	75. (B)	95. (C)
16. (B)	36. (A)	56. (C)	76. (D)	96. (A)
17. (B)	37. (D)	57. (B)	77. (C)	97. (D)
18. (A)	38. (C)	58. (A)	78. (A)	98. (C)
19. (C)	39. (C)	59. (C)	79. (D)	99. (D)
20. (C)	40. (A)	60. (B)	80. (B)	100. (C)

TEST 4

1. (A)	21. (B)	41. (C)	61. (C)	81. (A)
2. (B)	22. (A)	42. (C)	62. (B)	82. (C)
3. (C)	23. (C)	43. (D)	63. (A)	83. (D)
4. (C)	24. (C)	44. (C)	64. (B)	84. (D)
5. (A)	25. (C)	45. (A)	65. (D)	85. (C)
6. (D)	26. (B)	46. (C)	66. (C)	86. (B)
7. (A)	27. (B)	47. (C)	67. (B)	87. (D)
8. (B)	28. (C)	48. (B)	68. (B)	88. (A)
9. (A)	29. (A)	49. (D)	69. (C)	89. (A)
10. (A)	30. (A)	50. (D)	70. (C)	90. (D)
11. (A)	31. (B)	51. (C)	71. (D)	91. (A)
12. (B)	32. (B)	52. (B)	72. (D)	92. (B)
13. (C)	33. (C)	53. (A)	73. (C)	93. (A)
14. (B)	34. (B)	54. (B)	74. (A)	94. (C)
15. (A)	35. (A)	55. (D)	75. (B)	95. (B)
16. (C)	36. (D)	56. (D)	76. (B)	96. (B)
17. (A)	37. (A)	57. (A)	77. (B)	97. (D)
18. (A)	38. (C)	58. (D)	78. (C)	98. (A)
19. (C)	39. (B)	59. (A)	79. (B)	99. (B)
20. (C)	40. (D)	60. (B)	80. (C)	100. (B)

TEST 5

1.	(B)	21.	(B)	41.	(A)	61.	(B)	81.	(C)
2.	(A)	22.	(A)	42.	(D)	62.	(D)	82.	(D)
3.	(A)	23.	(A)	43.	(B)	63.	(A)	83.	(A)
4.	(C)	24.	(C)	44.	(C)	64.	(D)	84.	(A)
5.	(C)	25.	(A)	45.	(D)	65.	(B)	85.	(D)
6.	(C)	26.	(B)	46.	(B)	66.	(C)	86.	(C)
7.	(C)	27.	(A)	47.	(A)	67.	(A)	87.	(A)
8.	(A)	28.	(B)	48.	(C)	68.	(C)	88.	(C)
9.	(C)	29.	(A)	49.	(A)	69.	(C)	89.	(C)
10.	(B)	30.	(A)	50.	(D)	70.	(D)	90.	(C)
11.	(C)	31.	(B)	51.	(B)	71.	(B)	91.	(C)
12.	(A)	32.	(C)	52.	(A)	72.	(A)	92.	(C)
13.	(B)	33.	(C)	53.	(B)	73.	(D)	93.	(A)
14.	(B)	34.	(C)	54.	(C)	74.	(A)	94.	(C)
15.	(B)	35.	(D)	55.	(C)	75.	(A)	95.	(C)
16.	(C)	36.	(B)	56.	(D)	76.	(B)	96.	(A)
17.	(C)	37.	(C)	57.	(A)	77.	(A)	97.	(A)
18.	(C)	38.	(A)	58.	(B)	78.	(D)	98.	(A)
19.	(A)	39.	(C)	59.	(A)	79.	(B)	99.	(C)
20.	(B)	40.	(C)	60.	(B)	80.	(A)	100.	(A)

TEST 7

1.	(C)	21.	(B)	41.	(C)	61.	(C)	81.	(B)
2.	(B)	22.	(A)	42.	(A)	62.	(B)	82.	(D)
3.	(D)	23.	(C)	43.	(C)	63.	(D)	83.	(D)
4.	(A)	24.	(C)	44.	(C)	64.	(B)	84.	(C)
5.	(D)	25.	(B)	45.	(B)	65.	(C)	85.	(B)
6.	(B)	26.	(A)	46.	(C)	66.	(C)	86.	(C)
7.	(B)	27.	(C)	47.	(C)	67.	(A)	87.	(A)
8.	(C)	28.	(A)	48.	(B)	68.	(B)	88.	(B)
9.	(B)	29.	(C)	49.	(C)	69.	(B)	89.	(B)
10.	(C)	30.	(C)	50.	(C)	70.	(C)	90.	(B)
11.	(C)	31.	(B)	51.	(B)	71.	(B)	91.	(C)
12.	(C)	32.	(C)	52.	(D)	72.	(C)	92.	(C)
13.	(A)	33.	(D)	53.	(B)	73.	(A)	93.	(C)
14.	(A)	34.	(C)	54.	(C)	74.	(B)	94.	(D)
15.	(B)	35.	(B)	55.	(C)	75.	(C)	95.	(B)
16.	(B)	36.	(C)	56.	(A)	76.	(A)	96.	(B)
17.	(C)	37.	(D)	57.	(C)	77.	(B)	97.	(D)
18.	(C)	38.	(C)	58.	(A)	78.	(C)	98.	(A)
19.	(B)	39.	(A)	59.	(C)	79.	(D)	99.	(B)
20.	(C)	40.	(B)	60.	(D)	80.	(A)	100.	(A)

TEST 6

1.	(C)	21.	(B)	41.	(D)	61.	(A)	81.	(A)
2.	(B)	22.	(C)	42.	(A)	62.	(A)	82.	(C)
3.	(C)	23.	(B)	43.	(A)	63.	(C)	83.	(B)
4.	(C)	24.	(A)	44.	(A)	64.	(B)	84.	(C)
5.	(D)	25.	(A)	45.	(A)	65.	(C)	85.	(B)
6.	(A)	26.	(B)	46.	(B)	66.	(C)	86.	(B)
7.	(B)	27.	(B)	47.	(B)	67.	(D)	87.	(A)
8.	(C)	28.	(B)	48.	(C)	68.	(C)	88.	(A)
9.	(B)	29.	(A)	49.	(B)	69.	(B)	89.	(C)
10.	(B)	30.	(B)	50.	(C)	70.	(D)	90.	(A)
11.	(C)	31.	(C)	51.	(A)	71.	(C)	91.	(A)
12.	(B)	32.	(B)	52.	(B)	72.	(D)	92.	(A)
13.	(B)	33.	(A)	53.	(A)	73.	(A)	93.	(B)
14.	(B)	34.	(C)	54.	(D)	74.	(B)	94.	(B)
15.	(A)	35.	(D)	55.	(C)	75.	(A)	95.	(A)
16.	(B)	36.	(A)	56.	(B)	76.	(D)	96.	(A)
17.	(B)	37.	(C)	57.	(D)	77.	(A)	97.	(D)
18.	(A)	38.	(C)	58.	(A)	78.	(C)	98.	(B)
19.	(B)	39.	(B)	59.	(C)	79.	(A)	99.	(C)
20.	(C)	40.	(B)	60.	(A)	80.	(D)	100.	(D)

TEST 8

1.	(C)	21.	(C)	41.	(C)	61.	(C)	81.	(C)
2.	(D)	22.	(C)	42.	(B)	62.	(D)	82.	(C)
3.	(B)	23.	(B)	43.	(C)	63.	(C)	83.	(C)
4.	(A)	24.	(B)	44.	(A)	64.	(B)	84.	(C)
5.	(C)	25.	(B)	45.	(C)	65.	(C)	85.	(D)
6.	(A)	26.	(B)	46.	(D)	66.	(A)	86.	(A)
7.	(B)	27.	(B)	47.	(B)	67.	(B)	87.	(B)
8.	(A)	28.	(B)	48.	(B)	68.	(A)	88.	(D)
9.	(A)	29.	(C)	49.	(C)	69.	(B)	89.	(A)
10.	(B)	30.	(C)	50.	(D)	70.	(A)	90.	(D)
11.	(B)	31.	(A)	51.	(A)	71.	(A)	91.	(B)
12.	(A)	32.	(B)	52.	(A)	72.	(D)	92.	(A)
13.	(B)	33.	(D)	53.	(D)	73.	(C)	93.	(D)
14.	(C)	34.	(C)	54.	(A)	74.	(A)	94.	(B)
15.	(C)	35.	(C)	55.	(B)	75.	(D)	95.	(C)
16.	(B)	36.	(A)	56.	(C)	76.	(A)	96.	(B)
17.	(A)	37.	(B)	57.	(B)	77.	(B)	97.	(A)
18.	(C)	38.	(A)	58.	(A)	78.	(C)	98.	(C)
19.	(B)	39.	(A)	59.	(C)	79.	(B)	99.	(C)
20.	(C)	40.	(B)	60.	(A)	80.	(D)	100.	(D)

ANSWER KEY

TEST 9

1.	(B)	21.	(B)	41.	(A)	61.	(A)	81.	(D)
2.	(B)	22.	(B)	42.	(B)	62.	(A)	82.	(B)
3.	(A)	23.	(C)	43.	(D)	63.	(A)	83.	(C)
4.	(C)	24.	(A)	44.	(C)	64.	(A)	84.	(D)
5.	(B)	25.	(A)	45.	(D)	65.	(D)	85.	(C)
6.	(C)	26.	(A)	46.	(B)	66.	(C)	86.	(B)
7.	(B)	27.	(C)	47.	(D)	67.	(D)	87.	(D)
8.	(B)	28.	(A)	48.	(B)	68.	(A)	88.	(C)
9.	(A)	29.	(B)	49.	(C)	69.	(C)	89.	(C)
10.	(A)	30.	(A)	50.	(D)	70.	(C)	90.	(B)
11.	(C)	31.	(A)	51.	(D)	71.	(D)	91.	(A)
12.	(C)	32.	(A)	52.	(A)	72.	(A)	92.	(B)
13.	(C)	33.	(B)	53.	(A)	73.	(D)	93.	(D)
14.	(B)	34.	(A)	54.	(A)	74.	(B)	94.	(D)
15.	(B)	35.	(B)	55.	(A)	75.	(B)	95.	(B)
16.	(C)	36.	(C)	56.	(B)	76.	(B)	96.	(D)
17.	(B)	37.	(D)	57.	(D)	77.	(D)	97.	(C)
18.	(A)	38.	(A)	58.	(A)	78.	(D)	98.	(A)
19.	(B)	39.	(A)	59.	(C)	79.	(C)	99.	(D)
20.	(B)	40.	(D)	60.	(B)	80.	(C)	100.	(A)

TEST 10

1.	(B)	21.	(A)	41.	(C)	61.	(D)	81.	(D)
2.	(D)	22.	(B)	42.	(C)	62.	(A)	82.	(D)
3.	(A)	23.	(C)	43.	(A)	63.	(B)	83.	(B)
4.	(C)	24.	(B)	44.	(D)	64.	(C)	84.	(D)
5.	(A)	25.	(C)	45.	(C)	65.	(D)	85.	(C)
6.	(D)	26.	(A)	46.	(A)	66.	(B)	86.	(D)
7.	(A)	27.	(C)	47.	(B)	67.	(D)	87.	(A)
8.	(B)	28.	(A)	48.	(C)	68.	(A)	88.	(C)
9.	(C)	29.	(C)	49.	(B)	69.	(B)	89.	(A)
10.	(C)	30.	(B)	50.	(C)	70.	(C)	90.	(B)
11.	(A)	31.	(C)	51.	(A)	71.	(A)	91.	(C)
12.	(B)	32.	(C)	52.	(D)	72.	(D)	92.	(B)
13.	(B)	33.	(B)	53.	(D)	73.	(A)	93.	(C)
14.	(A)	34.	(A)	54.	(B)	74.	(D)	94.	(A)
15.	(A)	35.	(C)	55.	(B)	75.	(B)	95.	(C)
16.	(B)	36.	(D)	56.	(C)	76.	(C)	96.	(C)
17.	(A)	37.	(B)	57.	(D)	77.	(B)	97.	(C)
18.	(B)	38.	(D)	58.	(A)	78.	(D)	98.	(B)
19.	(B)	39.	(A)	59.	(A)	79.	(C)	99.	(C)
20.	(C)	40.	(A)	60.	(C)	80.	(A)	100.	(D)

1회

1.	(D)	21.	(A)	41.	(D)	61.	(D)	81.	(C)
2.	(B)	22.	(C)	42.	(B)	62.	(A)	82.	(C)
3.	(B)	23.	(B)	43.	(C)	63.	(C)	83.	(A)
4.	(A)	24.	(B)	44.	(C)	64.	(C)	84.	(A)
5.	(D)	25.	(C)	45.	(D)	65.	(C)	85.	(B)
6.	(B)	26.	(A)	46.	(B)	66.	(C)	86.	(A)
7.	(A)	27.	(B)	47.	(A)	67.	(D)	87.	(B)
8.	(C)	28.	(C)	48.	(B)	68.	(D)	88.	(C)
9.	(A)	29.	(C)	49.	(C)	69.	(D)	89.	(C)
10.	(C)	30.	(B)	50.	(D)	70.	(B)	90.	(A)
11.	(C)	31.	(A)	51.	(A)	71.	(A)	91.	(D)
12.	(A)	32.	(A)	52.	(C)	72.	(D)	92.	(C)
13.	(C)	33.	(B)	53.	(B)	73.	(B)	93.	(C)
14.	(B)	34.	(D)	54.	(D)	74.	(D)	94.	(D)
15.	(B)	35.	(C)	55.	(B)	75.	(B)	95.	(D)
16.	(C)	36.	(C)	56.	(A)	76.	(B)	96.	(A)
17.	(B)	37.	(A)	57.	(C)	77.	(C)	97.	(B)
18.	(C)	38.	(D)	58.	(A)	78.	(B)	98.	(C)
19.	(B)	39.	(D)	59.	(B)	79.	(B)	99.	(D)
20.	(A)	40.	(B)	60.	(A)	80.	(B)	100.	(D)

Part 1

1. (A) She's throwing a ball.
   (B) She's appreciating the paintings.
   (C) She's leaning against the wall.
   (D) She's painting the wall.

2. (A) People are singing together.
   (B) People are playing different instruments.
   (C) People are facing each other.
   (D) People are marching in formation.

3. (A) Bicycles are being assembled.
   (B) Bicycles are attached to bicycle racks.
   (C) The road is being paved.
   (D) Bicycles are against the wall.

4. (A) There is merchandise on the shelves.
   (B) The people are all carrying a backpack.
   (C) One of the women is paying for some items.
   (D) One of the women is mopping the floor.

5. (A) The frame is being cut.
   (B) The man is removing his gloves.
   (C) The ladder is being made.
   (D) The man is welding.

6. (A) An airplane is landing.
   (B) An aircraft is parked at the airport.
   (C) People are waving their hands from the airplane.
   (D) People are exiting the plane.

Part 2

7. Are you satisfied with your new wallet?
   (A) Absolutely! I'm very happy with it.
   (B) Yes, for our customer satisfaction.
   (C) No, it's hanging on the wall.

8. Do you happen to know who's in charge of revising the budget report?
   (A) Yes, I was overcharged.
   (B) No, you don't need to go over the report.
   (C) I guess Mr. Carter is responsible for that.

9. Who will be making the first speech?
   (A) Mr. Hernandez from the Singapore branch.
   (B) Yes, I will make a phone call to you later.
   (C) Melanie missed the first class.

10. What's the weather like there in Toronto?
    (A) She likes living in Toronto.
    (B) I don't know whether it will rain tomorrow.
    (C) It's cold and snowy.

11. When is the next flight scheduled to leave?
    (A) No, he left 10 minutes ago.
    (B) I think we're behind schedule.
    (C) At 7:30 P.M. sharp.

12. Where is the instruction manual for the new copier?
    (A) I guess it's in the bottom drawer.
    (B) I don't like coffee.
    (C) I think he is a good instructor.

13. How long have you worked for this company?
    (A) Approximately 30 years ago.
    (B) Around 11 P.M.
    (C) About 5 years.

14. Why did Christine cancel her trip to Hawaii?
    (A) She was born in Hawaii.
    (B) She had the flu.
    (C) The meeting was canceled.

15. Which caterer is supplying food for the wedding reception?
    (A) A small amount of food.
    (B) The same one we used last month.
    (C) The orders have come in online.

16. I think we'd better get there by subway.
    (A) Okay, I'll pick it up.
    (B) I left my bag in the subway.
    (C) Yes, if you want to avoid traffic.

17. You're going to the concert after work, aren't you?
    (A) Sorry, I didn't watch the concert last night.
    (B) No, I have some overtime work.
    (C) No, tickets are still available.

18. Do you happen to know how I can access the company's files?
    (A) At the accessory shop.
    (B) You can accompany me.
    (C) You should enter the code first.

19. Which do you prefer, a table in the middle or by the window?
    (A) A table for three, please.
    (B) I don't have a preference.
    (C) Yes, that sounds great.

20. What was J&J Company's final offer for a bid?
    (A) Approximately 10 million dollars.
    (B) It's a really good offer.
    (C) At the final stage.

21. Was it a long journey?
    (A) It certainly was.
    (B) Yes, hurry up.
    (C) No, he has a long beard.

22. I strongly believe she wears contact lenses.
    (A) I swear I'll accept your offer.
    (B) I don't wear perfume at all.
    (C) How can you tell?

23. Why don't we go over the résumés over lunch?
    (A) We'll review the applications tonight.
    (B) That sounds great.
    (C) Lunch was terrific.

24. Wouldn't this platter be good for a wedding gift?
    (A) It's really good for your health.
    (B) I think it couldn't be better.
    (C) Yes, he is planning to go there.

TEST 01

25. Should I send this package by regular mail or by courier?
    (A) No, your career is excellent.
    (B) Yes, you've got mail.
    (C) It depends on how urgent it is.

26. Who will accompany you to the airport?
    (A) My colleague at work is taking me.
    (B) It's a publishing company.
    (C) My friend will pick me up at the airport.

27. Did you consider applying for the job in marketing?
    (A) A ten percent discount applies to this item.
    (B) Why? Do they have an opening?
    (C) No, I don't need to purchase office supplies.

28. When is your company planning to announce the merger?
    (A) It's an emergency meeting.
    (B) Three days ago.
    (C) We're holding a press conference until next month.

29. The train left on time, didn't it?
    (A) At the training session.
    (B) No, he didn't.
    (C) Yes, like always.

30. Where can I find Professor Eugene's office?
    (A) Mondays between 1 and 3.
    (B) I'm afraid he's on vacation.
    (C) Did you check the lost and found?

31. Haven't you found your briefcase yet?
    (A) No, I failed to find it.
    (B) It will be a brief meeting.
    (C) Yes, it was founded two years ago.

Part 3

Questions 32-34 refer to the following conversation.

M   Which flight do you think we should take?
W   Well, there are two to Detroit. One is at 9 A.M., and the other leaves at 11:30 A.M.
M   Let's take the one at nine o'clock. That way, we'll have time to grab some lunch before that noon meeting starts.
W   That sounds like a nice plan. I'll make the reservations.
M   Okay, thank you.

32. What mode of transportation will the speakers use?
    (A) Aircraft
    (B) Car
    (C) Boat
    (D) Train

33. What time do the speakers plan to travel?
    (A) At 5:00 A.M.
    (B) At 9:00 A.M.
    (C) At 11:30 A.M.
    (D) At 12:00 P.M.

34. What will the woman probably do next?
    (A) Attend a meeting
    (B) Have lunch
    (C) Travel to Detroit
    (D) Book tickets

新 Questions 35-37 refer to the following conversation with three speakers.

W   Did you hear the news? Jim got that promotion he applied for. He's going to be the senior manager of human resources at the head office. I just heard about it from Jane in accounting.
M1   Wow, he must be really excited. When will he be starting the new position?
W   They need him there in three weeks. The previous manager will be retiring then.
M2   Good for Jim.
M1   Why don't we throw him a party?
W   That sounds like a great idea.

35. What is the main topic of the conversation?
    (A) An upcoming corporate merger
    (B) A round of layoffs
    (C) The promotion of a coworker
    (D) Plans for summer vacation

36. When will the discussed event happen?
    (A) Immediately
    (B) In a week
    (C) In three weeks
    (D) In the New Year

37. What is the timing of the event dependent upon?
    (A) Someone's retirement
    (B) The opening of a location
    (C) The redecoration of an office
    (D) The completion of training

Questions 38-40 refer to the following conversation.

M   Future World Home Furnishings and Appliances. This is Gary speaking. How can I help you today?
W   Um, yeah, I bought a bread maker machine at your downtown store. It's the Happy Home brand, model 435. I read the manual, but I can't seem to figure out how to set the auto-start timer.
M   Okay, let me just access the manual for that item. Let's see… first you need to press the "Mode" button until "Auto-Start" appears in the lower right of the LCD screen. Then press the "Set" button until the display shows the number of hours later you want the unit to start.
W   Okay, here we go… Oh, that was easy; I can't believe I couldn't figure that out. Thanks so much.

38. Why is the woman calling?
    (A) To request a refund
    (B) To request a service visit
    (C) To ask for directions to the store
    (D) To get help with a product

39. What did the woman have trouble with?
    (A) Activating the lighting display
    (B) Deciding what ingredients to add
    (C) Assembling the product
    (D) Setting the timer

40. What did the woman say she had already done?
    (A) Spoken to a service technician
    (B) Looked over the manual
    (C) Turned the product off and on
    (D) Exchanged the product

Questions 41-43 refer to the following conversation.

M How are you doing with the final project for our new promotional event?
W Not good at all. I've only just glanced at the proposal. I've just got so much other stuff going on right now. I really don't think I'll finish it in time.
M No kidding. I'm busy too. It's due this Monday morning, isn't it? Why don't you ask to get an extension?
W It's hard to say, but I'll stop by now and ask the director. You should come with me.
M I'm afraid I can't. I have a doctor's appointment.

41. What is the main topic of the conversation?
    (A) Arranging a date
    (B) Seeing a doctor
    (C) Signing up for a training
    (D) Finishing an assignment

42. What is the due date?
    (A) Friday
    (B) Monday
    (C) Tuesday
    (D) Thursday

43. What will the woman probably do next?
    (A) Send an e-mail
    (B) Finish an assignment
    (C) Visit a director
    (D) Go to a movie

Questions 44-46 refer to the following conversation.

M Hi Jinny, this is Sam Billings calling. I need to have Dr. Jones take a look at my foot. When do you think I would be able to get in to see him? I'd like to get in as soon as possible.
W Well, he's available this Friday at 3 P.M., next Monday at 2 P.M., or next Wednesday at 5:30.
M I can't really get in during the work day, so I guess I'll have to come in on Wednesday.
W Wednesday it is then. Please let us know as soon as possible if anything comes up that won't let you make the appointment.

44. What job does Jinny most likely do?
    (A) Factory worker
    (B) Dental assistant
    (C) Doctor's receptionist
    (D) Personal trainer

45. What day can the man come in?
    (A) Friday
    (B) Monday
    (C) Tuesday
    (D) Wednesday

46. What does the woman ask the man to do?
    (A) Call another branch of the business
    (B) Call to advise them of any changes
    (C) Consult a specialist
    (D) Pay a deposit in advance

Questions 47-49 refer to the following conversation.

M Hey, Betsy, this note on my desk says that the CEO of the company wants to meet with me. Do you have any idea what that's all about?
W Apparently, he's bringing in all the heads of the departments to discuss ideas to save money. He's going to want to know what you think you can do here in maintenance.
M I'm not sure how much we can do here. I think I run a pretty tight ship. I suppose I could try to see if I can find cheaper suppliers for some of the cleaning products we use.
W That's a good idea. We could also cut back a bit more on heating and air conditioning on the weekends. Maybe restrict it to some special work areas for the few people who do come in.

47. What is the man asking about?
    (A) Why the CEO wants to see him
    (B) Where to buy cleaning supplies
    (C) The date and time of a meeting
    (D) The status of a utility bill

48. What department is the man the head of?
    (A) Marketing
    (B) Maintenance
    (C) Accounting
    (D) Public relations

49. What idea does the woman have?
    (A) Having a meeting with the CEO
    (B) Reorganizing the department
    (C) Reducing air conditioning and heating
    (D) Finding cheaper suppliers for cleaning supplies

Questions 50-52 refer to the following conversation.

M Jessica, we're supposed to have that staff dinner the day after tomorrow, aren't we? What time is that supposed to start?
W I booked a room at the Red Dragon Chinese Restaurant for 7:30. I know you requested that we have it at that Mongolian buffet place, but they were all booked up that day. I ate at the Red Dragon not too long ago, and it was really good.
M That sounds fine to me. Just make sure we get a big enough room. When I was there last, we were packed into one that should have had about six fewer people in it.
W I've already checked; the room has plenty of space for us all.

50. What event will happen the day after tomorrow?
    (A) A training seminar
    (B) A management meeting
    (C) A cooking lesson
    (D) A meal with employees

51. Where will the event most likely happen?
    (A) At a Chinese restaurant
    (B) At a Mongolian buffet
    (C) At the company cafeteria
    (D) In the manager's home

52. What does the man mean when he says, "When I was there last, we were packed into one that should have had about six fewer people in it"?
    (A) The food was not good.
    (B) Some of the staff didn't show up.
    (C) The room was too small.
    (D) The wait staff was not polite.

Questions 53-55 refer to the following conversation.

W: Darren, I thought you told me that the flyers with the new phone number for the delivery service were supposed to be ready today.
M: They were, but the printing company has a backlog of orders. They've promised to get them to us sometime tomorrow afternoon.
W: I guess that will be alright, but they definitely need to be sent out before the old number is deactivated. If not, we'll lose a lot of business.
M: No worries. I'll double-check with the printer now, and I'll arrange for the delivery service to be ready as soon as the flyers are.

53. What is the main topic of the conversation?
(A) A retirement party
(B) A printing order
(C) An employee training seminar
(D) The promotion of a colleague

54. What is the company in the process of doing?
(A) Signing a contract
(B) Hiring new employees
(C) Relocating its offices
(D) Changing its phone number

55. What will the man probably do next?
(A) Order lunch
(B) Contact a company
(C) Go home for the day
(D) Arrange a meeting

Questions 56-58 refer to the following conversation.

W: Hey, John, what do you think of the new head of accounting, Mr. Aimes? He just started yesterday.
M: He seems like a really capable guy. I heard he just finished an MBA program at the same time as holding down his full-time job. That's quite impressive.
W: Right. There's no way I could do that. It's all I can do to change out of my work clothes at the end of the day. How do you think he'll handle the department?
M: I imagine he'll make a few changes. People coming out of MBA programs often have been studying very up-to-date approaches to things. He'll probably want to try out a few of the ideas that he has been working on.

56. What is the main topic of the conversation?
(A) A new staff member
(B) A rescheduled meeting
(C) An office relocation
(D) A new training program

57. What does the man mean when he says, "He'll probably want to try out a few of the ideas that he has been working on"?
(A) Company travel will be reduced.
(B) New office furniture will be ordered.
(C) New ideas will be implemented.
(D) Staff numbers will be reduced.

58. What has Mr. Aimes recently done?
(A) Completed his MBA
(B) Fired a poorly performing employee
(C) Canceled a sales seminar
(D) Trained a new secretary

Questions 59-61 refer to the following conversation.

M: Hi, I'd like to get this letter to my sister in Manila before the end of the week. Is that possible?
W: Yes, that would be our express service. It's guaranteed to be there within three days. It's not cheap, though. The cost for that is $15.65. Will that be okay?
M: Wow, that certainly isn't cheap. How much does it cost to have a confirmation of her receiving the letter?
W: Oh, that's actually included in the cost of our express service. Please fill out this form.

59. Where does the woman most likely work?
(A) At a doctor's office
(B) At a post office
(C) At a ski resort
(D) At a health club

60. How much extra does the receipt confirmation cost?
(A) $0.00
(B) $5.00
(C) $10.75
(D) $15.65

61. What does the woman ask the man to do?
(A) Attend a seminar
(B) Submit a report
(C) Deliver a letter
(D) Complete a form

Questions 62-64 refer to the following conversation and list.

M: Jessie, I'm very excited about the concert our company is supporting. A lot of fans will be joining it. So it definitely will be great publicity.
W: Thanks for reminding me. Have you checked the list of graphic design firms we are considering to design the concert souvenirs? We need to hire one soon so the souvenirs will be ready in time.
M: Oh, sorry, I was busy with the budget report, but I can look at it now. I think Hoo Design is great to work with, but that we need a company that's a little less expensive. As you know, we have a tight budget.
W: You're right. Why don't we go for the one in New York? I'm pretty sure this firm has a good reputation, and its prices are very reasonable.

62. What type of event is the company sponsoring?
(A) A musical event
(B) An auction
(C) A theater performance
(D) A sporting event

63. What is the man concerned about?
(A) A lack of volunteers
(B) A customer complaint
(C) A limited budget
(D) A delayed concert

64. Look at the graphic. Which company do the speakers choose?
(A) Great View Art
(B) Hoo Design
(C) Supreme Design
(D) Modern Art

Questions 65-67 refer to the following conversation and floor plan.

M Catherine, I know you're heading to the express bus terminal soon to visit a client in Boston, but do you have time to approve the room assignment for our improvement?
W No problem. So, what are we looking at here?
M Rooms A and B have been assigned to the human resources department. And you've got the office next to the Information Desk.
W That's good for me. So, that leaves the corner office for you, right?
M Yes, I thought it would be good for me to be close to both the HR team and you.
W That sounds like a great idea. I think our members of staff will be very happy to hear about the assignments at the meeting next Wednesday.

65. According to the man, what will the woman be doing today?
(A) Shopping for some office supplies
(B) Reporting a renovation plan
(C) Taking public transportation
(D) Preparing a press release

66. Look at the graphic. Which office has been assigned to the man?
(A) Room A
(B) Room B
(C) Room C
(D) Room D

67. What does the woman say will take place next week?
(A) A new product launch
(B) A retirement party
(C) A conference call
(D) A staff meeting

Questions 68-70 refer to the following conversation and map.

W I'm so glad I ran into you, Mark. This rest area is quite confusing. I'm on my way to the airport, but I'm not sure which highway I should take. I usually take highway 11, but it's closed for repaving the road.
M Well, I have a highway map with me. I always take this route. Even though it's not an expressway, it doesn't take that long. And you can stop at Urban Crossing if you want to.
W Thanks for the tip. I don't want to miss my flight to Seoul.
M Why are you going there?
W Actually, I'm going to my cousin's wedding. I'll tell you all about it at our next regular staff meeting.
M I'll look forward to it. Have a great trip!

68. Where does the conversation take place?
(A) At an airport
(B) At a business office
(C) At a hotel
(D) At a rest area

69. Look at the graphic. Which route does the man suggest the woman take?
(A) Highway 7
(B) Highway 11
(C) Highway 13
(D) Highway 15

70. Why is the woman going to Seoul?
(A) To attend a meeting
(B) To visit a relative
(C) To interview for a job
(D) To buy a car

Part 4

Questions 71-73 refer to the following report.

Welcome to CKDU's Homeward Bound traffic report. Traffic is moving surprisingly well for a long weekend Friday. The McKay and McDonald bridges are both busy but steady. The one area where commuters will encounter some delays is the downtown area near Barrington Street. Traffic is still moving but is being hampered by a group of protesters. Apparently, the group is protesting new reductions to unemployment benefits. Try to avoid that area if at all possible. The construction that was slowing down Bay Road has finally been completed, and that road is also moving well. Enjoy the long weekend. This is Debra Bartlett for CKDU, your best source for news and information. Stay tuned for Joe Haskins with the weather.

71. What is the report mainly about?
(A) Traffic
(B) Political protests
(C) The weather
(D) Transportation costs

72. According to the announcer, what has caused a problem?
(A) Closed bridges
(B) Bad weather
(C) Construction
(D) A rally

73. What will the listeners probably hear next?
(A) A music program
(B) The weather report
(C) A game show
(D) The local news

Questions 74-76 refer to the following advertisement.

Are you a university student? Are you looking for something different than the average summer job? Backwoods Tours is looking for physically fit and outgoing people to serve as guides on river rafting excursions in the British Columbia interior. Our clientele includes people from all over the world and we offer trips with varying levels of challenge. Experience is preferred; however, we can provide full training. If you think you have what it takes to fill this satisfying and challenging position, call us today at 406-755-1244 to arrange an interview, or send your résumé and cover letter to application@backwoodstours.com. Make that call today and get ready for the adventure of a lifetime.

74. What is the advertisement about?
(A) An exercise program
(B) A rafting tour
(C) A holiday sale
(D) A job opportunity

75. What qualifications should applicants have?
(A) Previous experience
(B) Physical fitness
(C) A pilot's license
(D) Their own vehicle

76. What are people interested in the job asked to do?
(A) Come to a job fair
(B) Contact the company
(C) Check the Web site
(D) Complete a test

Questions 77-79 refer to the following telephone message.

Hi, this is Dana calling from the Downtown Health Clinic. According to your file, you are due for your annual physical. We have an appointment available next Tuesday at 2:00. Please give me a call at 555-7414 to let me know if this would be suitable for you. Don't forget that the clinic has moved since you were last here. We're still in the State Building, but we're on the ninth floor now and not the twelfth floor.

77. Where does the speaker most likely work?
(A) At a pharmacy
(B) At a dentist
(C) At a doctor's office
(D) At a beauty salon

78. Why is the woman calling?
(A) To request a payment
(B) To arrange an appointment
(C) To cancel a test
(D) To book a surgery

79. What does the woman mean when she says, "don't forget that the clinic has moved since you were last here"?
(A) To let the customer know the appointment has been changed
(B) To remind the customer of the new location of the hospital
(C) To let the listener know the doctor is not available
(D) To confirm that the customer must not be late

Questions 80-82 refer to the following announcement.

Ladies and gentlemen, this is your captain, Vincent McKenzie, speaking. On behalf of myself and the entire crew, I would like to welcome you aboard Eva Air flight 867 from Taipei to Bangkok. We will be departing shortly, and we'll touch down in Bangkok at approximately 8:15 P.M. with a total flying time of approximately three hours and fifteen minutes. The weather today in Bangkok is hot and humid at 32 degrees Celsius. Your flight attendants will go through the safety procedures with you shortly. And about 30 minutes after takeoff, meals will be served. While you may feel free to move about the cabin while the seatbelt light is off, please return to your seat immediately when you see the seatbelt light activated. Thanks for flying with Eva Air and enjoy your flight.

80. Who most likely is the speaker?
(A) A flight attendant
(B) An aviator
(C) A customs officer
(D) A businessman

81. Where are the listeners going?
(A) Tokyo
(B) Taipei
(C) Bangkok
(D) Havana

82. What most likely will happen next?
(A) Passengers will get off the plane.
(B) The plane will land.
(C) Safety procedures will be demonstrated.
(D) The passengers will receive lunch.

Questions 83-85 refer to the following talk.

Greetings, everyone. Welcome to the World Technology Conference. Over the course of the weekend, you will have the chance to learn about some of the most amazing breakthroughs in technology that have been made over the last year. Companies and institutes from over 30 countries are represented here. You will have the chance to experience demonstrations, roundtable debates, and presentations. The first order of business, however, will be a welcome banquet followed by a cocktail party, where those of you who already know each other can get reacquainted and those of you who have not met yet can make your introductions. Dinner will be served in about 30 minutes in the Paradise Room.

83. What is the talk mainly about?
(A) Events at the conference
(B) The dinner menu
(C) Accommodation arrangements
(D) Rules for the conference

84. What does the man mean when he says, "Welcome to the World Technology Conference"?
(A) Scientists are attending the conference.
(B) Musicians are attending the conference.
(C) Construction workers are attending the conference.
(D) Fitness coaches are attending the conference.

85. What is the first event of the conference?
(A) A technology demonstration
(B) A meal with attendees
(C) An award presentation
(D) A roundtable debate

Questions 86-88 refer to the following talk.

I'd like to welcome our research interns to the summer program at Healthcom Technologies. I've been a researcher here at Healthcom for more than 15 years now. During that time, I never learned more than when I was an intern here in the summer program myself. Through the course of that summer I became acquainted with technologies far ahead of what I was exposed to at my university. More importantly, I developed a work ethic that has served me well throughout my research career. I learned the ability to do more than one thing at the same time and to work in a team environment with other researchers. You will all work very hard over the next 2 months and you will not be paid a great deal of money, but I believe that you will take something away from here that money cannot buy.

86. What type of work will the interns be doing?
(A) Laboratory research
(B) Navigation
(C) Advertising
(D) Police work

87. What does the man mean when he says, "I learned the ability to do more than one thing at the same time"?
(A) He has lab techniques.
(B) He is good at multitasking.
(C) He has an ability to keep the records accurately.
(D) He is available 24-hours a day.

88. How long is the internship program?
(A) Two weeks
(B) One month
(C) Two months
(D) Three months

Questions 89-91 refer to the following talk.

Ladies and gentlemen, thank you for attending this celebration. I am very pleased to announce that this has been the most profitable year in the history of HighTechno Computers. We could not have done it without each and every one of you. Thanks to your efforts, profits are up 27% over last year. Furthermore, we are ready to release our newest computer program package, Super Bits, more than a month ahead of schedule. Now, here to present the highly coveted award for Employee of the Year is Dean Anderson, head of human resources. Everyone, let's give Dean a warm welcome.

89. Who is the intended audience of this talk?
(A) Potential clients
(B) Law enforcement officers
(C) Company employees
(D) Company shareholders

90. What does the company probably sell?
(A) Software
(B) Cars
(C) Carpet
(D) Appliances

91. What will Mr. Anderson probably do next?
(A) Submit a report
(B) Conduct an interview
(C) Have dinner
(D) Award a prize

Questions 92-94 refer to the following talk.

Welcome to the Museum of Modern Art, or MOMA, as we like to call it around here. Today's tour will last approximately thirty minutes and will focus primarily on our current exhibition of some of the pioneers of modern painting. This includes some of the works of Edvard Munch, Gustav Klimt, Toulouse-Lautrec, and Kandinsky. We will also touch on some of the works of some important sculptors and lithograph makers. After the tour, please don't forget to visit the gift shop. There are some excellent books that deal with some of the individual artists that we have here as well as others that deal with specific areas of our permanent collection. If you follow me, first off, we have a collection of some of the works of Edvard Munch.

92. Who most likely is the speaker?
(A) A bank teller
(B) A cafeteria employee
(C) A museum guide
(D) A marketing manager

93. How long will the tour be?
(A) 20 minutes
(B) 45 minutes
(C) A half hour
(D) An hour and a half

94. What will the tour members probably do last?
(A) Go to the airport
(B) Fill out a form
(C) Book a tour
(D) Visit the souvenir shop

Questions 95-97 refer to the following report and map.

Attention, Central Apartment residents. This is a reminder that the city's annual marathon race will be taking place on April 15. The road that runs in front of the main entrance will be closed for the competition from 9:00 A.M. to 3:00 P.M. The other streets around our apartment complex will still remain open. So drivers who use that road should think about taking an alternate road. Whatever route you decide to take to work, you have to allow more time to commute. Otherwise, you will be stuck in heavy traffic because of this event. We'll keep you updated.

95. What will take place on April 15?
(A) A flea market
(B) A job fair
(C) Some road construction
(D) A sporting event

96. Look at the graphic. Which street will be closed?
(A) Kane Avenue
(B) Madison Road
(C) Maple Road
(D) Parkland Avenue

97. What does the speaker suggest?
(A) Heading for the office late
(B) Making a detour
(C) Using public transportation
(D) Considering joining a car pool

Questions 98-100 refer to the following telephone message and expense report.

Hello, Cathy. This is Eugene from accounting. I'm examining the expense report you submitted for your recent business trip to Seattle, but I can't find one of your receipts. I see you are requesting reimbursement for an expense of $250 on May 10th, but I can't find the receipt for it. It looks like it was missing when you submitted the paperwork. I'll need that to process your request for the reimbursement. If you don't have it now, can you call me at extension 3 and then I'll tell you what the procedure is for requesting reimbursement without a receipt. I'm looking forward to hearing from you soon.

98. Why is the speaker calling?
(A) Some paperwork did not have a signature.
(B) A reservation has changed.
(C) A certain receipt was not included.
(D) The dates of the business trip were wrong.

99. Look at the graphic. Which expense needs to be confirmed?
(A) Car rental
(B) Meal
(C) Parking
(D) Accommodations

100. What does speaker say he can do?
(A) Cancel a reservation
(B) Handle a complaint
(C) Hire a new employee
(D) Explain a process

2회

1.	(D)	21.	(A)	41.	(C)	61.	(C)	81.	(A)
2.	(A)	22.	(C)	42.	(C)	62.	(B)	82.	(C)
3.	(D)	23.	(C)	43.	(B)	63.	(D)	83.	(A)
4.	(B)	24.	(A)	44.	(B)	64.	(A)	84.	(D)
5.	(B)	25.	(B)	45.	(C)	65.	(B)	85.	(B)
6.	(C)	26.	(A)	46.	(D)	66.	(C)	86.	(B)
7.	(C)	27.	(C)	47.	(B)	67.	(B)	87.	(D)
8.	(A)	28.	(C)	48.	(C)	68.	(A)	88.	(A)
9.	(A)	29.	(B)	49.	(D)	69.	(D)	89.	(D)
10.	(C)	30.	(C)	50.	(A)	70.	(C)	90.	(B)
11.	(B)	31.	(A)	51.	(A)	71.	(C)	91.	(C)
12.	(B)	32.	(B)	52.	(C)	72.	(D)	92.	(C)
13.	(C)	33.	(A)	53.	(C)	73.	(B)	93.	(B)
14.	(A)	34.	(B)	54.	(D)	74.	(A)	94.	(A)
15.	(C)	35.	(B)	55.	(A)	75.	(C)	95.	(B)
16.	(C)	36.	(B)	56.	(C)	76.	(C)	96.	(C)
17.	(A)	37.	(A)	57.	(D)	77.	(C)	97.	(D)
18.	(A)	38.	(B)	58.	(B)	78.	(A)	98.	(A)
19.	(B)	39.	(C)	59.	(A)	79.	(D)	99.	(A)
20.	(A)	40.	(A)	60.	(C)	80.	(D)	100.	(B)

Part 1

1. (A) A man is looking for some ads in the newspaper.
   (B) A man is standing next to the column.
   (C) A street is crowded with many people.
   (D) A man is examining a newspaper.

2. **(A) Some people are waiting at a traffic light.**
   (B) There are many vehicles on the road.
   (C) There are benches in front of the building.
   (D) Some people are resting on the grass.

3. (A) Buildings are being torn down.
   (B) Cars are being inspected by a mechanic.
   (C) Some people are fishing from a boat.
   (D) Cars are parked along the pier.

4. (A) All seats are occupied in an office.
   (B) People are gathered in an office.
   (C) The woman is taking notes.
   (D) A group of people has gathered in a laboratory.

5. (A) People are watching a performance.
   (B) A man is paying for a purchase.
   (C) A man is signing up for a conference.
   (D) One of the women is buying a present.

6. (A) Food is being served to the guests.
   (B) Glasses are being filled.
   (C) There are utensils on the table.
   (D) Meat is being roasted on the grill.

Part 2

7. Are you supposed to be in Prague?
   (A) Prague is in the Czech Republic.
   (B) They will supposedly arrive in Prague.
   (C) The conference was put off until next month.

8. Would you like to go to the beach with me?
   (A) I'm afraid I don't have enough time.
   (B) I'd like to go out.
   (C) Yes, I'll go tomorrow.

9. Who is going to chair the meeting on the recruitment plans?
   (A) Andrew Park from human resources.
   (B) They are new recruits.
   (C) I don't know the person sitting there.

10. What does a one-way ticket from Shanghai to Beijing cost?
    (A) All tickets were sold out.
    (B) Sorry, the deadline has passed.
    (C) I'm afraid I have no idea.

11. When will the sales meeting take place?
    (A) In the boardroom.
    (B) In two weeks.
    (C) For three hours.

12. Where does Susan work?
    (A) It's on her desk.
    (B) In an office building downtown.
    (C) From 8:30 to 6:00.

13. How often do you visit Singapore on business?
    (A) Usually just to show my wares.
    (B) Last June, I think.
    (C) A couple of times a year.

14. Why is it so humid in this room?
    (A) There is no air conditioning in here.
    (B) Yes, it's quite cold, isn't it?
    (C) Because the argument was heated.

15. Which novel are you reading in your book club?
    (A) You should read it carefully.
    (B) The health club is on the 5th floor.
    (C) The one you also read last week.

16. Jane always arrives at work at eight o'clock sharp.
    (A) Her desk is near the entrance.
    (B) Is the walk tiresome?
    (C) Are all your staff as punctual?

17. This firm was established about 7 years ago, wasn't it?
    (A) Yes, by Stephen Lee.
    (B) Yes, I work at a law firm.
    (C) It was built in Switzerland.

18. Can you please tell me where I can buy tickets for a baseball game?
    (A) Proceed to a box office.
    (B) Tickets were sold out.
    (C) I know where Ms. Kim is.

19. Should I put these boxes on your desk or put them somewhere else?
    (A) Let me put them down first.
    (B) Either is fine.
    (C) No, the package hasn't arrived yet.

20. What did you do with the extra folders?
    (A) I put them in the warehouse.
    (B) No, I didn't.
    (C) I did it myself.

21. Were you supposed to leave for L.A. yesterday?
    (A) Yes, but I changed my mind.
    (B) No, it was yesterday.
    (C) Where are you heading?

22. Feel free to call us if you have any queries.
    (A) Perhaps I could.
    (B) No, that might happen.
    (C) Thanks, I'll do that.

23. Why don't you think the offer over before you make a decision?
    (A) Two days wasn't enough.
    (B) The disagreement occurred yesterday.
    (C) Actually, I've already made up my mind.

24. Have you just been promoted?
    (A) Yes, I'll start in my new position on Monday.
    (B) Yes, the clothing promotion was a success.
    (C) Yes, I am.

25. Which carpet do you think matches this floor, blue or black?
    (A) I don't think so.
    (B) I think either would be nice.
    (C) I watched a tennis match on TV.

26. Who is the new employee at our office?
    (A) His name is Leonardo.
    (B) We are all employed here.
    (C) In the office.

27. Could you assist Mr. Johnson with the coffee machine?
    (A) Yes, he needs four copies.
    (B) Yes, my assistant did it.
    (C) I'd be glad to.

28. When are the sales figures for last month coming out?
    (A) 300 million dollars.
    (B) Yes, if they are wrong.
    (C) In about three days.

29. You've printed out the minutes from the last meeting, haven't you?
    (A) It took three hours.
    (B) No, I'll do it first thing tomorrow.
    (C) The printer takes a minute to warm up.

30. Where should I put my signature?
    (A) Your sign goes here.
    (B) In the drawer, please.
    (C) At the bottom of the page.

31. Wasn't Ms. Tucker supposed to lead the investigation?
    (A) It was decided she lacked the experience.
    (B) I've already been considered.
    (C) The investment was sound.

Part 3

Questions 32-34 refer to the following conversation.

W Hello, this is Surf and Turf Restaurant. How can I help you?
M I'd like to make a reservation for this Friday evening for four people at 8:15.
W Oh, I'm afraid we're full at that time. I could fit you in at 8:45, though. Would that be suitable for your party?
M I'll have to get in touch with my friends and get back to you. I'm not entirely sure if that will work for everyone else.

32. Why is the man calling?
    (A) To invite the woman to an event
    (B) To book a table
    (C) To order takeout food
    (D) To cancel a reservation

33. What is the problem?
    (A) No tables are available at 8:15.
    (B) The business closes at eight o'clock.
    (C) The restaurant is out of lobster.
    (D) The woman has lost her job.

34. What does the woman suggest?
    (A) Coming another day
    (B) Coming half an hour later
    (C) Trying another location
    (D) Eating at home

Questions 35-37 refer to the following conversation.

M Cindy, could you give me a hand with this Internet connection? I can't seem to figure out what's wrong with it. And I can't even get online to see what the problem might be.
W I have to go to a meeting right now, but I could help you when I get back in about an hour.
M Actually, I have to be able to get online right away. I'll call someone in the IT department and see if they can send someone to help me.
W Okay. Sorry I couldn't help you.

35. What does the man need help with?
    (A) A printer
    (B) Internet access
    (C) A filing system
    (D) An answering machine

36. When will the woman most likely return from her meeting?
    (A) The next day
    (B) In an hour
    (C) At 7 P.M.
    (D) On Thursday

37. What will the man probably do to solve the problem?
    (A) Call the IT department
    (B) Consult the manufacturer's Web page
    (C) Buy a new router
    (D) Use the fax machine

Questions 38-40 refer to the following conversation with three speakers.

W1 Hi, Bill. We were wondering if there was a filing cabinet in here.
M   Actually, we have a few. What size were you looking for?
W1 We were hoping to get one of those ones that's about four and a half feet tall and has four drawers.
M   Oh, I don't think we have one that big. All of the ones that we have only have three drawers and are a lot shorter than that.
W2 I'm sorry to hear that. However, we definitely need it for storing some office supplies.
M   In that case, I could order one for you from our supplier, and it would probably be here by the end of the week.

38. What are the women looking for?
    (A) An order form
    (B) A filing cabinet
    (C) A measuring tape
    (D) A wardrobe

39. Where most likely are the speakers?
    (A) In a restaurant
    (B) In a church
    (C) In an office storeroom
    (D) On an airplane

40. What does the man offer to do?
    (A) Place an order
    (B) Build something
    (C) Go home early
    (D) Ask his assistant

Questions 41-43 refer to the following conversation.

M	Wendy, I thought you were supposed to be at that training session in Los Angeles by now.
W	I was supposed to be, but they postponed it by a week because they had a problem with one of the speakers.
M	Oh, that must be a real hassle. You had to change your entire schedule around to accommodate this training session.
W	Yeah, I won't even be able to go now. My schedule is just too packed.
M	Cheer up! It happens all the time.

41. Where did the man expect the woman to be?
(A) In the conference room
(B) In San Francisco
(C) At a training session
(D) At a job interview

42. Why is the woman at the office?
(A) She had a meeting there.
(B) Her conference was canceled.
(C) Her conference was pushed back.
(D) She had to pack her bags.

43. Why won't she take a trip next week?
(A) She has to move to a new office.
(B) Her schedule will be too busy.
(C) She has to talk with a client.
(D) Her office will be renovated.

Questions 44-46 refer to the following conversation.

W	Driver, how long do you think it will be before we get to the Empire State Building?
M	Well, ma'am, usually it would be about fifteen minutes, but with this traffic it might take us closer to an hour.
W	Oh, that's just too long. I'm sorry; I'm going to have to get you to let me out at a subway station.
M	No problem at all. You're in luck; the station's right over there. That'll be $11.50, please.
W	Here you are. Keep the change.

44. What does the woman ask about?
(A) Directions to the subway
(B) The duration of a trip
(C) The cost of a ticket
(D) The bus schedule

45. Where most likely is the woman?
(A) In a bakery
(B) In a museum
(C) In a cab
(D) At an airport

46. What will the woman probably do next?
(A) Arrange a meeting
(B) Take a taxi
(C) Collect her change
(D) Go into the subway station

Questions 47-49 refer to the following conversation.

M	Hello, Hillcrest Properties.
W	Hello, my name is Dana Wilkins. My friend George Perry recommended you. My company is relocating me to Houston, and he mentioned that you would be able to help me find a new home there. He said you gave him excellent service and got him a fair price for his house.
M	Oh, yes. I remember George. That's very kind of him. We helped him sell his house when he moved from here to Los Angeles. What sort of home are you looking for?
W	I'm looking for a studio apartment somewhere near the downtown area. I'll be in town next week. Would you have time to show me some units?

47. Why is the woman calling?
(A) She wants a new job.
(B) She wants to buy a home.
(C) She wants to arrange a flight.
(D) She wants to ask for directions.

48. Where does the man most likely work?
(A) At a software company
(B) At a moving company
(C) At a real estate agency
(D) At an interior decorating company

49. What will the man most likely do next?
(A) Apply for a job
(B) Travel to Los Angeles
(C) Buy a house
(D) Arrange a meeting time

Questions 50-52 refer to the following conversation.

W	James, I just got a call from Mtech. They want to know when the marble flooring they ordered will be in. Do you know?
M	I just talked to the supplier on the phone. Hopefully I'll hear back within the hour. Do you want me to give them a call when I hear back?
W	No, that's okay. Let me know when you hear, and I'll call them. I have to give them a price for some wallpaper as well.
M	No problem.

50. What does the man say he just did?
(A) Made a telephone call
(B) Filed a report
(C) Finished his work
(D) Canceled an order

51. Why did Mtech call?
(A) To check on an order
(B) To cancel a meeting
(C) To confirm a price
(D) To hire a new employee

52. What does the man mean when he says, "No problem"?
(A) He doesn't understand the problem.
(B) He can't cancel the order.
(C) He will advise the woman.
(D) He will help the woman install the material.

Questions 53-55 refer to the following conversation.

W Dave, I was wondering if it would be okay if I came along to work at the kitchen appliance tradeshow next week.
M Umm... I had already assigned everybody to the tradeshow that I thought we would need. Why?
W Well, it's in Las Vegas, and my cousin lives there. I haven't seen him in a while. I could stay with him and we wouldn't have to pay for a hotel.
M I guess that should be okay. Just remember that you'll be there to get some work done.
W I'll keep that in mind.

53. What does the woman ask the man to do?
(A) Give her the weekend off
(B) Suggest some kitchen appliances
(C) Allow her to work at a tradeshow
(D) Pay for her hotel costs

54. Why does the woman want to go to Las Vegas?
(A) She wants to apply for a job.
(B) She wants to stay at a hotel.
(C) She wants to enjoy some tradeshows.
(D) She wants to see her relative.

55. What does the man remind the woman about?
(A) That she will have to work
(B) That she must arrive on time
(C) That she has a meeting this weekend
(D) That her brother no longer lives in Las Vegas

Questions 56-58 refer to the following conversation.

M Wow, that musical was fantastic! I'm really surprised there were so few people here.
W I'm not particularly surprised. It got terrible reviews in the paper, and I wasn't very impressed with it myself.
M Well, I don't care what you or the reviews say; I loved it. Anyway, would you like to stop for a drink before we head home? We could swing by Jenny's Bar and Grill on 5th Street. We haven't been there in ages.
W That sounds like a good idea. The babysitter isn't expecting us home for at least another hour and a half, and we could even have a game of pool.

56. What are the speakers discussing?
(A) Their favorite actors
(B) The movie they are watching
(C) The performance they've just seen
(D) A rock concert

57. What does the woman mean when she says, "I'm not particularly surprised"?
(A) She thought it was very sad.
(B) She thought it was excellent.
(C) She thought it was too long.
(D) She didn't like it.

58. What will the speakers most likely do next?
(A) Hire a babysitter
(B) Go to a pub
(C) See a movie
(D) Go to a musical

Questions 59-61 refer to the following conversation.

M Hello, Wharton residence.
W Hello, is Diane Wharton available?
M I'm afraid not. She's out right now. I'm her husband. I'll definitely let her know.
W My name is Jenny Felling, and I'm calling from the human resources department of Growtech Pharmaceuticals. She interviewed with us last week. We'd like to offer her the position, and we were wondering if she would be able to come in next Tuesday to sign the contract, if she is still interested in the job.
M Really? That's great. She'll be very happy about the news. I'll definitely let her know. Thanks.

59. Why is the woman calling?
(A) To make a job offer
(B) To order food
(C) To cancel a meeting
(D) To collect an outstanding bill

60. When does the woman want to meet with Ms. Wharton?
(A) This Monday
(B) Next Monday
(C) Next Tuesday
(D) Over the weekend

61. What does the man say he will do?
(A) Arrange an interview
(B) Receive a delivery for Ms. Wharton
(C) Give Ms. Wharton a message
(D) Come to the office to meet Ms. Felling

Questions 62-64 refer to the following conversation and chart.

M Welcome to Samson Electronics. What can I do for you?
W I just bought this digital camera last month from your store. But when I try to save the photos I've taken, an error code displays on the screen.
M Oh, really? Let me take a look first. I have a chart here of all the codes. Perhaps it'll tell us what's going on. I think I found the problem. According to the chart, it seems that there is something wrong with the memory card.
W Oh, do I need to purchase a new memory card?
M Well, let me change it for a new one for free because it is under warranty.

62. Who most likely is the man?
(A) A mechanic
(B) A store clerk
(C) An electrician
(D) A photo artist

63. Look at the graphic. Which error code is the camera displaying?
(A) E-1
(B) E-2
(C) E-3
(D) E-4

64. What will the man most likely do next?
(A) Replace an item
(B) Purchase a new item
(C) Read a manual
(D) Wrap up a camera

Questions 65-67 refer to the following conversation and map.

M Amy, the hospital will be closing the parking lot in front of our research lab for construction next month. Can you send an e-mail to tell the rest of your staff members?

W No problem. Did they find a place to park for everyone until the construction is finished?

M Yes. I think we're supposed to use the West Parking lot instead.

W That's quite far from the lab. It is very inconvenient for everyone to get there on foot. In addition, it is winter now.

M Don't worry. The board of directors decided to provide free shuttle buses from the West Parking lot to our building. Could you let your team members know this decision as well?

65. Look at the graphic. Which parking area will be closed?
   (A) North
   (B) East
   (C) South
   (D) West

66. What is the woman concerned about?
   (A) Encountering road construction
   (B) Paying parking fees
   (C) Walking a long distance
   (D) Facing heavy traffic

67. What does the man say the board will do?
   (A) Change the company's policy
   (B) Offer complimentary shuttles
   (C) Provide a bonus
   (D) Reimburse employees

Questions 68-70 refer to the following conversation and building directory.

M Hi, I have an appointment with my accountant at 2:00 P.M. I just parked at the outdoor parking lot. And I want to know where I should pay for parking.

W Oh, actually, according to this building's parking policy, visitors can park in our garage at no cost. I just need you to present the ticket you received when you entered the parking garage.

M That sounds great; I appreciate it. Also, this is my first time visiting Mr. Smith's office. I can't find his name on the building directory. Could you tell me where his office is?

W Mr. Smith just moved in three days ago, and we haven't had time to change the directory yet. His office is on the third floor.

68. What is the purpose of the man's visit?
   (A) He is meeting with an accountant.
   (B) He has to pay for parking.
   (C) He will work out.
   (D) He is eating some food.

69. What does the woman say about the parking policy?
   (A) It has a time restriction.
   (B) It isn't available for residents.
   (C) It is for visitors only.
   (D) It is complimentary for visitors.

70. Look at the graphic. Which office name has to be updated on the building directory?
   (A) Kim's Stationery
   (B) P&T Restaurant
   (C) Miracle Fitness Center
   (D) Jane's Clinic

Part 4

Questions 71-73 refer to the following message.

Hi, this is Janet Wilson. I bought a washing machine at your store yesterday. My husband's hooked it up, but it's just not working properly. It just keeps beeping and displaying some sort of error code. Could you send someone over right away to look at it? I don't want to have to bring it back to the store, and the warranty says that home service is included for the first year. You can reach me at 555-1254. Thanks very much.

71. Why is the woman calling?
   (A) To buy an appliance
   (B) To cancel a delivery
   (C) To report a problem
   (D) To order food

72. What product is the woman discussing?
   (A) An exercise bike
   (B) A microwave oven
   (C) A stereo system
   (D) A washing machine

73. What does the speaker want the store to do?
   (A) Send spare parts
   (B) Send a service person
   (C) Order a part
   (D) Deliver a replacement

Questions 74-76 refer to the following announcement.

Good morning, everyone. Thanks so much for coming to this residents' meeting. My name is Angela Tiller, and I am the new director of the Shady Acres retirement home. As I am sure you have heard by now, Dan Green, the previous director, has left Shady Acres for personal reasons. I understand that he was very popular with all the residents here, and I'll do my best to fill his shoes. At this point, I have no intention of changing any of the policies or programs that Dan set up; however, I may make some modifications as time goes on. In the meantime, I want you to know that my door is always open for questions or to hear your concerns.

74. What is the purpose of the meeting?
   (A) To announce new management
   (B) To announce a new building project
   (C) To explain a change in policies
   (D) To announce the closure of the facility

75. What type of businesses does Angela Tiller work for?
   (A) A building supply company
   (B) A hospital
   (C) A retirement home
   (D) A delivery service

76. Why did Ms. Tiller's predecessor leave?
   (A) He was transferred.
   (B) He went into retirement.
   (C) He had a personal matter.
   (D) He was dismissed.

Questions 77-79 refer to the following talk.

Hi, everyone, and welcome to our yearly sales review meeting. As I'm sure you're all aware, this year's results have been somewhat mixed. We have significantly expanded our overseas sales; however, domestic sales have stagnated and in some areas actually declined. Overall sales levels have remained almost the same as last year's, so we definitely did not hit our growth targets for the year. Over the next month, we are going to have a series of meetings to hammer out a plan to improve our position over the next year.

77. What is the purpose of the talk?
    (A) To order new equipment
    (B) To announce layoffs
    (C) To discuss the sales results
    (D) To discuss tax returns

78. According to the speaker, what positive results were there?
    (A) Overseas sales increased.
    (B) Domestic sales have hit a target.
    (C) Expenses were reduced.
    (D) The sales force was increased.

79. What course of action does the speaker announce?
    (A) Restrictions on corporate travel
    (B) Taking over another company
    (C) Hiring additional employees
    (D) A series of planning meetings

Questions 80-82 refer to the following telephone message.

Hello, Mr. Wilson. This is Dave calling from Ace Couriers. We've received a package with your name and phone number on it, but there appears to be a problem with the address. Our driver stopped at the address we have this afternoon, but the woman there said that she did not know you. Could you please give me a call as soon as possible at 555–7142 and confirm your address for us? I'm sure you're anxious to have your package. Thanks.

80. What is the speaker calling about?
    (A) Car rental
    (B) Emergency arrangements
    (C) Airline tickets
    (D) A package delivery

81. What information does the speaker require?
    (A) A shipping address
    (B) A telephone number
    (C) A family member's name
    (D) A list of contents

82. How does the speaker request that Mr. Wilson contact him?
    (A) By online chat
    (B) By mail
    (C) By telephone
    (D) By e-mail

Questions 83-85 refer to the following talk.

Good afternoon, and thanks for tuning in. We have a fascinating lineup for you today. My first guest will be Dr. Sandra Beard. Dr. Beard has just returned from Mozambique, where she was coordinating a program that gives young doctors experience in hospitals in developing nations in Africa. This program both benefits the hospitals and provides the doctors with a different perspective. Dr. Beard will tell us about her program, and then we're going to open up the phone lines and invite any questions from our listeners.

83. Where would this talk most likely be heard?
    (A) On the radio
    (B) In a supermarket
    (C) At a construction site
    (D) In a hospital

84. What field does Sandra Beard work in?
    (A) Geology
    (B) Chemistry
    (C) Environmental science
    (D) Medicine

85. What did Sandra Beard do recently?
    (A) Started a company
    (B) Returned from Africa
    (C) Wrote a book
    (D) Invented a product

Questions 86-88 refer to the following telephone message.

Hello, Mr. Harrison. This is Andrea Phelps, the senior editor at the Herald Tribune. I've just been going over your writing samples and reviewing your résumé and cover letter. Your experience is quite impressive, and the writing work you've submitted is excellent as well. While we don't have any full-time staff writer positions available at this time, I think I can offer you some freelance assignments. If you're interested, I'd like you to come in for an interview and to discuss some of our upcoming projects. Please give me a call at 555–1244 to let me know when you can come in. If I don't pick up, dial three to talk to my secretary; she knows my schedule.

86. Who is Mr. Harrison?
    (A) A professional athlete
    (B) A journalist
    (C) A magazine editor
    (D) A photographer

87. What does the caller want to discuss with Mr. Harrison?
    (A) Political issues
    (B) Sporting events
    (C) Current affairs
    (D) Writing assignments

88. What should Mr. Harrison do if Ms. Phelps does not answer the phone?
    (A) Press 3
    (B) Leave a message
    (C) Call back later
    (D) Send a letter

Questions 89-91 refer to the following introduction.

Hello, everyone. As you all know, we are here tonight to honor our colleague and friend Abdel Pratha on the occasion of his retirement after 25 years of devoted service to our company. Mr. Pratha was one of the first employees of this company when we were just starting out. He stuck with us through thick and thin and is now ready for a well-earned rest. Those of you who haven't been here that long and only know Mr. Pratha as the vice-president of marketing might be surprised to know that he actually started out doing clerical work for the company all those years ago. Here is Mr. Pratha to say a few words.

89. Who is Mr. Pratha?
(A) The CEO of the company
(B) A shipping manager
(C) A clerical worker
(D) One of the executives of the company

90. What does the speaker say about Mr. Pratha?
(A) He is being offered a promotion.
(B) He was with the company for 25 years.
(C) He recently joined the company.
(D) He has not been very reliable.

91. What does the man mean when he says, "Here is Mr. Pratha to say a few words"?
(A) Mr. Pratha will install a new word processor software.
(B) Mr. Pratha will type on a keyboard.
(C) Mr. Pratha will make a speech at the ceremony.
(D) Mr. Pratha will talk to guests one-on-one.

Questions 92-94 refer to the following announcement.

Attention, everyone. This is Dan Wilson, the building safety officer, with an important announcement. This afternoon at 3:00 we will have a fire drill. When the fire alarm goes off, please proceed out of the building in an orderly fashion and congregate out in front of the building. Please do not use the lifts. Once we are in front of the building, I will take attendance and then we will all be able to return back to our workstations. Thanks very much.

92. Who most likely is the speaker?
(A) A human resources director
(B) A computer programmer
(C) A safety worker
(D) A salesperson

93. What is the announcement about?
(A) A problem with the plumbing
(B) A fire drill
(C) The elevators being serviced
(D) A staff meeting

94. What does the man mean when he says, "I will take attendance"?
(A) The activity is mandatory.
(B) The activity was postponed.
(C) The activity was canceled.
(D) The activity will go smoothly.

Questions 95-97 refer to the following talk and graph.

Good afternoon, folks. I'd like to start off our monthly sales meeting by looking at our progress in attracting new customers here at Lucky Seven Appliances. As you can see, July was our most successful month. We can probably attribute this to the launch of the cutting-edge washing machine, Wind Wind, which came out that month. You will also see that the second-highest increase in new customers occurred during our special promotional event. This sale was a smash hit. We're now planning to hire a Web designer to make our Web site be more user-friendly for our patrons. I'm sure everything will go well.

95. Where most likely does the speaker work?
(A) At an insurance company
(B) At a home appliance company
(C) At a supermarket
(D) At a design company

96. Look at the graphic. When was the promotional event held?
(A) In June
(B) In July
(C) In August
(D) In September

97. According to the speaker, what is the company going to do to improve their Web site?
(A) Hold an emergency meeting
(B) Launch a new product
(C) Conduct a promotional event
(D) Employ some experts

Questions 98-100 refer to the following telephone message and work schedule.

Hello, Jason. It's Thomas. I was pleased to hear that our company will recruit three employees. We really need more people to take care of all of our clients' claims about delayed shipping. But we haven't hired anyone new for a long time. So I think we should meet to talk about the application process in detail. I'm looking at my work schedule at the moment, and actually I have some free time this Thursday. Since we'll both be at the staff meeting that morning, why don't we meet right after that meeting, which will probably take about an hour? I have time between that meeting and a lunch appointment with my client at 1:00. Please, let me know whether this is fine with you. Thanks!

98. Where most likely does the speaker work?
(A) At a shipping company
(B) At an accounting firm
(C) At an event planning agency
(D) At a law firm

99. What would the speaker like to discuss with the listener?
(A) A recruiting process
(B) A staff layoff
(C) A project budget
(D) A client claim

100. Look at the graphic. What time does the speaker want to meet?
(A) At 9:00
(B) At 11:00
(C) At 12:00
(D) At 14:00

3회

1.	(A)	21.	(A)	41.	(C)	61.	(D)	81.	(A)
2.	(B)	22.	(A)	42.	(B)	62.	(C)	82.	(D)
3.	(D)	23.	(A)	43.	(A)	63.	(A)	83.	(B)
4.	(C)	24.	(C)	44.	(D)	64.	(B)	84.	(C)
5.	(A)	25.	(A)	45.	(A)	65.	(B)	85.	(A)
6.	(A)	26.	(B)	46.	(D)	66.	(C)	86.	(C)
7.	(C)	27.	(A)	47.	(B)	67.	(D)	87.	(B)
8.	(B)	28.	(B)	48.	(C)	68.	(B)	88.	(A)
9.	(A)	29.	(B)	49.	(D)	69.	(D)	89.	(B)
10.	(A)	30.	(A)	50.	(C)	70.	(C)	90.	(A)
11.	(B)	31.	(B)	51.	(B)	71.	(D)	91.	(B)
12.	(C)	32.	(B)	52.	(A)	72.	(C)	92.	(A)
13.	(B)	33.	(B)	53.	(A)	73.	(C)	93.	(C)
14.	(A)	34.	(C)	54.	(B)	74.	(D)	94.	(C)
15.	(C)	35.	(C)	55.	(D)	75.	(B)	95.	(C)
16.	(B)	36.	(A)	56.	(C)	76.	(D)	96.	(A)
17.	(B)	37.	(D)	57.	(B)	77.	(C)	97.	(D)
18.	(A)	38.	(C)	58.	(A)	78.	(A)	98.	(C)
19.	(C)	39.	(C)	59.	(C)	79.	(D)	99.	(D)
20.	(C)	40.	(A)	60.	(B)	80.	(B)	100.	(C)

Part 1

1. **(A) The man is walking to the right.**
   (B) The clock is hanging on the wall.
   (C) The men are working on the street.
   (D) The man is looking at the bulletin board.

2. (A) The man is walking up the stairs.
   (B) The man is holding a newspaper.
   (C) The windows are being opened.
   (D) The man is putting on a hat.

3. (A) The boat is being docked.
   (B) The people are walking away from each other.
   (C) The women are swimming in the ocean.
   (D) The man is carrying a plastic bag.

4. (A) The people are looking at each other.
   (B) The women are clapping their hands.
   (C) One of the women is smiling.
   (D) The people are having a serious conversation.

5. **(A) The cars are parked along the street.**
   (B) The building is being renovated.
   (C) The windows are all open.
   (D) The men are crossing the street.

6. **(A) There are no people in the restaurant.**
   (B) There are five tables outside.
   (C) There is art being hung on the columns.
   (D) There are several trees on the terrace.

Part 2

7. Who is working out of the Miami office today?
   (A) I am working out of Boston.
   (B) He is always working.
   (C) I think Ms. Gonzales is.

8. What do you say to a game of poker after dinner?
   (A) Yes, I will be eating dinner.
   (B) I'm afraid I'll be out of town.
   (C) I enjoyed the game very much.

9. Did you register online or in person at the school?
   (A) I did it on the school's Web site.
   (B) I registered last night.
   (C) Because the school is far from my house.

10. Do you have time to help me this morning?
    (A) If there's no other work to do.
    (B) Yes, I helped him yesterday.
    (C) It is ten o'clock.

11. When was the last time you went to Dallas?
    (A) A little over 400 kilometers.
    (B) About 4 months ago.
    (C) Every year for the past ten years.

12. Did you decide which television you want to buy?
    (A) I am watching television with my friend.
    (B) No, it is $750.
    (C) The one with the largest screen.

13. Would you please give this letter to Mr. Graham?
    (A) I am writing the letter now.
    (B) No problem.
    (C) Yes, please hold.

14. I heard we hired a new secretary.
    (A) Yes, you heard right.
    (B) No, my secretary is away on leave.
    (C) I am on my way.

15. Let's get together for lunch tomorrow.
    (A) It tastes a bit strange.
    (B) They will be meeting for lunch.
    (C) Sounds good to me.

16. Did you know Mary is retiring next week?
    (A) Mary worked here for almost 30 years.
    (B) I thought you knew.
    (C) I am having lunch with Mary tomorrow.

17. I heard that you only accept cash.
    (A) I have a little bit of cash.
    (B) We accept credit cards as well.
    (C) That is acceptable.

18. The assignment is due tomorrow, isn't it?
    (A) That's what I heard.
    (B) Sure, I am available tomorrow.
    (C) I was assigned to write the report.

19. Where did you go for dinner yesterday?
    (A) I am having dinner at home today.
    (B) I wasn't very hungry.
    (C) I tried a new restaurant.

20. Are you available for a meeting this afternoon?
    (A) Yes, I have lunch plans.
    (B) No, the copy machine is broken.
    (C) Unfortunately, I will not be in the office.

21. Do you have Ms. Jensen's home address?
    (A) I'm afraid I don't have it.
    (B) I think she leaves around 5.
    (C) I will be going to a party there tomorrow.

22. Would you hand out these free samples?
    (A) Okay, I will do it now.
    (B) Down in the lobby.
    (C) I have sampled the food before.

23. Didn't you borrow books from the library this morning?
    (A) Yes, I just got back.
    (B) No, I quit my job at the library.
    (C) No, we don't.

24. How do I turn off this television?
    (A) No, there is nothing interesting on.
    (B) It's a right turn.
    (C) There should be a button on the left side.

25. When was the carpet in the lobby replaced?
 (A) Yesterday, when you were out.
 (B) I was planning on washing it this afternoon.
 (C) You can try next door.

26. Are you comfortable using chopsticks?
 (A) I am a fan of pork chops.
 (B) Yes, I've used them before.
 (C) Our reservation is for seven o'clock.

27. Why are they rearranging the furniture?
 (A) They're making room for a new workstation.
 (B) No, the movers are on their way now.
 (C) We're going to throw them away.

28. Should we buy additional equipment for the office this month?
 (A) No, we already hired someone this month.
 (B) We don't have the budget.
 (C) We can meet this afternoon at three o'clock.

29. Did Mr. Maynor assign you to the Cohen project?
 (A) He likes giving assignments.
 (B) Yes, just this morning.
 (C) No, in the desk drawer.

30. Should we have chocolate cake or apple pie for dessert?
 (A) Whichever you want.
 (B) Help yourself.
 (C) I made a reservation at the Dessert Café.

31. This is the malfunctioning copy machine, isn't it?
 (A) There are a number of functions.
 (B) Yes, the repairman is on his way.
 (C) I need thirty copies for the meeting.

Part 3

Questions 32-34 refer to the following conversation.

M Hi. I'm here to see Dr. Paulson. I don't have an appointment, but I've had a sharp pain in my knee since yesterday. Will I have to wait long?
W I'm sorry to say Dr. Paulson is out of town at a conference and will not be in today. I can make an appointment so you can see her at 10 A.M. tomorrow morning.
M I don't think I can wait until tomorrow. Is there another doctor available to see me?
W Dr. Chung is in and seeing patients. There is an opening at 3 P.M. today. How does that sound?

32. Why is the man talking to the woman?
 (A) To deliver a package
 (B) To see a doctor
 (C) To reserve a spot at a conference
 (D) To make an appointment for tomorrow

33. Why does the man decide not to see Dr. Paulson the next morning?
 (A) He will be at the conference with Dr. Chung.
 (B) He needs prompt assistance.
 (C) He has a meeting.
 (D) He will be out of town.

34. What will the man most likely do?
 (A) Come back tomorrow morning
 (B) Visit a nearby pharmacy
 (C) Meet with a different physician
 (D) Call Dr. Paulson on the phone

Questions 35-37 refer to the following conversation.

W Hello. My name is Jessica Smith. Is Ms. Maeda in? I'm one of her clients.
M Unfortunately, she is out of the country until next week. If it is regarding something urgent, I can try to reach her on her mobile phone.
W No, it's not urgent. I was just dropping off these signed legal documents. Can I leave them with you?
M Of course. I will see that Ms. Maeda gets these as soon as she's back. It would help me if you would leave a note for Ms. Maeda saying what this is in regard to.

35. Why does the woman want to see Ms. Maeda?
 (A) To ask about a court date
 (B) To sign a contract
 (C) To give her some documents
 (D) To tell her she is leaving the country

36. Where is Ms. Maeda?
 (A) Overseas
 (B) At home
 (C) At a legal conference
 (D) In her office

37. What will the man do next?
 (A) Write a note
 (B) Call Ms. Maeda
 (C) Go home
 (D) Deliver a message

Questions 38-40 refer to the following conversation.

M Hi, Judy. You're preparing the agenda for the board meeting tomorrow morning, right? Let me take a look at it before you send it around to the board members.
W Sure, I'm still working on it. I'm waiting to hear from Cathy regarding her presentation on next year's budget. Once I insert that item, it will be ready. I'll let you know. It shouldn't be later than 2 P.M.
M That sounds fine. Please make sure to note on the agenda who will be speaking about each item at the meeting as well. Thanks.

38. What is the woman working on?
 (A) Next year's budget
 (B) A set of presentation slides
 (C) A meeting agenda
 (D) A speech

39. What does the woman promise to do?
 (A) Reassign some work to Cathy
 (B) Make a copy of the agenda
 (C) Update the man on her work progress
 (D) Meet the man at the board meeting

40. What does the man ask the woman to do?
 (A) Include names on the agenda
 (B) Rehearse for a speech
 (C) Send the agenda out before speaking to Cathy
 (D) Let her revise the agenda

Questions 41-43 refer to the following conversation.

M Hey, Jane! Are you on your way to French class? I just heard that Professor Van Saint's class has been canceled today.
W Really? Do you know why? She did look like she might be coming down with something when I saw her yesterday at the library.
M Apparently, her brother is getting married, and she's at the ceremony. I heard from someone else in the class.
W I'm glad to hear it's not something bad. Do you want to go grab an early lunch?
M That sounds great. Now we have a free hour!

41. What does Professor Van Saint teach?
(A) Spanish
(B) Business marketing
(C) French
(D) Accounting

42. Why is the class canceled?
(A) Bad weather
(B) Marriage of the professor's relative
(C) Sickness of the professor
(D) Public holiday

43. How long was the class supposed to be?
(A) 60 minutes
(B) 90 minutes
(C) 30 minutes
(D) 2 hours

Questions 44-46 refer to the following conversation.

W Hi there. I was hoping you could help me find a book that was recommended to me by a friend. It's going to be a present for my husband for his birthday. He loves a good mystery, and my friend told me about one of the current best-sellers.
M Can you let me know the title or author of the book?
W Unfortunately, I can't. I can't remember anything about the book, except that it takes place in London in the 19th century.
M Oh, I think I know that one. It must be the new novel by John Garvin. I haven't read it yet, but I've heard it's very good. The reviews have all been very positive. Garvin is a great writer. Well, it just so happens that we have a copy still in stock. If you wait here just a minute, I'll go get it for you.

44. Where does the conversation take place?
(A) At a museum
(B) At a department store
(C) At a library
(D) At a bookstore

45. What does the man imply when he says, "Oh, I think I know that one"?
(A) He knows what she is talking about.
(B) The store has only one copy remaining.
(C) The man knows the woman well.
(D) The man will show the woman a review.

46. What will the woman most likely do?
(A) Go to another store
(B) Buy two copies
(C) Ask the man to call her husband
(D) Purchase a gift

Questions 47-49 refer to the following conversation with three speakers.

M1 Hi, Sam! Hello, Laura! Did you hear they're going to be giving us Korean classes starting next week?
M2 I hadn't heard that.
W Oh, I thought it wasn't until next month. I'm really excited to get started.
M1 I just heard it from the manager. The first class is next Monday, the 10th.
M2 Yeah, there have been a lot of tourists from Korea staying at our hotel in recent months. I've had trouble communicating with some of them.
W I agree. Picking up a few key phrases in Korean should help ease communications and improve our service.
M1 You know, the manager also told me that the classes are going to be mandatory. They're even going to grade us on class participation!
M2 That doesn't sound like much fun.

47. What are the speakers discussing?
(A) A trip to Korea
(B) A language course
(C) Lecture schedules
(D) A management meeting

48. When will the classes start?
(A) The middle of next month
(B) Tomorrow
(C) Next week
(D) On Tuesday

49. What is mentioned about the hotel?
(A) It is located in Korea.
(B) Its marketing has focused on Korea recently.
(C) It has only three employees.
(D) It has been accommodating many foreign guests.

Questions 50-52 refer to the following conversation.

W Greg, do you have a second? I've got Micron Technologies on the phone. They want to make a reservation for three single rooms from next Wednesday to Friday.
M Sure, hold on. Yes, we can accommodate that. I'll put that in the system right now. They're lucky to be calling now because we're expecting to have a large wedding here next week, and we may be all booked up.
W Greg, they also want to reserve a car and driver for Thursday.
M I'm going to have to call our usual limo service. Just tell them you'll call them back in about 15 minutes.

50. Where most likely do the speakers work?
(A) At a restaurant
(B) At a limo service
(C) At a hotel
(D) At a wedding hall

51. Why is Micron Technologies calling?
(A) To book a wedding
(B) To reserve rooms for next week
(C) To ask about a car service
(D) To complain about poor service

52. What will the man probably do next?
(A) Contact a car company
(B) Call Micron Technologies back
(C) Reschedule a wedding
(D) Clean a hotel room

Questions 53-55 refer to the following conversation with three speakers.

W: Hi, guys. Did you guys check out the review in the paper yesterday?
M1: No, I missed it. What did it say?
W: The article was extremely positive, and our restaurant got a perfect four stars!
M2: That's fabulous!
W: The critic who wrote the article described our appetizers as "delicacies from heaven" and went on and on about how creative our menu choices were—food combinations he had never seen before.
M1: I want to get my hands on a copy of that review for our kitchen wall.
M2: Definitely. I can't wait to read the article myself.
W: You're in luck! I brought an extra copy with me in my bag.

53. What type of business do the speakers probably work in?
(A) A restaurant
(B) A hotel
(C) A newspaper
(D) A travel agency

54. According to the woman, what did the critic say?
(A) He is friends with the chef.
(B) The menu was innovative.
(C) The service was fantastic.
(D) The food was ordinary.

55. What does one of the men say he will do?
(A) Close down the business
(B) Write something on the wall
(C) Think of new menu items
(D) Post the article

Questions 56-58 refer to the following conversation.

W: I was hoping we would be able to do all of the tests right here.
M: Unfortunately, we're only equipped here to perform some of the specialized tests that you'll need. You should go to one of the larger facilities, like the municipal hospital on Gray Street. You will be able to save time and money if you have all the tests done in one place.
W: I've had a bad experience at the municipal hospital. I prefer the general hospital across the bridge. Please write me a referral that I can take there.
M: Of course. You can pick it up from the receptionist on your way out.

56. Where does the conversation probably take place?
(A) At a university
(B) At a large hospital
(C) At a clinic
(D) At an exam center

57. What does the man propose that the woman do?
(A) Come back tomorrow
(B) Go to a different institution
(C) Decide which tests she wants
(D) Take medicine regularly

58. What will the man probably do next?
(A) Prepare a document
(B) See another patient
(C) Call the general hospital
(D) Conduct a specialized test

Questions 59-61 refer to the following conversation.

M: Jenny, did you hear the news? The price of strawberries is soaring because of the snowstorm last weekend. The price has almost doubled! We should consider raising the price of our strawberry pies. They are really our only product right now.
W: That's too much. I'm worried we'll lose customers, though, if we reflect that cost increase in the price of our pies. Customers buy our pies because of their reasonable pricing. Let's first think of other ways to cut back on costs.
M: Okay, let's see… I'll spend some time tonight reviewing our recent expenses. Maybe we can cut back on some other ingredients.

59. What does the man mention about the snowstorm?
(A) It covered the bakery in snow.
(B) The bakery is not doing very well.
(C) The price of strawberries nearly doubled.
(D) The price of strawberry pies has gone up.

60. What does the woman imply?
(A) They may need to close down the bakery.
(B) They should apply cost-cutting measures.
(C) The price of strawberries is going to continue to rise.
(D) They have already started losing customers.

61. What does the man say he will do tonight?
(A) Call a few customers
(B) Cut down on the number of ingredients
(C) Buy more strawberries
(D) Review financial records

Questions 62-64 refer to the following conversation.

M: Mandy, I need 30 copies of the presentation for the meeting this afternoon.
W: I'm way ahead of you. Rachael will have the 30 copies ready and placed in the meeting room before the meeting starts.
M: That's great. It would also be a good idea to have some snacks and drinks set out in the meeting room, enough for 30 people. Most of them will be flying in for this meeting, and there will probably be some hungry people in the room.
W: No problem. I'll get right on it. How about light sandwiches and sodas?
M: That should work. You should also get some waters and juices for those who don't drink soda.
W: Got it. Do you have someone helping you with the projector?
M: I already told Rachael to do that.

62. What are the speakers trying to do?
(A) Organize a group lunch
(B) Choose between soda and juice
(C) Prepare for a presentation
(D) Reserve a meeting room

63. What does the woman imply when she says, "I'm way ahead of you"?
(A) She already took care of it.
(B) She is in front of the man.
(C) She is almost done.
(D) She will win the race.

64. What will the woman do next?
(A) Distribute copies of the presentation
(B) Order snacks and drinks
(C) Give a presentation
(D) Help the man with the projector

Questions 65-67 refer to the following conversation and schedule.

W Michael, you're going to be up last today, right?
M No, I just noticed there's a mistake in the program. Martha should be performing after me.
W Why the change?
M She told me she's worried she won't be able to finish playing both of her pieces within the given 30 minutes.
W Oh, okay then. I guess you're going on after me then.
M That's right. I still need practice on the Mozart sonata. I'm just not fast enough yet.

65. Look at the graphic. Who will be performing right before Michael?
    (A) Henry
    (B) Melissa
    (C) Martha
    (D) Nobody

66. What kind of performance will Martha do?
    (A) Dancing
    (B) Singing
    (C) Musical instrument
    (D) Monologue

67. Why did the program change?
    (A) The show has been postponed.
    (B) Martha still needs to practice her piece.
    (C) Melissa is sick.
    (D) Martha will go over the allotted time.

Questions 68-70 refer to the following conversation and list.

W Can you help me order a new desk for the head of the accounting department?
M Sure, what kind of desk is he looking for?
W It would need to be a large one with drawers. He likes to stack a lot of documents on his desk. But it's going to need to be less than $800.
M There are plenty of good office desks for that price. We should be able to find one that he likes. Here is the catalog we usually use to order office equipment. I just used it yesterday to order some staplers.
W Great! Let me take a look.
M What do you think about this one?

68. What does the department head want?
    (A) A stapler
    (B) A desk
    (C) A new job
    (D) A comfortable chair

69. What did the man last order from the catalog?
    (A) Staples
    (B) Printer paper
    (C) An office desk
    (D) Staplers

70. Look at the graphic. What item will the woman probably order?
    (A) A
    (B) B
    (C) C
    (D) D

Part 4

Questions 71-73 refer to the following announcement.

Okay, everyone. Gather around. Before we go through the main entrance, I want to remind you about a few things. The museum does not allow any touching of the artwork. Please do not make contact with any of the sculptures, artifacts, paintings, or other items on display. By that, I mean not just your hands, but your clothes and anything that you're carrying. You are allowed to take pictures, but no flash photography. Also, no eating, drinking, or smoking, unless in specially designated areas in the lobby. Those areas will close at 3:00 P.M. today. Lastly, please remember that we will be meeting back here, where we are standing now, at exactly 4:00 P.M. That gives you about four hours to enjoy the museum before we leave. Now, please follow me through the main entrance. I know you will all have a great time.

71. Where is the announcement being made?
    (A) At a stadium
    (B) At a restaurant
    (C) At a university library
    (D) At a museum

72. What does the speaker ask the listeners to do?
    (A) Be careful when touching the sculptures
    (B) Not eat but feel free to drink anywhere
    (C) Be at the appointed place on time
    (D) Go directly home after viewing the exhibits

73. When must the listeners leave the building?
    (A) 12:00 P.M.
    (B) 3:00 P.M.
    (C) 4:00 P.M.
    (D) 8:00 P.M.

Questions 74-76 refer to the following announcement.

Attention, all monorail passengers heading to Hotel Candle Lake. This is your conductor speaking. I've just received an alert saying that the section of the track just before the hotel has been shut down due to ice from the recent snowstorm. Workers have already begun trying to defrost the track, but I understand it will take at least another two hours to have the track up and running again. Because of this, we are planning on reversing course and heading back to the last monorail station. You are all welcome to wait at the station until the track is up again. Alternatively, you are free to take the local bus or a taxi to get to the hotel if you are in a hurry. Apologies for the inconvenience, and thank you all for your patience.

74. Where is the announcement being made?
    (A) On a local bus
    (B) At a monorail station
    (C) At a hotel
    (D) On a monorail train

75. Why was the announcement made?
    (A) The train will stop and wait.
    (B) The train will head back.
    (C) The train will continue on to the hotel.
    (D) The train needs to be repaired.

76. According to the speaker, what can listeners do?
    (A) Wait two hours on the train
    (B) Walk back to the monorail station
    (C) Help the workers repair the track
    (D) Take a bus or taxi to the hotel

Questions 77-79 refer to the following advertisement.

Do you have trouble getting out of bed in the morning? Is it a struggle just to get through your day? If so, the experts at Cottonwood Clinic may be able to help you. James Cotton, our owner and chief therapist, is the author of the book Energize Your Life, which discusses his methods for helping you cope with stress and breathing new energy into your daily routine. Dr. Cotton has been featured in numerous health magazines and has won a number of awards for his unique treatment methods, including one last month at the Annual Conference of National Psychologists. The clinic has witnessed hundreds of patients find new meaning and vigor in their lives. Our hours are from 10 A.M. until 8 P.M., Monday through Friday, including holidays. Please give us a call at 555-1821 to meet with one of our therapists. If you set up an appointment this week, we'll take 20% off the cost of your initial consultation.

77. Who is James Cotton?
(A) A pastor
(B) A cotton farmer
(C) A therapist
(D) A magazine editor

78. What happened to James Cotton last month?
(A) He won an award.
(B) He was featured in a magazine.
(C) He opened the Cottonwood Clinic.
(D) He was out of town.

79. How can patients get a discount?
(A) By calling next Monday
(B) By presenting a coupon
(C) By bringing a copy of a book
(D) By making an appointment this week

Questions 80-82 refer to the following radio broadcast.

Welcome back, everyone. You are listening to Radio Classics this beautiful morning. We've invited into our studio today renowned performer Dimitry Olanov, a cellist who hails from Moscow. He first grabbed a cello when he was four years old, and he spent his youth winning numerous competitions. He first performed on the stage at Carnegie Hall at the young age of 16. He has traveled the world, delighting audiences everywhere, from as far west as Canada to as far east as Japan. He will perform for us here in a few minutes—Vivaldi. Now, with that introduction, I give you Mr. Olanov.

80. Where can this morning's recital be heard?
(A) In the auditorium
(B) On the radio
(C) In Japan
(D) At Carnegie Hall

81. What does the speaker say about Dimitry Olanov?
(A) He lives in Russia.
(B) He does not perform outside Canada.
(C) He does not play a musical instrument.
(D) He won only one competition.

82. What will Dimitry Olanov most likely do this morning?
(A) Talk about his childhood
(B) Travel to Canada
(C) Discuss his love for Vivaldi
(D) Play a musical instrument

Questions 83-85 refer to the following talk.

I truly appreciate all of your hard work on the project. Thanks to you, it was a huge success. The client just called to tell me that we have the best team of consultants he's ever worked with. We were able to lower their costs by over 40%, and we increased their sales by over 20% in less than one year! I know many of you are exhausted from the long hours you put into this project. I am confident that we could not have achieved this level of success without each and every one of you. Each of you will be receiving an extra bonus for your superb efforts. I know none of you were able to take any time off this summer, but you can now enjoy some time off. The next project we have lined up is not until next month, November. Nothing for any of you to do until then.

83. Who most likely are the listeners?
(A) Clients
(B) Consultants
(C) Salespeople
(D) Children

84. Why does the speaker say, "we could not have achieved this level of success without each and every one of you"?
(A) She wants to achieve success.
(B) She has a new project for the team.
(C) She wants to praise the team members.
(D) She is ready for a vacation.

85. What will the listeners do in October?
(A) Go on vacation
(B) Finish up the project
(C) Lower costs
(D) Start on a new project

Questions 86-88 refer to the following talk.

Hello, guys. Thank you all for coming. As I told you yesterday, we're going to be moving our office down the street to the Conway Center in a couple of weeks. The new space will be a lot bigger than what we're using now. Also, you all know how famous and prestigious the Conway Center is. We're a boutique law firm, and the new address should help to better publicize us. Our monthly rent will be going up, but I think we're getting back solid value. Another bonus is that both the subway and the commuter train stations are connected through the basement of the Conway Center. That'll make commuting much easier for all of you who don't drive. I'll get back to you later this week with details about packing and hiring a moving company.

86. What is the speaker mainly talking about?
(A) A subway station
(B) A boutique law firm
(C) An office relocation
(D) A prestigious building

87. What is the merit of the change?
(A) Smaller space
(B) More publicity
(C) Increased rent
(D) Parking

88. What does the speaker say about the Conway Center?
(A) It is on top of a train station.
(B) It is next to a shopping mall.
(C) It is the tallest building in the city.
(D) It is on the other side of town.

Questions 89-91 refer to the following report.

Good morning, everyone. You are watching Today in Business. I'm your host, Spencer Hawes. Our first story is about a blockbuster merger that was announced yesterday—GenuSoft and Softech. These are currently the two largest software companies in the United States, and after the merger, they will be the largest software company in the world. Yesterday's announcement stated that the reason for the merger is so that they can compete against Veriline, which is the world's largest software company today. The two merging companies have already laid out plans to come up with new global marketing strategies using social media platforms. The merger will become official this July. The new company will be called GenuTech, and it will be led by Valerie Wood, the current CEO of GenuSoft.

89. What is the report mainly about?
(A) A new construction project
(B) A business merger
(C) An innovative software product
(D) Social media platforms

90. What can be inferred about GenuTech's future plans?
(A) It will focus more on online marketing.
(B) It will seek to merge with Veriline.
(C) It will market only in the United States.
(D) It will hire someone new as its first CEO.

91. What does the speaker suggest about the reason behind GenuTech's formation?
(A) To increase sales revenues
(B) To deal with a market competitor
(C) To streamline costs
(D) To come up with global marketing strategies

Questions 92-94 refer to the following request and information.

I need your help with editing this video that I am hoping to upload onto the Internet. There is this new Web site that allows anyone to post clean, original works. I shot this video myself, but I'm having trouble getting rid of some of the noises in the background. I could really use your help with deleting those and also with adding in background music. Here is a list of the points in the video where I'd like you to insert music. Do you think you can do this? I need to make one change, though. I've decided I want BGM 2 to be the opening music, rather than BGM 1. If you can get this done by Thursday, I'll give you $100!

92. Why does the speaker say, "I need to make one change, though"?
(A) He wants to revise the chart.
(B) He has to change his background.
(C) He needs change for the vending machine.
(D) He wants to make a new song.

93. What does the speaker expect the listener to do?
(A) Pay him $100
(B) Compose background music
(C) Complete the task by Thursday
(D) Help him shoot a video

94. Look at the graphic. What can you tell about the speaker's request?
(A) BGM 4 should be the opening music.
(B) BGM 2 comes after BGM 4.
(C) BGM 2 should be played in two spots.
(D) Background music should be inserted 5 times.

Questions 95-97 refer to the following notice.

Thanks for coming, everyone. Let's get right to it. I'm going to explain to you what you need to do when picking classes this semester at Mi Amore Italian. As you know, our school is only open on Mondays and Tuesdays, and all of our classes are 120 minutes long. Students who are joining us for the first time are allowed only to take up to two classes per semester. This restriction is based on experience so you don't burn out too early. Returning students are free to take as many classes as they'd like. But some of the classes will require you to have taken another class first. For example, if you want to take Italian 201, you must already have completed Italian 101. The same thing applies to Italian 301; you must have completed Italian 201. Any questions?

95. Who are the listeners?
(A) Italian teachers
(B) Foreigners
(C) Students
(D) Employees

96. What is mentioned about the classes?
(A) New students can take up to two classes.
(B) Students may take Italian 201 and Italian 301 simultaneously.
(C) The first day of classes is on Saturday.
(D) No more than ten students are allowed in one class.

97. Look at the graphic. Which of the following combinations is possible for a new student?
(A) Italian 101 (Mon), Singing in Italian (Mon), and Italian Cuisine (Tues)
(B) Italian 101 (Mon) and Italian 301 (Tues)
(C) Italian 101 (Mon) and Italian 201 (Tues)
(D) Italian Cuisine (Mon) and Italian 101 (Tues)

Questions 98-100 refer to the following telephone message and schedule.

Hey, this is Megan calling. You know I was supposed to be flying back tomorrow, but I just got a call saying that my flight from Hawaii to Seattle has been canceled because of some unexpected bad weather. I called the airline, and they told me the soonest I can leave here is not going to be until tomorrow afternoon. But if I leave that late, by the time I land in Seattle and take public transportation to Tacoma, it's going to be after midnight. I think it makes more sense if I just enjoy this great place one extra night and fly back early the day after tomorrow. That should bring me into Tacoma that same evening. Anyway, Hawaii is just amazing. We should come together next time. I'll see you soon!

98. Why did Megan make a phone call?
(A) To say she is going to be leaving early
(B) To say she has lost some luggage
(C) To report that her flight schedule got delayed
(D) To say she will be traveling next to Boston

99. What does Megan say about her schedule?
(A) She was originally scheduled to leave today.
(B) She is transferring in Hawaii.
(C) Her final destination is Seattle.
(D) She can depart from Hawaii tomorrow if she wants to.

100. Look at the graphic. Which day will Megan go home?
(A) Saturday
(B) Sunday
(C) Monday
(D) Tuesday

4회

1.	(A)	21.	(B)	41.	(C)	61.	(C)	81.	(A)
2.	(B)	22.	(A)	42.	(C)	62.	(B)	82.	(C)
3.	(C)	23.	(C)	43.	(D)	63.	(A)	83.	(D)
4.	(C)	24.	(A)	44.	(C)	64.	(B)	84.	(D)
5.	(A)	25.	(C)	45.	(A)	65.	(D)	85.	(C)
6.	(D)	26.	(B)	46.	(C)	66.	(C)	86.	(B)
7.	(A)	27.	(B)	47.	(C)	67.	(B)	87.	(D)
8.	(B)	28.	(C)	48.	(B)	68.	(B)	88.	(A)
9.	(A)	29.	(A)	49.	(D)	69.	(C)	89.	(A)
10.	(A)	30.	(A)	50.	(D)	70.	(C)	90.	(D)
11.	(A)	31.	(B)	51.	(C)	71.	(D)	91.	(A)
12.	(B)	32.	(A)	52.	(B)	72.	(D)	92.	(B)
13.	(C)	33.	(A)	53.	(A)	73.	(C)	93.	(A)
14.	(B)	34.	(B)	54.	(B)	74.	(A)	94.	(C)
15.	(A)	35.	(A)	55.	(D)	75.	(B)	95.	(B)
16.	(C)	36.	(D)	56.	(D)	76.	(D)	96.	(B)
17.	(A)	37.	(A)	57.	(A)	77.	(B)	97.	(D)
18.	(A)	38.	(C)	58.	(D)	78.	(C)	98.	(A)
19.	(C)	39.	(B)	59.	(A)	79.	(B)	99.	(B)
20.	(C)	40.	(D)	60.	(B)	80.	(C)	100.	(B)

Part 1

1. (A) He is wearing a backpack.
   (B) He is leaving the building.
   (C) He is lifting the bag off the floor.
   (D) He is getting into the vehicle.

2. (A) They are boarding the aircraft.
   (B) They are loading luggage on the conveyor belt.
   (C) They are rolling the suitcase.
   (D) They are transporting the cartons.

3. (A) Trees are being planted in front of a building.
   (B) Lines are being painted on the road.
   (C) Shadows are being cast on the pavement.
   (D) Lampposts are being installed by the sign.

4. (A) One of the women is sitting on the grass.
   (B) They're standing in line for a bus.
   (C) They're gathered together outdoors.
   (D) A man is taking a picture in the park.

5. (A) A flag has been hung on the exterior of the building.
   (B) A car is being parked on the road.
   (C) Some windows have been left opened.
   (D) The stairway leads to the balcony.

6. (A) A server is taking off an apron.
   (B) Patio umbrellas have been folded.
   (C) They are having a conversation with a cashier.
   (D) Some seats are taken at an outdoor restaurant.

Part 2

7. Do you have a concert ticket?
   (A) I left it in my office.
   (B) Please take your seat.
   (C) I booked the table.

8. Could we discuss this after lunch?
   (A) No, every 30 minutes.
   (B) I'm meeting some clients.
   (C) About launching the product.

9. Who can open the office supply room?
   (A) I have the key.
   (B) I report to Joanne.
   (C) Some new supplies.

10. What kind of products does your company make?
    (A) Sportswear mostly.
    (B) The production department.
    (C) I'll accompany you.

11. When did Henry tidy the office?
    (A) After we left.
    (B) Soon, I hope.
    (C) She cleaned the floor.

12. Where is your new restaurant located?
    (A) In a couple of hours.
    (B) It's right around the corner.
    (C) I had the chicken.

13. How often do you visit your parents in Brisbane?
    (A) For a decade.
    (B) It's in Sydney, I think.
    (C) They don't live there anymore.

14. Why is the library closing early?
    (A) I checked out the books.
    (B) There's a foundation day event.
    (C) At ten o'clock on weekends.

15. Which plant produces these umbrellas?
    (A) The one in Westville.
    (B) It's going to rain.
    (C) Yes, water the plants.

16. You can pick up your car after one o'clock.
    (A) You are a mechanic.
    (B) I can deliver it for you.
    (C) Okay, I'll drop by then.

17. The prototype will be ready by next Monday, won't it?
    (A) We're still working on it.
    (B) Yes, I can type.
    (C) I already read the novel.

18. Do you think the new handbook contains enough information?
    (A) I would have liked more pictures.
    (B) No, thanks. I've had enough.
    (C) I think it can be handled properly.

19. Are you starting your new job immediately or taking some time off?
    (A) Yes, I applied for that online.
    (B) Yes, I'm interested in the position.
    (C) I'm going on vacation first.

20. What did the supervisor say about the annual report?
    (A) Once a year.
    (B) At the staff meeting.
    (C) She's satisfied with it.

21. Do you mind reviewing this budget proposal for me?
    (A) You proposed to me.
    (B) Sure, I'd be happy to.
    (C) She has a different view.

22. Our advertising budget was increased this month more than we expected.
    (A) Yes, by 15 percent.
    (B) Every Monday afternoon.
    (C) By decreasing advertisements.

23. Let's move to a quieter place for our efficiency.
    (A) Of course, the movie was great.
    (B) A new apartment building.
    (C) Room 81 is available.

24. Don't we need to set another table?
    (A) Employees from the sales team won't be coming.
    (B) I've never been to that place.
    (C) Yes, it's a famous restaurant.

25. Should we leave now, or can we wait a bit?
    (A) I was a little bit late.
    (B) You can leave it here, thanks.
    (C) How are the traffic conditions at this time?

26. Who can show me how to install the new program?
    (A) I just saw this month's figures.
    (B) I will, in a few minutes.
    (C) I'm not sure how to get there.

27. Will our proposal get to the Paris branch on time?
    (A) In the city council.
    (B) I sent it by overnight mail.
    (C) A 20 percent increase.

28. When can I receive the shipment of dress shoes?
    (A) From the shoe store.
    (B) A couple of months ago.
    (C) It's delayed at the airport.

29. Our train will be an hour late, right?
    (A) We should push back the client meeting.
    (B) We really enjoyed the training.
    (C) Platform 6 or 8.

30. Where should we place the new file cabinets?
    (A) It depends on Ms. Park.
    (B) Just across the street.
    (C) I ordered more a few days ago.

31. Wasn't the budget report supposed to be completed this morning?
    (A) I'm supposed to work.
    (B) There was a mistake on page 10.
    (C) By decreasing the budget.

Part 3

Questions 32-34 refer to the following conversation.

W   Good morning, Steve. This is Stella. I just came in and turned my computer on, but my screen is not working. I'm sure it's turned on because I can hear the fan blowing.
M   Are you sure the monitor is turned on? The computer and the monitor should be plugged into two separate outlets.
W   I'm not sure. I just pushed the power button and didn't touch anything else. I have to submit the weekly report first thing in the morning, so I am in real trouble now.
M   Calm down. Can you see the power light on? I mean, the one on the monitor.
W   Yes, both the computer and monitor are on. One is red and the other is blue.
M   Ah! That must be the problem. The indicator is blue if the monitor is connected to the computer properly.
W   So, you mean it's already turned on, right? What should I do to check now?
M   Do you see a blue cable coming out from the monitor? That must be plugged into the back of the computer. No, wait a minute. I'm coming to the 2nd floor. Just don't touch anything. I'll do it.

32. Why did the woman call the man?
    (A) To get help fixing a problem
    (B) To replace a device with a new one
    (C) To send him an urgent document
    (D) To connect the monitor properly

33. According to the woman, what did she do in the morning?
    (A) Turned on her computer
    (B) Came in earlier than usual
    (B) Tried connecting her monitor again
    (C) Printed the weekly report from her computer

34. What will the man probably do next?
    (A) Submit the report for Stella
    (B) Meet Stella in her office
    (C) Bring his computer to the 2nd floor
    (D) Try plugging the computer into another outlet

Questions 35-37 refer to the following conversation.

W   Hi, James. One of our drivers who usually delivers our merchandise to the Arcade Bakery is off sick today. So could you fill in for him this afternoon?
M   Sure, but this would be my first time delivering to that store. I need to know how to get there. Do you have the directions?
W   Okay, here you are. Just follow the map! One more thing, when you're there, remember to have the store manager sign the delivery confirmation form.

35. Why does the woman ask the man for help?
    (A) A coworker is not feeling well.
    (B) She is very sick.
    (C) She is out of town this afternoon.
    (D) She will take some time off.

36. What does the man need?
    (A) A key to a truck
    (B) A telephone number
    (C) A director's contact information
    (D) Directions to a store

37. What does the woman remind the man to do?
    (A) Get a signature
    (B) Notify his manager
    (C) Become a member
    (D) Sign the contract

Questions 38-40 refer to the following conversation.

M   Hello, this is Robert from SM Telecom. I'm supposed to visit you around two to upgrade the router.
W   Oops, I didn't expect you today. I thought you would come over tomorrow.
M   Oh, I'm sorry. There seems to be a mix-up in the information. Can I have your name, please?
W   I'm Ella Spencer in unit 503, Mainwell Apartments. And if possible, I'd rather have the service today because my Internet connection has been lagging all day.
M   Sure, Ms. Spencer. Your appointment was at 2:30 P.M. on Wednesday, but I can reschedule it right away. Is it okay to visit you at two?
W   Two sounds fine. I'll be staying home around that time, but I need to go out at three o'clock.
M   No problem. The work will take no longer than twenty minutes. I'll see you then.

38. Why will the man visit the woman's house?
    (A) To verify her name and address
    (B) To reschedule an appointment
    (C) To improve the network speed
    (D) To sell a telecommunication device

39. Why does the man ask the woman's name?
    (A) He is trying to be polite.
    (B) Some information is not accurate.
    (C) He'll write her a letter afterwards.
    (D) He wants to record the woman's voice.

40. What time does the woman want the upgrade to be finished by?
(A) By 2:00 P.M.
(B) By 2:20 P.M.
(C) By 2:30 P.M.
(D) By 3:00 P.M.

Questions 41-43 refer to the following conversation.

M Hi, Jessica. I was just looking over the building you designed for Mr. Bradley's law firm, and you did a great job!
W Thanks, I did my best! It was a wonderful design to work on!
M Why don't you join my team for our new account with Commonwealth Bank? You know, maybe they could be one of the biggest banks. They're expanding the business to open new branches nationwide.
W It sounds really interesting. But, at this time, I really can't say. I'm having a meeting with my manager to discuss another big project tomorrow, though.
M Okay. Is it possible to stop by your meeting and go over the details with both of you? This way, your manager will know how important this bank's project is as well.
W That sounds good!

41. Where are the speakers working?
(A) At an advertising agency
(B) At a law firm
(C) At an architectural company
(D) At a design school

42. What does the woman mean when she says, "I really can't say"?
(A) She is not allowed to reveal certain information.
(B) She should cancel the appointment.
(C) She cannot make a commitment yet.
(D) She has to revise some mistakes.

43. What does the man propose?
(A) Making an itinerary
(B) Preparing a negotiation
(C) Delaying a meeting
(D) Reviewing the project together

Questions 44-46 refer to the following conversation.

W I got a call from Mark Dice this morning. He eventually confirmed he cannot deliver the keynote address due to an important meeting. However, he still wants to present his opinion about recent changes in the market, he said.
M We were expecting this from the beginning, weren't we?
W Yes, we were. He hesitated to take it, saying he has another commitment that can't be missed. I should've found someone else.
M That's fine, and it was worth a try. Then, we can list him on the last day of the conference and ask the president to take the keynote speech.
W It's a relief that we have an alternative. I'll tell the president about this change. What else should we prepare?
M The timetable on the Web site should be revised, too. And we'll have to send text messages to those registered in advance and notify them of this change. I'll take care of it.

44. What problem are the speakers mainly discussing?
(A) They must launch a Web site in a hurry.
(B) There are not as many participants as they expected.
(C) They have make a change in a plan.
(D) The president won't be able to deliver a speech.

45. Why does the man say, "it was worth a try"?
(A) He is comforting the woman.
(B) He doesn't want to take the risk.
(C) He knew that Mr. Dice would turn them down.
(D) He regrets he had to meet the speaker in person.

46. What does the woman say she will do?
(A) Send text messages
(B) Update a Web page
(C) Contact the president
(D) Convince Mr. Dice to attend the event

Questions 47-49 refer to the following conversation.

M Good afternoon. This is Pablo Ortega. I called you to ask for a prescription for glasses.
W Hello, Mr. Ortega. I've checked your voice message. By the way, you should visit us again. We have a record saying that you saw Dr. Jenkins for a checkup in April, but it is no longer valid for a new prescription. You should get your eyes checked again, which will take about 30 minutes.
M Oh, I see. Can I see the doctor tomorrow morning?
W I'm afraid all the doctors have a full schedule on Thursday morning. How about Friday instead? We are open from 10 A.M. to 8 P.M.
M You close at 8? Then I can come in after work. Can I stop by this evening?
W Sure. I can schedule an appointment with the same doctor as last time. She's available from 6 to 7:30.
M Thank you. I'll be there by 7.

47. Who most likely is the woman?
(A) A pharmacist
(B) An optician
(C) A receptionist
(D) An appraiser

48. When is the man supposed to come?
(A) Wednesday morning
(B) Wednesday evening
(C) Thursday morning
(D) Thursday evening

49. What is suggested about the clinic?
(A) Dr. Jenkins is the only doctor working there.
(B) This is the first time Mr. Ortega has contacted it.
(C) It is open from 10 A.M. to 8 P.M. on weekends.
(D) It keeps some patients' medical records.

Questions 50-52 refer to the following conversation with three speakers.

M1 Thanks for coming, Chris and Nancy. I'm pleased you decided to come to take a look at this shop. As I told you yesterday, this property has a reasonable price because the seller wants to put the store up for sale so quickly.
W Yes, we really like the property, but we have some concerns.
M2 We're worried about the cost of refurbishment. We think everything needs to be changed.
M1 Don't worry about that. I can recommend an interior design company that provides low prices with high quality.
M2 That's good news. I'm just wondering why the owner decided to sell at short notice.
M1 Well, she'll start a new business out of the city.
W All right, could we sign the contract now?

50. Who most likely are Chris and Nancy?
(A) Apartment managers
(B) Interior designers
(C) Realtors
(D) Potential buyers

51. What are Chris and Nancy concerned about?
(A) The placement of smoke detectors
(B) The size of a property
(C) The expense of renovation
(D) The range of interior design companies

52. What is mentioned about the owner?
(A) She owns several stores.
(B) She'll start a new business.
(C) She can recommend qualified workers.
(D) She wants to change the interior.

Questions 53-55 refer to the following conversation.

W Hi Lucius. I've been trying to register for the workshop, but it said I'm using an incorrect password on my computer. I don't know what the problem is. What about your computer?
M Really? I already signed up for it. I think the tech support team upgraded some servers last night, so it was affected by this change.
W Oh. I guess I need to contact a technician from tech support. Who should I speak to about this?
M I don't know, but I think the best way is to submit a request form for service first. Let me do that for you here on my computer.

53. What is the woman unable to do?
(A) Log on to her computer
(B) Organize a workshop
(C) Print a document
(D) Create a password

54. According to the man, what happened yesterday?
(A) The power went out.
(B) Some servers were changed.
(C) Some equipment was broken.
(D) Computers were installed.

55. What does the man say he will do?
(A) Restart a computer
(B) Install new software
(C) Call a coworker
(D) Put in a help request

Questions 56-58 refer to the following conversation.

M Natalie, I just got your e-mail. The proposal looks pretty good, but we need to modify something.
W What do you think we should revise? Do we need to increase the estimates for the overhead?
M I think that is fine. The quotes for expenditure in Rome seemed a little low, though. There have been some cost-of-living increases over the past few months.
W Oh. Actually, I used the estimates from last year. I'll check that online and have that revised before I leave today.

56. What are the speakers mainly talking about?
(A) The cost of living
(B) Overseas branches
(C) An online business
(D) A proposed budget

57. What does the man say about the Rome expenses?
(A) They have been underestimated.
(B) They are the same as last year's.
(C) The quotes look good.
(D) The living costs were not in the budget.

58. What does the woman say she will do?
(A) Spend less money
(B) Estimate a price
(C) Use last year's records
(D) Update some information

Questions 59-61 refer to the following conversation.

W Hi, Edward! This is Jody from the personnel department. I just wanted to let you know that the projector in meeting room 5B is out of order.
M Yes, I can come down immediately and take a look at it.
W Right now? Umm, I'm interviewing someone here in 10 minutes. I don't use the equipment at all for that, so can you wait until I finish?
M No problem. In that case, I'll visit when you're done. Is there anything else you need to set up in the room?
W No, thanks. Nowadays, I try to talk to candidates in person without using equipment like video conferencing. It is important to know them well for a change.

59. Why is the woman calling the man?
(A) To report an equipment malfunction
(B) To check a device
(C) To request personal information
(D) To set up a meeting

60. What does the woman imply when she says, "I'm interviewing someone here in 10 minutes"?
(A) She needs help urgently.
(B) She does not want to be interrupted.
(C) She is not satisfied with an assignment.
(D) She will not attend another meeting.

61. What does the woman say is unique about the interview?
(A) It will be recorded.
(B) It will be filmed.
(C) It will be conducted face-to-face.
(D) It will last for more than an hour.

Questions 62-64 refer to the following conversation and sign.

W Thomas, have you already checked in your baggage? You'll stay three days for the conference, won't you?
M I'm afraid I can't stay for the whole conference. I have to return for an important client meeting. It was difficult to reschedule it. So I'll be returning right after my presentation the day after tomorrow.
W That's too bad. Anyway, don't we have to hurry if we want to catch the flight? My boarding pass says it's gate B14.
M Let's check the departure gate. Gate B14, there it is! It says our flight's on time. We do have time to have some drinks and snacks while we're walking over there.

62. Where is the conversation taking place?
(A) At a bus terminal
(B) At an airport
(C) At a business conference
(D) At a train station

63. Why isn't the man staying for the entire conference?
(A) He has a scheduling conflict.
(B) He is about to go on holiday.
(C) He has a presentation.
(D) He could not find a later flight.

64. Look at the graphic. What city are the speakers going to?
(A) Melbourne
(B) Sydney
(C) Perth
(D) Brisbane

Questions 65-67 refer to the following conversation and floor plan.

M Tracy, do you know when the floor plan will be posted? I'd like to check it before I leave. I'm taking the afternoon off.
W Actually, it came out last night. Here it is.
M Thank you. I should've asked sooner. Let's see. Hmm… The biggest room on the floor has been assigned to the sales department. Where are we going to move into?
W We're going to take the one between the copy room and the staff lounge. It's near the elevator.
M The members would be glad to hear about this, wouldn't they?
W Not exactly. As you know, the staff lounge is quite noisy in the afternoon.
M Since they have said they are adding some soundproof insulation this time, we'll see how it turns out. I'm leaving now. I have to see a doctor at 2.
W Alright, see you on Monday. We should come earlier because there is a lot of stuff to move.

65. Look at the graphic. Which room are the speakers moving into on Monday?
 (A) Room 302
 (B) Room 303
 (C) Room 304
 (D) Room 305

66. According to the woman, what would her colleagues say about their new room?
 (A) They're glad to take the biggest room.
 (B) They are pleased to be situated near the stairs.
 (C) They're not happy to be located near the staff lounge.
 (D) They enjoy the advantages of sound proof insulation.

67. Why does the man have to leave early today?
 (A) He has to meet a client at two o'clock.
 (B) He has an appointment in the afternoon.
 (C) He has to pack up his belongings in advance.
 (D) He has to pick up something in the staff lounge.

Questions 68-70 refer to the following conversation and list.

M Hey, Ms. Jennings, is the Internet working on your computer? I really need to check my e-mail.
W Yeah, I'm not having any problems at all.
M Well, whenever I log on to the Internet it freezes, so I can't see my e-mail. Have you received the data about the quarterly sales figures yet?
W Hmm, let me see… yes! Do you want me to send you the information?
M Thanks a lot, but could you print it out for me? I just need a copy of the quarterly sales figures for the meeting this afternoon.

68. Why is the man unable to access his e-mail?
 (A) He's using an incorrect password.
 (B) His Internet connection isn't available.
 (C) He forgot to update some software.
 (D) His computer is malfunctioning.

69. Look at the graphic. Who sent the e-mail the speakers are referring to?
 (A) Brian Swann
 (B) Yianni Ellenikiotis
 (C) Helen Yang
 (D) Brittany Seymour

70. What does the man ask the woman to do?
 (A) Call the technician
 (B) Present the quarterly sales figures
 (C) Print out a document
 (D) Arrange a meeting this afternoon

Part 4

Questions 71-73 refer to the following talk.

Thank you for visiting the opening of the new American Art exhibition at the Whitney Museum. This exhibit has some modern American art. Before we see the exhibition, I'd like to hand out some audio devices to you. This player can help you to hear background information about the art. Also, we'll have a great lecture from one of the famous artists at 2 P.M. I hope you'll enjoy the talk.

71. What is the purpose of the talk?
 (A) To ask for donations
 (B) To publicize the museum
 (C) To discuss modern art
 (D) To introduce an exhibit

72. What will the speaker distribute?
 (A) Entrance tickets
 (B) A brochure
 (C) A map of the museum
 (D) An audio player

73. According to the speaker, what will begin at two o'clock?
 (A) An auction
 (B) A concert
 (C) A talk
 (D) A reception

Questions 74-76 refer to the following telephone message.

Good morning, Sarah. This is Paul Grant from Furniture Depot. I regret to inform you that the chairs you wanted for your conference room are sold out. I ordered them for you, but they will take 4 weeks to get here. We do have similar style chairs in stock. If you want, I can have those delivered to you tomorrow. Give me a call and let me know what you decide. I'm going to be out all day today making deliveries, so either leave me a message or send me a text message. After returning to the store, I'll get back to you.

74. Why did the speaker leave a message?
 (A) To talk about a problem with an order
 (B) To find out when to make a delivery
 (C) To get more information about furniture
 (D) To ask for help choosing a new chair

75. When does the speaker say he can deliver similar chairs?
 (A) In 4 weeks
 (B) Tomorrow
 (C) This evening
 (D) In two days

76. What does the speaker say he will do today?
 (A) Work at the store all day long
 (B) Record some messages
 (C) Send the package
 (D) Deliver items

Questions 77-79 refer to the following advertisement.

If you're looking for a reliable travel agency with a good reputation and professional, knowledgeable staff, then look no further than Modu Travel Agency, located in heart of Chicago. Modu has been in business for twenty years, helping customers book reasonably priced trips worldwide. We specialize in European package tours, particularly to Italy. We are currently offering discount airfares on ten-day guided trips to Venice, Florence, and Rome. All trips include accommodation and sightseeing tours. Or, if you are planning a trip to Asia or other countries in Europe, our capable staff can assist you with all of your travel arrangements. Just give us a call at 978-6418 or visit our office.

77. How long has the business been operating?
(A) For twelve years
(B) For two decades
(C) For a decade
(D) For fifteen years

78. What type of business is being advertised?
(A) An airline
(B) A bus company
(C) A travel agency
(D) A bookstore

79. What special offer is the business making now?
(A) Free calling cards
(B) Reduced rates on certain flights
(C) Package tours to Asia and other countries in Europe
(D) Free accommodation in Venice and Florence

Questions 80-82 refer to the following news report.

This is Channel Five News. I'm Marco DeGrassi. At this morning's press conference, Milton City Council announced a plan to build more bus lanes to solve the traffic problems all over the city. Construction on the project is scheduled to begin at the end of this month. It'll take about 3 months. According to the city mayor, Tom Kenny, new bus lanes on the main roads will reduce the traffic congestion. Many citizens have already voiced their strong support for new lanes, although they will experience inconvenience during the construction. Stay tuned for news on the governor's race after the commercial break.

80. What does the speaker say will happen at the end of the month?
(A) A new City Hall will be built.
(B) Traffic congestion will take place.
(C) Construction on new bus lanes will commence.
(D) A hotel association will select a new president.

81. Who is Tom Kenny?
(A) A local politician
(B) A news reporter
(C) A bus driver
(D) A city spokesperson

82. What will listeners probably hear next?
(A) A sports game
(B) A local news report
(C) A sponsor's message
(D) A weather forecast

Questions 83-85 refer to the following announcement.

Good morning, everyone. Welcome to the Jeremy OA Training Center. We specialize in helping office employees make good use of various software and work more efficiently and conveniently. It's your first day today. You'll team up with three or four people from the same department. For each group, we'll assign a teaching assistant who is an expert in all kinds of office software and also understands the general workflow of each department. As you can see, we have an attendance book in front. Please check which training group you are in and sign next to your name on the list. This will take some time because we have many participants today. And for those who didn't turn in the copy of your photo ID card with the application, would you please submit it now? The copier is in room 305.

83. What type of business does the speaker work for?
(A) A recruiting agency
(B) A computer retailer
(C) An office equipment manufacturer
(D) An education center

84. Why does the speaker say, "the copier is in room 305"?
(A) He was asked if a copier is available.
(B) The attendees will learn how to make copies today.
(C) The teaching assistants need to copy the roll book.
(D) Some people should go to another room to prepare some document.

85. What does the speaker ask the listeners to do?
(A) Sign the contract
(B) Introduce themselves
(C) Team up with their colleagues
(D) Submit their applications in advance

Questions 86-88 refer to the following excerpt from a meeting.

Thanks for coming today on such a short notice. As I told you in the e-mail, we've been trying to help young students who are struggling to get through their lives without their parents' support. Thanks to the enthusiastic help and the donations from local businesses and the city council, we finally opened the Child Welfare Center last month, where we are providing meals and basic education services free of charge. Most of the beneficiaries are in their late teens; therefore, we need more education programs that are suitable for them. But unfortunately, we have insufficiency of funds and are unable to pay for this quality education. So, above all, I think we need to receive help from the current and former teachers in the area. I'll hand out a list of local schools. Please make sure to contact them, asking for help. I hope this project will be a great help for disadvantaged children, and more people join this meaningful cause.

86. What does the speaker mainly talk about?
(A) Building a welfare center
(B) Drawing more volunteers
(C) Organizing a fundraising event
(D) Becoming a teacher

87. What problem does the welfare center have?
(A) There are not many schools in the area.
(B) It cannot afford free meals for the beneficiaries.
(C) The center hasn't launched any education programs yet.
(D) They don't have enough money for a plan.

88. What are the listeners asked to do?
(A) Contact the schools in the area
(B) Look for a suitable contractor
(C) Attract more young teens
(D) Ask for their parents' support

Questions 89-91 refer to the following talk.

Hello, Ms. Shirley. This is Vanessa Adams from Rich Real Estate. I got the message you left while I was out of the office. It said that you need to change the moving date to earlier than you had indicated before. That means I have less time to look for an apartment that meets your requirements. But it's not a problem. We do have many rental apartments in our listings. By the way, can you tell me when you will visit our office? I think it would be better, if you like one of the properties, to sign a rental contract on that day. Please call back as soon as possible. Thank you.

89. What is the speaker doing for Ms. Shirley?
 (A) Finding a place to live
 (B) Reserving a hotel room
 (C) Buying an office building
 (D) Renovating an interior design

90. What does the speaker imply when she says, "But it's not a problem"?
 (A) She wants to recommend a moving company.
 (B) She asks for a specific reason.
 (C) She feels disappointed.
 (D) She thinks that she can resolve the issue.

91. What does the speaker ask Ms. Shirley to do?
 (A) Arrange an appointment
 (B) Sign the contract
 (C) Choose the color of the wallpaper
 (D) Update contact information

Questions 92-94 refer to the following telephone message.

Mr. Reece, this is Darius Stanton from the Colorado office. I'm calling to confirm your attendance at the board meeting here in March. The meeting is scheduled for the 10th. Your secretary mentioned last week that you might not be able to attend. So, I was wondering if this is still the case. If you are not able to come, please let me know whether you can participate in a conference call. I'll send you an e-mail with possible times for a call. With the time difference, however, please understand if they seem a little inconvenient. I'll also be attaching the proposed agenda for the meeting. I am looking forward to hearing from you.

92. Why is the speaker calling?
 (A) To schedule a meeting
 (B) To confirm the listeners' presence at a conference
 (C) To arrange suitable travel date
 (D) To reschedule a conference call

93. What did Mr. Reece's secretary tell Mr. Stanton?
 (A) His availability is uncertain.
 (B) His interest is negligible.
 (C) His attendance is mandatory.
 (D) His schedule is canceled.

94. What does the speaker say he will do?
 (A) Mail the proposed agenda
 (B) Arrange a flight
 (C) Send information electronically
 (D) Check the time difference

Questions 95-97 refer to the following instructions and seating chart.

Hello, everyone. I'm so glad that all you musicians are here to perform at the City Pop Festival. I want to give everyone some instructions briefly before you perform on the stage today. We don't have designated seats, so before and after each groups performance, please feel free to take any seats in the crowd if you want to watch the rest of the show. But I recommend you get a seat close to exit 2 to avoid disturbing the rest of the audience when you make your way from the stage. One more thing, could you stay a bit longer to take pictures after the performance? These pictures will be in the next issue of *City News Magazine*.

95. Who most likely are the listeners?
 (A) Photographers
 (B) Performers
 (C) Ushers
 (D) Audience members

96. Look at the graphic. What section does the speaker want the listeners to sit in?
 (A) Area 1
 (B) Area 2
 (C) Area 3
 (D) Area 4

97. What are listeners asked to do when the show ends?
 (A) Have some refreshments
 (B) Sign autographs
 (C) Revise a magazine
 (D) Attend a photo shoot

Questions 98-100 refer to the following excerpt from a meeting and survey.

I'd like to begin today's staff meeting by sharing some results of the customer survey of our running shoes recently conducted to satisfy customers. These results are very important. As you can see, what they like the most is the shoes' design. So we don't need to improve this. Here are the top four answers to the question, "What features of the product did you like most?" As you can see, the durability is the biggest problem we should upgrade. I'll let the product development team know about this. In the meantime, we can discuss the second-most-common answer. If you have any ideas, please let me know.

98. According to the speaker, why did the company conduct the survey?
 (A) To satisfy consumers
 (B) To release the running shoes
 (C) To cut operating expenses
 (D) To correct a questionnaire

99. Look at the graphic. Which survey result does the speaker want to address now?
 (A) Design
 (B) Color Scheme
 (C) Durability
 (D) Material

100. What does the speaker ask the listeners to do?
 (A) Conduct safety inspections
 (B) Give some feedback
 (C) Mention some potential employees
 (D) Contact the product development team

5회

1.	(B)	21.	(B)	41.	(A)	61.	(B)	81.	(C)
2.	(A)	22.	(A)	42.	(D)	62.	(D)	82.	(D)
3.	(A)	23.	(A)	43.	(B)	63.	(A)	83.	(A)
4.	(C)	24.	(C)	44.	(C)	64.	(D)	84.	(A)
5.	(C)	25.	(A)	45.	(D)	65.	(B)	85.	(D)
6.	(C)	26.	(B)	46.	(B)	66.	(C)	86.	(C)
7.	(C)	27.	(A)	47.	(A)	67.	(A)	87.	(A)
8.	(A)	28.	(B)	48.	(C)	68.	(C)	88.	(C)
9.	(C)	29.	(A)	49.	(A)	69.	(C)	89.	(C)
10.	(B)	30.	(A)	50.	(D)	70.	(D)	90.	(C)
11.	(C)	31.	(B)	51.	(B)	71.	(B)	91.	(C)
12.	(A)	32.	(C)	52.	(A)	72.	(A)	92.	(C)
13.	(B)	33.	(C)	53.	(B)	73.	(D)	93.	(A)
14.	(B)	34.	(C)	54.	(C)	74.	(A)	94.	(C)
15.	(B)	35.	(D)	55.	(C)	75.	(A)	95.	(C)
16.	(C)	36.	(B)	56.	(D)	76.	(B)	96.	(A)
17.	(C)	37.	(C)	57.	(A)	77.	(A)	97.	(A)
18.	(C)	38.	(A)	58.	(B)	78.	(D)	98.	(C)
19.	(A)	39.	(C)	59.	(A)	79.	(B)	99.	(C)
20.	(B)	40.	(C)	60.	(B)	80.	(A)	100.	(A)

Part 1

1. (A) A woman is changing into a swim suit.
   (B) A woman is walking along the beach.
   (C) A woman is surfing in the ocean.
   (D) A woman is picking up some seashells.

2. (A) A man is taking notes on the paper.
   (B) A man is walking in the forest.
   (C) A man is lying on the grass.
   (D) A man is sitting on the bench.

3. (A) Food is being prepared in the kitchen.
   (B) A man is washing dishes.
   (C) A man is wearing gloves.
   (D) A bowl is being filled with water.

4. (A) Some people are watching a movie.
   (B) Some people are sitting in a line.
   (C) A woman is speaking to a group of people.
   (D) A woman is arranging a document.

5. (A) A customer is ringing a bell.
   (B) A woman is trying on a ring.
   (C) Some jewelry is on display.
   (D) A telephone is ringing.

6. (A) The armchairs are facing the artwork.
   (B) The rug is being rolled up.
   (C) The sitting area is brightened by lamps.
   (D) Books are being stacked on the table.

Part 2

7. How do you come to the office every day?
   (A) By the post office.
   (B) No, I didn't go there.
   (C) I just walk.

8. I think you really liked the volunteer we met yesterday, didn't you?
   (A) Yes, we should give him a better position.
   (B) He'll do it tomorrow.
   (C) I received a copy of his application.

9. Is the shareholders' meeting scheduled to be held on April 5?
   (A) We should have shared them last year.
   (B) To discuss our new products.
   (C) No, it has been delayed.

10. Who do I have to inform of my change of address?
    (A) No, it doesn't change at all.
    (B) Anderson, at the reception desk.
    (C) Tom will give an address.

11. Why are your office supplies moved to another room?
    (A) We will move to Chicago.
    (B) An old piece of furniture, thanks.
    (C) Water is leaking through the ceiling.

12. The new products will be ready by next Friday, right?
    (A) No, we need more time to finish them.
    (B) Yes, it makes a lot of products.
    (C) I will read newly-published books.

13. The door to the supply room has been locked.
    (A) We supply tickets.
    (B) I'll call the manager.
    (C) I can lock the window for you.

14. When will the headquarters on Main Street be remodeled?
    (A) A quarter of a mile.
    (B) Work begins next Monday.
    (C) Yes, I enjoy walking down the street.

15. Do you know who is carrying out the survey today?
    (A) In Ashton's division.
    (B) Winston Bale is.
    (C) Please fill in the survey form.

16. Could you give me a ride when you leave the office?
    (A) I just placed an order for office supplies.
    (B) I dropped off and missed the show.
    (C) Today, I took a taxi to work.

17. Which store sells these lunch boxes?
    (A) Probably last year.
    (B) Yes, it's going to snow heavily.
    (C) The one between 5th and 6th Avenue.

18. Doesn't Mindy generally leave at six o'clock?
    (A) Actually, I believe she has little.
    (B) She won't take long.
    (C) Yes, but she will work late into the night.

19. Should we walk or drive to the shop?
    (A) My car is in the parking lot right here.
    (B) A few blocks from your home.
    (C) The grocery store, please.

20. What did Mr. Clyne say about the plan?
    (A) At the press conference.
    (B) He finally approved it.
    (C) He plans to decline an interview.

21. How often do you check your e-mail?
    (A) Yes, I'll do that.
    (B) Twice a day.
    (C) By express mail.

22. Are you getting back to work or going on a vacation?
    (A) I'm taking some time off.
    (B) I need to get it back quickly.
    (C) I applied for the job.

23. When does your order arrive?
    (A) It is being held up at customs.
    (B) He arrived at the airport.
    (C) A new product.

24. You could use a larger font for the presentation.
    (A) The projector is ready.
    (B) We need a wider space to accommodate them.
    (C) I think that would help.

25. Where should we take our clients for the meeting?
    (A) I decided yesterday.
    (B) The airplane will arrive soon.
    (C) He sent the file.

26. Do you mind reviewing the budget report for me?
    (A) A weather report.
    (B) Oh, I was about to get off work.
    (C) He has a different viewpoint.

27. Are the clients satisfied with the proposal we revised?
    (A) They'll let us know later today.
    (B) In the December issue.
    (C) A few suggested scenarios.

28. Who has the survey results?
    (A) Jamison will meet there soon.
    (B) Let me check the file.
    (C) The survey form, I think.

29. Did you go to the festival last weekend?
    (A) I don't like crowded areas.
    (B) When is the last day?
    (C) They're in good condition.

30. Can you show me how to fix the copy machine?
    (A) Lucy learned about that last month.
    (B) A copy of the contract will be ready.
    (C) A copy machine was installed in the conference room.

31. What should we do to celebrate Mr. Dickson's promotion?
    (A) In 2 years, probably.
    (B) Let's go to the Oliver's restaurant.
    (C) He is starting his new business.

Part 3

Questions 32-34 refer to the following conversation.

M Hi, I saw your store advertised on the Internet, so I dropped by. Your shop is having a clearance sale at the moment. Is that right? Is the sale applicable to home appliances, too?
W Sure, the products on display are all 50 percent off the retail price. Did you download the coupon that came with the ad?
M Actually, I downloaded it on my mobile phone, but I left it at home. It might be better to go back there and come again to get a discount.

32. Why does the man choose to shop at the store?
    (A) It is conveniently located.
    (B) The staff is very kind.
    (C) He saw an online advertisement.
    (D) One of his colleagues recommended the store.

33. What does the woman ask about?
    (A) An identification card
    (B) A receipt
    (C) A discount coupon
    (D) An advertisement flyer

34. Why does the man say he will go home?
    (A) He wants to come with his parents.
    (B) He has to answer the phone.
    (C) He left something behind.
    (D) He doesn't want to buy this product.

Questions 35-37 refer to the following conversation.

W Hi, Mr. Bacon. I have a blouse that should be dry-cleaned. I would like you to remove a coffee stain from it.
M We can definitely get rid of the stain on your shirt. It will be ready by Saturday. I'll also have the skirt you requested earlier ready by then, too.
W It would be great if I could wear the blouse and skirt for my important job interview on Friday. So... um... I was wondering if this could be done sooner.
M I could do that. I'll start working on it immediately so both will be ready by Thursday evening.

35. Where is the conversation most likely taking place?
    (A) At a coffee shop
    (B) At an office
    (C) At a clothing factory
    (D) At a dry cleaner's

36. What is the woman doing on Friday?
    (A) Meeting a client
    (B) Interviewing for a job
    (C) Going on a vacation
    (D) Visiting relatives

37. What does the man offer to do?
    (A) Exchange a defective product
    (B) Cancel a reservation
    (C) Offer an express service
    (D) Place a special order

Questions 38-40 refer to the following conversation.

M Hello, this is Harvey Harris from United Electric Service. I was scheduled to visit your office to install some refrigerators this afternoon, but what I'm doing now is taking longer than planned. Unfortunately, I won't be able to make it until 7 P.M.
W Thank you for the information. Our office closes at 6 P.M., but our security guard in the building is on duty for 24 hours. I'll ask the one on duty to let you in.
M Thank you. And when I finish the installation, how can I send the invoice?
W I would appreciate it if you could just leave it with him.

38. Why will the man visit the woman's office?
    (A) To set up appliances
    (B) To make a repair
    (C) To deliver a speech
    (D) To get a refund

39. What does the woman say she will do?
    (A) Cancel an appointment
    (B) Meet with a client
    (C) Talk to a security officer
    (D) Provide a receipt

40. What does the woman ask the man to leave with the security guard?
    (A) An estimate
    (B) A manual
    (C) An invoice
    (D) An agreement

新 Questions 41-43 refer to the following conversation with three speakers.

M1 Hi. Welcome to Burton Store. How can I be of assistance?
W   Well, I wonder if you could help me. I am looking for colored pencils for my daughter.
M1 Hmm… I'm not sure if we have them for children. As far as I know, we have them only for professionals, but let me check on this. Hey, Christopher, do we have children's colored pencils?
M2 Yes, we do, but just not on this floor. They're upstairs. Let me show you. Please follow me.
W   That's good news. And do you know where I can get them gift-wrapped? They are for my daughter's birthday present.
M2 Actually, we offer a gift-wrapping service for free.
W   That's perfect. Thanks!

41. What is the woman shopping for?
    (A) Stationery
    (B) Wrapping paper
    (C) Children's book
    (D) Paint

42. What does Christopher say about the items?
    (A) They're sold out.
    (B) They're offered at a discounted price.
    (C) They've already been delivered.
    (D) They're on a different floor.

43. What additional service does Christopher mention?
    (A) Express delivery
    (B) Free packaging
    (C) A free estimate
    (D) On-site repair

Questions 44-46 refer to the following conversation.

W   I talked to Hugo Robbins on the phone yesterday. We were going to have him as our keynote speaker for the April conference, but he confirmed that he is unable to participate.
M   Really? That's bad news. We have to find a replacement for him as soon as possible. We don't have much time because the schedule for the conference program will be out next week.
W   Do you have any alternatives to recommend?
M   As a matter of fact, I know a qualified candidate; Tim Lee. He's a very attractive speaker and will pull in huge crowds. I'll call him and let you know if he is available.

44. What are the speakers organizing?
    (A) A job interview
    (B) A music concert
    (C) A conference
    (D) A wedding party

45. What problem does the woman mention?
    (A) An event has been delayed.
    (B) A flight was canceled.
    (C) Hotels are all booked up.
    (D) A speaker has canceled.

46. What most likely will the man do next?
    (A) Send an invitation card
    (B) Make a phone call
    (C) Make a reservation
    (D) Prepare a meeting

Questions 47-49 refer to the following conversation.

W   Hi, Dennis. Did you check on the schedule for next month's sports program? I rearranged the schedule for you to teach two classes.
M   Great! Thanks. Hmm… The two classes are back-to-back.
W   Right. Isn't that what you want?
M   Well, we have to put the equipment away and prepare the next class in just ten minutes because the basketball class is scheduled to begin right after my table tennis class is over. Who can help me? I can't do it alone.
W   I understand. How about changing the start time of the basketball class? If it starts 10 minutes later, there'll be no problem.

47. Where do the speakers most likely work?
    (A) At a fitness center
    (B) At a police station
    (C) At a department store
    (D) At a heavy equipment facility

48. What does the man imply when he says, "I can't do it alone"?
    (A) He is asking for a pay increase.
    (B) He wants to know the exact number of members.
    (C) He thinks that a task is impossible.
    (D) He is satisfied with his current position.

49. What does the woman offer to do?
    (A) Change the schedule
    (B) Move the equipment
    (C) Clean up the facility
    (D) Recruit more members

Questions 50-52 refer to the following conversation.

W   Jason, I should wrap up the quarterly sales report for the presentation on Friday. Please check to see if you need to revise it.
M   Actually, I'm still correcting some of the figures. The computer system was down for maintenance yesterday, so I'm terribly behind on my work. When do you need it by?
W   By tomorrow morning, if possible. I have to get the presentation ready by then because the shareholders' meeting is scheduled to be held on Friday.

50. What are the speakers discussing?
    (A) Selecting a new computer system
    (B) Checking maintenance information
    (C) Starting a business
    (D) Finishing a report

51. Why was the man unable to complete a task?
    (A) Sales revenue has decreased.
    (B) A system was not working properly.
    (C) A colleague was out of town.
    (D) A meeting was canceled.

52. What does the woman say she will do?
    (A) Prepare for a meeting
    (B) Change a reservation
    (C) Contact the maintenance department
    (D) Email a report

Questions 53-55 refer to the following conversation with three speakers.

M   Hi, I'm Richard Rose. I made a phone call yesterday to get my medical records as I need a copy of them when I go on a business trip to Singapore next month.
W1 All right, I'll check on this. Who's your doctor?
M   Doctor Mitchell.
W1 Okay, I think my colleague printed them in the morning. One second, sir. Jennifer?
W2 Yes?
W1 You printed Mr. Rose's records in the morning, right?
W2 Yes. Please just sign this form before I give them to you.
M   Sure. Could I borrow a pen?

53. What does the man say he will do next month?
    (A) Participate in a medical forum
    (B) Go away on business
    (C) Move to a different city
    (D) Finish a medical course

54. According to the conversation, what did Jennifer do in the morning?
    (A) She rescheduled an appointment.
    (B) She prescribed some medicine.
    (C) She printed some documents.
    (D) She treated a patient.

55. What does Jennifer ask the man to do?
    (A) Make a payment
    (B) Wait for a while
    (C) Sign a form
    (D) Call a doctor's office

Questions 56-58 refer to the following conversation.

M   Hello, I placed an order for a wireless speaker on your Web site on May 5th. My credit card statement said that I was charged two times for the purchase.
W   I'm really sorry to hear that, sir. Actually, we had a problem with our electronic payment system on that date. So, online transactions were repeated automatically.
M   Oh, is that so?
W   Yes, the refund procedure is currently underway, but I can deal with yours immediately if you wish.
M   Okay, that's a relief. Thank you.
W   After I put this through… um… if you don't mind, could you take part in our survey?
M   Sure, no problem.

56. Why is the man calling?
    (A) He wants to buy another product.
    (B) His order has not yet been delivered.
    (C) He needs to know the store's Web site address.
    (D) He was charged twice for a purchase.

57. What does the woman explain about?
    (A) A technical issue
    (B) A renovation project
    (C) An inventory shortage
    (D) A credit card expiration date

58. What does the woman ask the man to do?
    (A) Return a product
    (B) Respond to a survey
    (C) Visit a Web site
    (D) Keep a receipt

Questions 59-61 refer to the following conversation.

W   Hey David, it's Green. I'm trying to enter the building, but the gate won't open when I swipe my ID badge.
M   That occurred to a few employees today. If you let me know your employee number, I'll reenter your information into the server right now. Then, the gate scanner should recognize you.
W   Okay, but can you let me in now? I have a meeting with a client.
M   It's against the company policy. It'll only take a few minutes.
W   I understand. Then I hope it can be done as quickly as possible.

59. Where most likely is the woman?
    (A) At a building entrance
    (B) In a meeting room
    (C) At an airport
    (D) In an elevator

60. What does the man ask for?
    (A) A department name
    (B) An employee number
    (C) A password
    (D) A telephone number

61. Why does the man say, "It's against the company policy"?
    (A) To postpone a meeting
    (B) To refuse a request
    (C) To ask for a help
    (D) To make up for a mistake

Questions 62-64 refer to the following conversation and seat map.

W   Excuse me, sir. You might be sitting in the wrong seat. According to my ticket, I'm supposed to sit in A.
M   No, I'm quite certain that I'm in 8A. Let's take a look at your ticket. Hmm… I understand what happened. You should be seated right ahead of me.
W   Oh. Thank you, and sorry about that. By the way, if you don't mind, could you change your place with me? My boyfriend is going to be sitting in 8B. It would be great if we could watch the film together.
M   Sure, that's no problem. I like a seat closer to the screen anyway.

62. What is the purpose of the conversation?
    (A) To explain refund regulations
    (B) To introduce a new film
    (C) To offer a special discount
    (D) To resolve a problem

63. Look at the graphic. What seat was the woman originally assigned to?
    (A) 7A
    (B) 7B
    (C) 8A
    (D) 8B

64. What does the woman ask the man to do?
    (A) Check the time when the movie starts
    (B) Choose another movie
    (C) Request a discount coupon
    (D) Change the seat

Questions 65-67 refer to the following conversation and schedule.

W: Hi, Tolisso. How's the renovation plan for the hotel going?
M: Great. Even though the hotel is somewhat old, it was structurally sound. The plan is well under way.
W: Good. I would like to put it up for sale on the first day of December. I think that it is the best time to sell. Will everything be finished by then?
M: Let me see. We've just finished the furniture, flooring, and lighting installation. And we're scheduled to start remodeling the fitness center next week. Yes, we could be done by the end of November.
W: Could you send me the details about the total expected cost? This will help me set a price for the hotel.

65. What most likely is the man's profession?
    (A) Engineer
    (B) Construction manager
    (C) Real estate agent
    (D) Salesperson

66. Look at the graphic. What stage of the renovation will begin next week?
    (A) Stage 1
    (B) Stage 2
    (C) Stage 3
    (D) Stage 4

67. What does the woman ask the man to send?
    (A) An estimated price
    (B) Some photos
    (C) A schedule
    (D) A hotel address

Questions 68-70 refer to the following conversation and pie chart.

M: Lauren, I have read the M&A report. Have you seen the file? We considered taking over Goldman Holdings last year.
W: Really? What else does it say?
M: The main topic is our company's market share. Even though we still wouldn't have the biggest market share in the industry, we're trying to improve our competitive edge.
W: So, it looks like we're already the third biggest and acquiring Goldman Holdings will definitely help our company overtake Ingram to rank second in the industry. I think taking over the company would be a good decision.
M: Well… I'm not sure. It isn't such a good idea. Now I'm reading the latest report. Goldman Holdings' profits has decreased for the past few months.

68. What are the speakers mainly discussing?
    (A) An annual plan
    (B) Unemployment rates
    (C) A business acquisition
    (D) A budget report

69. Look at the graphic. Where do the speakers work?
    (A) Lowe
    (B) Ingram
    (C) Morgan Express
    (D) Goldman Holdings

70. Why does the man say he is not convinced?
    (A) He didn't read the report.
    (B) Some information is inaccurate.
    (C) The man is not good at analyzing data.
    (D) The company's profits have reduced recently.

Part 4

Questions 71-73 refer to the following advertisement.

Do you have old electronic products that you never use, such as old computers and TVs? Why don't you bring them to Avnet Electronics? We'll make a visit to pick up your devices and recycle them. If you donate your old devices to us, you'll get a 10 percent discount coupon for any products sold in our stores. To get information on our locations or the donation process, please feel free to visit our Web site at www.avnetelectronics.com.

71. What service is being advertised?
    (A) Home delivery
    (B) A recycling program
    (C) Product repair
    (D) An education course

72. How can listeners get a discount?
    (A) By making a donation
    (B) By taking a class
    (C) By purchasing a certain item
    (D) By recommending a company

73. What does the speaker say is available on a Web site?
    (A) A product line
    (B) Information on a company
    (C) A promotional video
    (D) A list of locations

Questions 74-76 refer to the following announcement.

Attention, ladies and gentlemen, the Frontier Airlines' non-stop flight from London to San Francisco has been delayed. We apologize for the inconvenience that this may have caused you. If you visit the information desk next to Gate 11 and speak to a Frontier Airlines representative, we will do our best to book you on a different flight to your final destination. While waiting, please enjoy complimentary beverages and snacks, courtesy of Frontier Airlines. Your understanding and patience are greatly appreciated. Thank you for flying Frontier Airlines.

74. Where is the announcement probably being made?
    (A) At an airport
    (B) At a bus station
    (C) At a taxi stand
    (D) At a ticket office

75. What does the speaker ask listeners to do?
    (A) Meet with a representative
    (B) Cancel a ticket
    (C) Visit the company's Web site
    (D) Book a hotel

76. According to the speaker, what will be offered?
    (A) A free dinner
    (B) Free refreshments
    (C) An itinerary
    (D) Maps

Questions 77-79 refer to the following telephone message.

Hi, it's Mia. Can we meet at noon? We have to interview the candidates for our new branch manager position. As you already know, we have only three months left before the opening of the new branch. I'll send you an e-mail shortly with a list of the most promising. Before we meet, please narrow the list down to three candidates. Thanks.

77. What is the purpose of the message?
 (A) To set up a meeting
 (B) To receive an order
 (C) To get an approval
 (D) To make a contract

78. What does the speaker imply when she says, "we have only three months left before the opening of the new branch"?
 (A) She should find a place to conduct an interview.
 (B) She wants the listener to visit a branch.
 (C) A branch office should be opened soon.
 (D) A decision should be made as soon as possible.

79. What most likely will the speaker do next?
 (A) Make a list of candidates
 (B) Email some documents
 (C) Call a branch office
 (D) Fill out an application

Questions 80-82 refer to the following talk.

Good morning, everyone. During your internship program, I hope you have gained a valuable experience at our museum. Today, I want you to help us promote the upcoming exhibition by Vincent Van Gogh. It will be one of the biggest exhibitions held in our museum, so I would like you all to distribute flyers not only to hotel guests and shoppers, but also to pedestrians. I'll give you a map where you can check the marked locations to visit. Please return to the museum at 6 P.M. See you then.

80. Where does the speaker work?
 (A) At a museum
 (B) At a hotel
 (C) At a store
 (D) At a coffee shop

81. What will the listeners be doing today?
 (A) Making a flyer
 (B) Going on a tour
 (C) Distributing leaflets
 (D) Taking pictures

82. What has the speaker done for the listeners?
 (A) Made a reservation for a restaurant
 (B) Ordered gifts
 (C) Provided complimentary tickets
 (D) Circled places on a map

Questions 83-85 refer to the following excerpt from a meeting.

As the head of the agency, I'm very delighted to announce that our agency has been named the 2017 ISAA Advertisement of the Year. It is attributable to your hard work and dedication. I personally think highly of the work that Emmy Kunis and her team did on the AVIS campaign. The company has actually increased its revenue by 15 percent due to this campaign. Please give Ms. Kunis and her team a big round of applause for what they have achieved.

83. What kind of business does the speaker work for?
 (A) An advertising agency
 (B) A furniture store
 (C) A library
 (D) A financial institution

84. What is the speaker announcing?
 (A) An award winner
 (B) A resignation
 (C) A promotion
 (D) A retirement

85. What does the speaker say about Emmy Kunis's work?
 (A) It made an agency increase in its value.
 (B) It led to changes in a company's regulations.
 (C) It took advantage of the latest technology.
 (D) It helped its client boost profits.

Questions 86-88 refer to the following talk.

Thank you for participating in the meeting. We'll review results from the customer survey for our new model, ASM-1700. As you already know, this microwave has various new features that our customers will really love. The survey showed that the most popular feature of the microwave is that it has an auto sleep mode, making it easier to save energy than our previous models. Due to all the features it has, the user manual increased to 30 pages, which is too many. So the related department is now editing this.

86. What is the main topic of the meeting?
 (A) A new department
 (B) A user manual
 (C) Survey results
 (D) Product defects

87. What feature of the product does the speaker mention?
 (A) An energy-saving function
 (B) A digital display
 (C) Its durability
 (D) A removable rack

88. What does the speaker imply when she says, "So the related department is now editing this"?
 (A) The manual can only be viewed online.
 (B) The manual is available in multiple languages.
 (C) The manual should be shortened.
 (D) Customers should read it thoroughly.

Questions 89-91 refer to the following excerpt from a meeting.

Welcome to the Morris Park project. As many of you know, we've made an effort to build a park in the center of the city. Sadly, even though we've received donations from a large number of community groups in this area to help purchase trees, we're still lacking in funds. That means we need more funds to build amenities and buy benches. Therefore, we should make contact with some local business owners to find out their willingness to make a donation. What I am asking you to do is simple. Just make a list of local business owners interested in taking part in this project.

89. What is the talk mainly about?
 (A) Attracting foreign companies
 (B) Opening an art gallery
 (C) Building a park
 (D) Solving traffic congestion

90. What problem does the speaker mention?
 (A) A delayed schedule
 (B) A transportation system
 (C) Lack of funds
 (D) A manpower shortage

91. What are the listeners asked to do?
 (A) Hold a meeting
 (B) Carry out a survey
 (C) Come up with a list of local businesses
 (D) Purchase items

Questions 92-94 refer to the following announcement.

Hello, everyone. I'm so glad you've taken time to visit the Union Staffing Agency. We specialize in finding the right position in various companies from law firms to hospitals. Today, you'll have an interview with our recruiters, who will find out which company would be best suited for you and match your professional expertise with its needs. As you may know, this process could take some time. While waiting, please help us make a copy of your ID card. The copy machine is on the second floor.

92. What type of business does the speaker work for?
(A) A law firm
(B) A hospital
(C) An employment agency
(D) A manufacturer

93. What does the speaker imply when he says, "this process could take some time"?
(A) He wants the listeners to be patient.
(B) He points out that the office is very busy.
(C) He says that the scheduled date could be canceled.
(D) He suggests that the listeners be ready anytime.

94. What does the speaker ask the listeners to do?
(A) Submit their application
(B) Receive a letter of recommendation
(C) Make a copy of their identification
(D) Fill out some documents

Questions 95-97 refer to the following recorded message and order form.

Hi, this message is for Elisha Stewart. I just received the order from your company. I was, however, surprised by the number of cups in the order form. You normally don't place an order like this. So, I will revise the number to be equal to your usual order. Please call me if you have any problems with this. By the way, I'll be away from work next week. John will cover my duties while I'm on leave. So please call John if you need anything.

95. Look at the graphic. Which quantity of the order form will be changed?
(A) 100
(B) 200
(C) 300
(D) 250

96. What is the speaker doing next week?
(A) She is going on a vacation.
(B) She is moving to a different country.
(C) She is remodeling her house.
(D) She is changing her job.

97. What does the speaker say about John?
(A) He will be dealing with some accounts.
(B) He will cancel an order.
(C) He will print some documents.
(D) He will introduce a new product.

Questions 98-100 refer to the following excerpt from a meeting and graph.

I'd like to start by expressing my sincere gratitude to all of you for participating in our survey. Here at Morgan Bookstore, we're dedicated to customer satisfaction. We have received many suggestions for improving our services. So, let's look into those results. As you can see, customers want lower prices, but we should comply with the government policy of fixed book prices. We can, however, accept the second-most-popular suggestion. So, we'll start working on that service right now. As an expression of our appreciation, those who participate in the survey will receive one of our best-selling novels for free.

98. Where does the talk take place?
(A) At a bookstore
(B) At a factory
(C) At a hotel
(D) At the airport

99. Look at the graphic. Which suggestions will the company begin to work on?
(A) Discount coupons
(B) More seats
(C) Free shipping
(D) Lower prices

100. What will the people receive for completing the survey?
(A) A complimentary book
(B) A discount coupon
(C) Refreshments
(D) A store gift card

6회

1. (C)	21. (B)	41. (D)	61. (A)	81. (A)
2. (B)	22. (C)	42. (A)	62. (A)	82. (C)
3. (C)	23. (B)	43. (A)	63. (C)	83. (B)
4. (C)	24. (A)	44. (A)	64. (B)	84. (C)
5. (D)	25. (A)	45. (A)	65. (C)	85. (B)
6. (A)	26. (B)	46. (B)	66. (C)	86. (B)
7. (B)	27. (B)	47. (B)	67. (D)	87. (A)
8. (C)	28. (B)	48. (C)	68. (C)	88. (A)
9. (B)	29. (A)	49. (B)	69. (B)	89. (C)
10. (B)	30. (B)	50. (C)	70. (D)	90. (A)
11. (C)	31. (C)	51. (A)	71. (C)	91. (A)
12. (B)	32. (B)	52. (B)	72. (D)	92. (A)
13. (B)	33. (A)	53. (A)	73. (A)	93. (B)
14. (B)	34. (C)	54. (D)	74. (B)	94. (B)
15. (A)	35. (D)	55. (C)	75. (A)	95. (A)
16. (B)	36. (A)	56. (B)	76. (D)	96. (A)
17. (B)	37. (C)	57. (D)	77. (A)	97. (D)
18. (A)	38. (C)	58. (A)	78. (C)	98. (B)
19. (B)	39. (B)	59. (C)	79. (A)	99. (C)
20. (C)	40. (B)	60. (A)	80. (D)	100. (D)

Part 1

1. (A) A man is reading the magazine.
   (B) A man is putting on a shirt.
   (C) A man is holding some reading material.
   (D) A man is boarding the plane.

2. (A) They are pushing the carts.
   (B) They are using the escalator.
   (C) They are riding the elevator.
   (D) They are going up the stairs.

3. (A) There are vehicles on the bridge.
   (B) The bridge is being built over the river.
   (C) The water is flowing under the structure.
   (D) The boats are passing the stadium.

4. (A) Some balloons are hanging from the ceiling.
   (B) All of the seats are occupied.
   (C) The restaurant is filled with the diners.
   (D) A waiter is holding the tray.

5. (A) Some instruments are being played on a stage.
   (B) The men are trying on their uniforms.
   (C) All of the people are facing each other.
   (D) There are mountains in the distance.

6. (A) An assortment of items is being displayed on the shop's shelves.
   (B) The clerk is assisting a customer.
   (C) A mask is being hung on the wall.
   (D) The lights are being turned on.

Part 2

7. Is there a pharmacy nearby?
   (A) There is a prescription.
   (B) It's one block away.
   (C) I don't know when it opens.

8. Can you pass me the scissors, please?
   (A) Sure, I'll have some.
   (B) They are sold out.
   (C) Here you are.

9. Who revised these documents?
   (A) He made some revisions.
   (B) My secretary did.
   (C) Yes, I'd be happy to.

10. What date would you like to reserve the table?
    (A) I prefer a non-smoking area.
    (B) On the 5th of this month, please.
    (C) It's upstairs.

11. When is the best time to contact Mr. Smith?
    (A) In the office.
    (B) Two days ago.
    (C) Any time before seven o'clock.

12. Where should I leave these office supplies?
    (A) At 3:30.
    (B) Take them to the storeroom.
    (C) To San Francisco.

13. How much time do you need to complete the report?
    (A) The reporter will be here soon.
    (B) I'm almost finished.
    (C) Three times a week.

14. Why did you recommend taking the subway instead of the bus?
    (A) Across a small bridge.
    (B) It will be much faster.
    (C) Because they lowered bus fares.

15. Which of you read this novel?
    (A) David and I did.
    (B) This book is really interesting.
    (C) Red is better.

16. I'm eagerly looking forward to this performance.
    (A) No not here. Over there, please.
    (B) Yes, we were lucky to get these tickets.
    (C) I need to fill out this form.

17. This meal comes with a free drink, doesn't it?
    (A) I'd like to come with you.
    (B) Let me check on that.
    (C) I'm very thirsty.

18. Do you know which customer ordered this sandwich?
    (A) The man at table 4.
    (B) I'd prefer fried chicken.
    (C) Yes, I know how to make the sandwich.

19. Are you ready to leave now, or do you need more time to pack?
    (A) It is packed with papers.
    (B) Our plane isn't until 7.
    (C) Is Kay leaving some for me?

20. Which part of the plant am I working in tomorrow?
    (A) The times are listed in the manual.
    (B) I watered the plant this morning.
    (C) Didn't your manager tell you?

21. Are you ready to get off work today?
    (A) Yes, I have to work late.
    (B) I just found out I have a conference call.
    (C) I read it.

22. I left my wallet at the hotel.
    (A) It's actually a right turn.
    (B) I prefer to stay at the Park View Hotel.
    (C) Don't worry. I can lend you some money.

23. Let's walk to the public library.
    (A) Not too fast.
    (B) It is too far to walk.
    (C) I didn't know the way.

24. Couldn't we put off the conference until March?
    (A) Maybe, but the hotel charges cancellation fees.
    (B) To the nearest post office.
    (C) Yes, that was a great conference call.
25. Would you like to make a presentation first, or should I?
    (A) I don't have much to say.
    (B) This is the first time.
    (C) Yes, I am.
26. Who will volunteer to organize the banquet next week?
    (A) Mr. Rossi has been helping me.
    (B) I'd be delighted to.
    (C) She is working next week.
27. Would you like to come in on Saturday the 15th?
    (A) No, our office is located on the 10th floor.
    (B) It would have to be toward the end of the working day.
    (C) What was her name again?
28. When will I receive the details about this product?
    (A) From the electronics store.
    (B) You will be hearing from the supplier soon.
    (C) The certification was issued last week.
29. Our advertising budget was increased this month, wasn't it?
    (A) Yes, by 30 percent.
    (B) Every Monday morning.
    (C) The advertisement was successful.
30. Where is the report from the accounting department?
    (A) Bring it to my office.
    (B) We are still compiling it.
    (C) I counted them yesterday.
31. Isn't there any more space at the Springfield warehouse?
    (A) Just a few kilometers down the main expressway.
    (B) Yes, we'll make a delivery on Friday.
    (C) I actually asked about the one in Watertown.

Part 3

Questions 32-34 refer to the following conversation.

W   Hello, I have a problem with the tablet PC that I bought here last week. Every morning I find it turned off, although the indicator says the battery is full.
M   Hmm… Let me take a look. This is the Astro 7. Did you leave it plugged into an outlet overnight?
W   Yes, I did. I never forgot to recharge it every night. I think there is a problem with the battery.
M   That sometimes happens when it's overcharged. Luckily, the company has noted this issue and released an update.
W   Oh, that's nice. Can I download the update from the Internet?
M   That's right. Let me do it for you. Just five minutes will do.

32. Why is the woman at the shop?
    (A) To buy a mobile phone
    (B) To ask about a device
    (C) To sell a computer
    (D) To charge a battery
33. What is the problem with the computer?
    (A) It turns off by itself.
    (B) It ran out of battery.
    (C) It is not connected to the Internet.
    (D) It was not fully charged.
34. What will the man probably do next?
    (A) Give a full refund
    (B) Replace the battery
    (C) Update the device
    (D) Report the problem to the manufacturer

Questions 35-37 refer to the following conversation.

M   Hello, I'm calling to ask about shipping items from New York to Tokyo. We have 80 framed pictures and 10 clay statues to ship to the Edo Museum here in Tokyo.
W   Sure. We specialize in shipping valuable items. They'll be handled carefully and will arrive on time. How early do you need them?
M   Well, these items are going to be displayed at the museum next month, so we'll need them by the 15th. But I was wondering how much it would cost.
W   I can't actually give you a final cost estimate without the exact dimensions of each item. Could you please email me this information at smith@kccshipping.com?

35. Why is the man calling?
    (A) To ask about a membership card
    (B) To sign up for an exhibition
    (C) To check a ticket reservation
    (D) To inquire about a delivery service
36. What will happen next month?
    (A) A museum exhibition
    (B) A book signing
    (C) An international music festival
    (D) A pottery-making demonstration
37. What additional information does the woman ask for?
    (A) A price estimate
    (B) An e-mail address
    (C) The sizes of some items
    (D) The man's seating number

Questions 38-40 refer to the following conversation.

M   Hi, Sharon. This is Tim Blanks. I interviewed you last week for the reporter position at NSL Newspaper Company. I'm calling to see when you are available to finalize the next step.
W   Hi, Mr. Blanks. Thanks for calling me. I have to work all day tomorrow, but I'm free on Tuesday and Wednesday.
M   Right. I want you to come in to write a short article as a sample so we can get a better sense of your writing skills. Could you come in at ten o'clock on Wednesday morning? It'll take about two hours to complete.

38. Why is the man calling the woman?
    (A) To return her résumé
    (B) To notify her of an interview
    (C) To ask her to visit him again
    (D) To give details about the job opening
39. Why is the woman unavailable tomorrow?
    (A) She will be traveling.
    (B) She will be working.
    (C) She will be giving a presentation.
    (D) She will be finishing an assignment.
40. What does the man ask the woman to do?
    (A) Submit a résumé
    (B) Write an article
    (C) Read an employee handbook
    (D) Write a novel

Questions 41-43 refer to the following conversation.

W: Carlos, now I'm leaving for the airport to pick up the vice-president. Are you done with the marketing report?
M: Several graphs need to be replaced. It's going to be tight for the four o'clock meeting.
W: I already revised all the figures in the tables and graphs. Is there any problem?
M: Some of the figures don't match the last quarterly report. So I'm verifying them over again and putting in the correct ones.
W: Oh, I see. I don't have time to go over it now, so I'll let you be the judge.
M: Don't worry, and be careful driving in the rain. Shall I make some copies when I'm finished?
W: You don't have to do that. Just send the file to the secretary's office. They'll bind it with other documents to make booklets.

41. What are the speakers mainly discussing?
(A) The details of a booklet
(B) Bad weather
(C) Driving to the airport
(D) Revising a document

42. What is suggested by the speakers?
(A) The woman revised the marketing report.
(B) The rain has finally stopped.
(C) The man has finished the report.
(D) There will be a meeting at three o'clock.

43. What will the woman probably do next?
(A) See an executive at the airport
(B) Correct errors in a paper
(C) Tell the man an e-mail address
(D) Book a flight

Questions 44-46 refer to the following conversation.

W: I'm really looking forward to hearing Steve Torre's speech today. I've already read many books about the financial crisis in the world. So I think this is one of the best finance conferences.
M: I think so. And there are so many attendees here! It looks like the only available seats are here in the back. Let's just sit in this row.
W: The last row? I think we can do better. I'd like to sit close to the presentation.
M: Oh, don't worry about that. Look over there! There are two seats left close to the front entrance. Let's go and sit quickly.

44. What type of event are the speakers attending?
(A) A professional conference
(B) An employee orientation
(C) A book signing
(D) A staff meeting

45. Why does the man say, "Let's just sit in this row"?
(A) He thinks they have no choice.
(B) He wants to encourage the woman to work harder.
(C) He is disappointed in the presentation.
(D) He thinks his team is more competent than other teams.

46. What does the man say about the seats?
(A) They are all occupied.
(B) They are available near the entrance.
(C) They are not enough for everyone.
(D) They are broken.

Questions 47-49 refer to the following conversation.

M: Jessica, this is Brian. I've just heard about the traffic congestion on Main Street. Will you be able to make it in time?
W: I was going to call you, Brian. I'm stuck here. I'm sorry for being late for the retirement ceremony for our president. And I have the present and flowers with me here in the taxi.
M: They are for the last part of the event. You still have an hour probably.
W: Perfect. The taxi driver says it'll take about 30 minutes. By the way, what about the congratulatory message? I was supposed to hand it to Elizabeth. It's on my computer.
M: Don't worry. She's with me, and we're almost there. I can stop by the 2nd floor and print it out from your computer.
W: Thank you so much. Just call me again when you turn on the desktop. You'll need the password.

47. Why will the woman probably be late?
(A) She is buying a present on the way.
(B) She is held up by a traffic jam.
(C) She had a computer malfunction.
(D) She needs to give a message to Elizabeth.

48. What does the woman recommend?
(A) Taking a taxi instead
(B) Going to her office
(C) Calling her again later
(D) Getting a message from Elizabeth

49. What does the man imply when he says, "They are for the last part of the event"?
(A) Jessica doesn't need to prepare the congratulatory message.
(B) Jessica doesn't need to be at the event from the beginning.
(C) Jessica doesn't need to tell him the password to her computer.
(D) Jessica doesn't need to meet Elizabeth at the ceremony.

Questions 50-52 refer to the following conversation.

M: Excuse me, I bought this book about gardening here last week, and it's missing several pages in the middle. Could I exchange it for another copy?
W: Sure, as long as it was purchased less than a month ago and you have the original receipt, it's not a problem.
M: I'm afraid I don't have the receipt. I threw it out when I got home. I just opened it today, though. It hasn't been used.
W: I'm sorry, sir. But store policy won't let me exchange it without a receipt.

50. What is suggested about the book?
(A) It is a used book.
(B) It is expensive.
(C) It has a defect.
(D) It was on sale.

51. What does the man ask the woman to do?
(A) Switch the item
(B) Make a copy
(C) Buy a book
(D) Give a discount

52. What does the woman ask for?
(A) A credit card number
(B) Proof of purchase
(C) A billing address
(D) An exchange

Questions 53-55 refer to the following conversation.

M Hello, this is Sato Aiko. I was a patient at your medical clinic, but I recently moved to Osaka. A few days ago, I asked that my medical records be sent to my new doctor here, but they haven't received them yet.

W Mr. Sato. Yes, let me check… I can see your request, but you didn't sign the form to transfer your records. We can't send them to your new doctor's office until that's done.

M Oh, I must have forgotten to sign it. Do I need to come in to do that?

W No, I can send you a form by e-mail. Just sign it and mail it back by express mail.

53. What has the man recently done?
(A) Relocated to a new place
(B) Sent a package
(C) Had a medical check-up
(D) Seen a doctor

54. What problem does the woman mention?
(A) An appointment was delayed.
(B) A payment was not received.
(C) An address is incorrect.
(D) A document has not been signed.

55. What does the woman say she will do?
(A) Sign the contract
(B) Update the contact information
(C) Email a document
(D) Send something by express mail

Questions 56-58 refer to the following conversation with three speakers.

W1 Thanks for coming to this interview, Mr. McCarthy. I'm Olivia Barash, head of the personnel department at KBC film production company.

W2 And I'm Jennie Finch. I'm a film producer. Nice to meet you.

M Nice to meet you both. And thanks for the interview opportunity.

W2 We've reviewed your résumé, and you seem to be highly qualified for the camera operator position. But we're just wondering about your requirements, since our film crews often get assigned tasks on short notice.

M I see. Don't worry. I can be available anytime.

W1 Okay, so can we take a look at a sample of your work? You said you brought a video. Is it possible to see it now?

M Sure, my file's right here on my laptop.

56. Where do the women most likely work?
(A) At an electronics store
(B) At a movie production company
(C) At a TV station
(D) At a movie theater

57. What job requirement do the speakers discuss?
(A) Being professionally certified
(B) Using the proper equipment
(C) Having camera operation skills
(D) Handling some urgent tasks

58. What will the man do next?
(A) Show his work sample
(B) Make a video
(C) Meet a director
(D) Buy a laptop

Questions 59-61 refer to the following conversation.

W Roy, I confirmed the cost to use Hyde Park for our company retreat next month. I think it's reasonable. So we'll probably choose this place. By the way, have you contacted the catering company yet?

M No, I haven't decided yet, and I'm just thinking about whether we should order food for our event. Since it's going to be at a park this year, perhaps everyone can bring their favorite food instead.

W That's a good point. However, we should make sure people are willing to bring their dishes to share before we make a final decision about not using a caterer.

M I agree. I'll forward an e-mail to the staff today and find out their opinions.

59. What will happen next month?
(A) A dedication
(B) A holiday party
(C) A company outing
(D) A retirement celebration

60. What is the man considering?
(A) Whether to use a catering company
(B) Where to hold an event
(C) When to begin the company function
(D) Who should be invited

61. What does the woman imply when she says, "That's a good point"?
(A) She agrees with the man's opinion.
(B) She wants to bring some food.
(C) She'll send an e-mail.
(D) She suggests ordering some food.

Questions 62-64 refer to the following conversation and chart.

W Max, I'm planning to see a new play at the City Theater this weekend. Don't you want to go with me?

M Absolutely! I've read good reviews from a recent article. It said it's a wonderful performance! How much is the ticket?

W It depends… Let's look at the information. I'm a member, and one more person can get an additional discount, so both of us can buy tickets at the member's price.

M Wow, that's good news. Would that be for Saturday or Sunday?

W Saturday at 7 P.M. Is it possible?

M Sure. Could you order the tickets for me?

W No problem. I'll visit the Web site and order them now.

62. What type of event are the speakers discussing?
(A) A theater performance
(B) A museum exhibition
(C) A new movie
(D) A live music concert

63. Look at the graphic. What ticket price will the speakers probably pay?
(A) $16
(B) $24
(C) $30
(D) $40

64. What does the woman say she will do?
(A) Leave work early
(B) Purchase the tickets
(C) Pay with a credit card
(D) Visit the theater

Questions 65-67 refer to the following conversation and list.

W: Hi, this is Linda from SummerMax advertising. We reserved the picnic area in Parramatta Park on April 19th for a company picnic. But I'm calling to see if we could change to another Saturday.
M: Let me check the schedule. I'm sorry, but all Saturdays are booked in April. What about in May?
W: No, it has to be in April because we're going to expand the production line in May. Is there another venue in the park that we could use in April?
M: I'm sorry, but wait. My coworker just told me that someone called this morning to cancel their reservation. Let me check it again.
W: Oh, that's perfect!
M: Yes, I can see the memo here that says Amax Accounting changed their event to June. So you can use their spot.

65. Why is the woman calling?
(A) To cancel the event
(B) To change the location
(C) To change the date
(D) To give an invitation

66. According to the woman, what will her company do in May?
(A) Relocate to a different city
(B) Expand a budget
(C) Enlarge a work area
(D) Hire additional workers

67. Look at the graphic. When will the woman use the park?
(A) April 5
(B) April 12
(C) April 19
(D) April 26

Questions 68-70 refer to the following conversation and map.

W: What should we do for our director's retirement party next week? I think we should do something to thank him for his dedication to our company.
M: Well, let's do more than just write thank-you cards. How about buying a special gift for him?
W: That's actually a good idea. In that way, he could always remember us every time he looks at the present. So, what kind of gift is the best for him?
M: I have an idea. I know a premium gift shop on George Street that handles personalized gifts such as cups and trophies. They're only a block away from us. I'll drop by their store this afternoon.
W: Actually, they just moved to a new location at the corner of Central Avenue and Broadway, across from AnZ bank.
M: Alright! I think I know it.

68. What do the speakers want to do?
(A) Plan a party for customers
(B) Celebrate a company's anniversary
(C) Express their gratitude
(D) Send out invitations

69. What does the man suggest doing?
(A) Making a presentation
(B) Purchasing a present
(C) Writing a report
(D) Giving an award

70. Look at the graphic. Where is the gift shop located?
(A) 1
(B) 2
(C) 3
(D) 4

Part 4

Questions 71-73 refer to the following telephone message.

Hi, Ms. Jade. This is David Foster calling from David's Garage. When I inspected your vehicle, I noticed a problem with a light bulb that cannot be turned on. So it needs to be replaced. I ordered the part this morning, but it won't arrive at the shop until next week. So if you'd like, we can lend you a car to use until your car is fixed. Please get back to me at 333-3033.

71. Where does the speaker work?
(A) At an electronics store
(B) At a hardware store
(C) At a car repair shop
(D) At a cleaning service

72. What does the speaker say he has done?
(A) Scheduled an appointment
(B) Completed a repair
(C) Replaced a light
(D) Ordered a part

73. What does the speaker offer?
(A) A rental car service
(B) An extended warranty
(C) A free inspection
(D) An express delivery

Questions 74-76 refer to the following excerpt from a meeting.

Last on the agenda today, I'd like to talk about using telephone conferencing more often this year. Computers with video cameras have been set up in all meeting rooms for use during teleconferences. Staff will be trained on how to use the equipment. Our group training is scheduled for next Wednesday after lunch in meeting room C, so please mark your calendars. One more important thing, before the training, you should read the manual I passed out. It'll help you to be much more familiar with the equipment. If you are not available next week, please let me know by the end of the week. I'll arrange other sessions at a later date.

74. What is the speaker mainly discussing?
(A) A change to project timelines
(B) Plans to use teleconferencing
(C) Some expected job opportunities
(D) Camera installation

75. According to the speaker, what will happen next week?
(A) Employees will learn new procedures.
(B) Salespeople will meet with clients.
(C) Designers will create video materials.
(D) Technicians will replace old computers.

76. What does the speaker ask the listeners to do?
(A) Distribute handouts
(B) Compile sales data
(C) Set up the equipment
(D) Refer to the instructions

Questions 77-79 refer to the following tour information.

Welcome to St. Cyres National Park. My name is Sean, and I'll be your guide on our hike to the top of Chester Point today. As we go, I'll show you many of the unique plants and flowers the park is famous for. I will also explain a little bit about its history. It will take about 2 hours to reach the top, but this will include several short breaks along the way. We should arrive at the top around noon and will stop for a picnic lunch there. I would ask you to please protect the environment by not throwing out your trash on the path. There aren't any trash bins on the top of the mountain, so you'll need to carry your garbage with you and discard it in the garbage cans in the parking area when we come back.

77. Where is the tour most likely taking place?
    (A) At a nature center
    (B) In a parking area
    (C) At a flower shop
    (D) At an outdoor market

78. Where will the group have lunch?
    (A) At a mountain cabin
    (B) At a waterfall
    (C) At the summit
    (D) In a parking lot

79. What are the listeners asked to do?
    (A) Throw away trash when they return
    (B) Refrain from picking flowers on the trail
    (C) Not interrupt while the speaker is talking
    (D) Take a group photo after the hike

Questions 80-82 refer to the following advertisement.

Do you want to get a driver's license at a reasonable price? Then look no further. The SimPit Driving School is the answer! We're currently offering a special for new drivers. If you sign up for our three-week introductory course anytime during March, you will receive a 20 percent discount. SimPit hires only certified instructors who are friendly, patient, and experienced, and our cars are fully insured and totally dependable. The three-week course includes one week of classroom instruction in traffic laws, one week of automobile safety and basic car maintenance, and one week of hands-on driving practice. For more information, or to register for a course, please visit our Web site at www.simpitdriving.com.

80. Who is this advertisement for?
    (A) Traffic police
    (B) Driving instructors
    (C) Auto mechanics
    (D) New drivers

81. What is being advertised?
    (A) A discount on driving instruction
    (B) A sale on used cars
    (C) Automobile insurance
    (D) A job opening for driving instructors

82. How can the listeners sign up for a service?
    (A) By visiting an office
    (B) By sending for a brochure
    (C) By visiting a Web site
    (D) By making a phone call

Questions 83-85 refer to the following excerpt from a meeting.

Thanks for attending today's meeting. I'd like to start by looking over some results of the customer survey we conducted last week. Last year, we introduced our new blender, the Brown 100. As you know well, it has many great features such as ice-grinding, low noise, and low power consumption. According to the survey, the biggest advantage of this model is that it can be disassembled into several parts so that users can wash it entirely. However, it has a higher failure rate at the same time. The most frequent problem is that customers cannot put the parts back together. Also, they may not be aware of the parts that shouldn't be washed with water, and often damage the motor. We'll be releasing the new model, the Brown 150, this year, and we ought to make it a better one. That is to say, we must strengthen the strengths and make up for the weaknesses.

83. What kind of business does the speaker work for?
    (A) A repair center
    (B) A home appliance company
    (C) A market research firm
    (D) A cleaning company

84. What is the most popular feature of the current model?
    (A) Waterproof motor
    (B) Self-cleaning
    (C) Detachable parts
    (D) High power consumption

85. What does the speaker imply when she says, "strengthen the strengths and make up for the weaknesses"?
    (A) She believes the new model has to be more expensive.
    (B) She doesn't want to give up the advantages of the previous model.
    (C) She regrets the Brown 150 model was designed too poorly.
    (D) She doesn't agree with the customers about their complaints.

Questions 86-88 refer to the following telephone message.

Hello, Ms. Cynthia. I just received your message about the problem you encountered with some of the office supplies we sent your company 3 days ago. I'm so sorry that your order arrived damaged. We'll of course stop by your office to pick up the supplies with new materials tomorrow. You don't need to do anything. We can just handle everything. Also, I'll give you a special offer on the next purchase. Again, we apologize for the inconvenience caused. We appreciate your understanding. Thank you for your continual business with us.

86. Why is the speaker calling?
    (A) To receive a message
    (B) To apologize to a customer
    (C) To order some items
    (D) To inquire about a product

87. What problem does the speaker mention?
    (A) Some items are faulty.
    (B) A machine is broken.
    (C) A shipment is late.
    (D) Some items are out of stock.

88. Why does the speaker say, "We can just handle everything"?
    (A) To make up for a mistake
    (B) To purchase the item
    (C) To provide a sample
    (D) To give a special gift

Questions 89-91 refer to the following news report.

Good morning, this is Duncan Piper reporting for Channel 7 local news. I'm here in the Strathfield Plaza, just standing in front of Ruda's Delicious Ice Cream, which is celebrating its grand opening. This is the first franchise location of Ruda's Delicious Ice Cream in our city, but the Sydney-based company is already famous nationwide. To celebrate the opening this morning, the company is giving away a complimentary ice cream cone to the first 100 people. But it's only available before noon. Just come by the store and enjoy a free taste. Even if you miss the free ice cream, you can try it anytime. It's very tasty!

89. What type of business is being discussed?
    (A) A fabric manufacturer
    (B) An ice cream factory
    (C) A local business
    (D) A cooking school

90. What can be inferred about the company?
    (A) It has never operated in this city before.
    (B) Its headquarters moved to another city.
    (C) It is celebrating its 10th anniversary.
    (D) It is expanding a building.

91. What will some customers receive before noon?
    (A) A free sample
    (B) Some coupons
    (C) A promotional brochure
    (D) Complimentary recipes

Questions 92-94 refer to the following announcement.

Many of you have probably seen the electricians in and around the office here this week. Apparently, there was a power failure on the fourth floor last week. This means that the electricity on that floor will have to be turned off for a few hours tomorrow while technicians try to solve this problem. So, please use your laptop computer to work on and we'll use the conference room on the fifth floor as a temporary office space. Before leaving the office today, remember that you should save any important documents.

92. What kind of work needs to be done?
    (A) Electrical maintenance
    (B) Computer system upgrades
    (C) Software installation
    (D) Floor cleaning

93. When will the work begin?
    (A) Tonight
    (B) Tomorrow
    (C) This weekend
    (D) Next week

94. What are some listeners asked to do?
    (A) Hire the technicians
    (B) Use personal electronics
    (C) Attend the meeting in the conference room
    (D) Remove important documents from the computer

Questions 95-97 refer to the following recorded message and order form.

Hello, this message is for Tim Falcon. I'm calling about the weekly order you just asked for, because I found you ordered a different one from what you usually do. I think you're still using the FX-Q1700, right? The one you've ordered doesn't work with the grayscale printer in your office. That's for the FX-Q2200C, which can print colored copies of various sizes. So I wonder whether I should change the item code to match your usual order. If you have a new printer now and this is what you want, please call me by the end of the day. We close at 9:30. Thank you for your business with us.

95. Look at the graphic. Which item does the speaker want to be checked?
    (A) FC505
    (B) PW74
    (C) HK250
    (D) DC303

96. What is suggested about Tim Falcon?
    (A) He has ordered from this store before.
    (B) He has a new printer in his office.
    (C) He works for a printing company.
    (D) He works until 9:30.

97. Why would Tim Falcon call back?
    (A) To check the working hours
    (B) To order more stationery
    (C) To receive a new printer
    (D) To confirm an item code

Questions 98-100 refer to the following talk and graph.

Good morning. I'd like to commence our quarterly sales meeting by reviewing our progress in expanding new customers here at Elena beauty hair salon. As you know, March was the most successful month. We can probably attribute this to promoting big discounts for the 15th anniversary celebration. You can also see that the second highest increase in new customers occurred during our free dyeing event. So, generally, this quarter was successful. Now, we have to prepare for next quarter to continue this trend. We're planning to make our Web site more user-friendly. Therefore, many customers can get more useful information like looking at the variety of hair styles. I think it is critical for sustaining and increasing our business success.

98. Where most likely does the speaker work?
    (A) At an advertising agency
    (B) At a beauty parlor
    (C) At a cosmetics store
    (D) At a supermarket

99. Look at the graphic. When was the discount event held?
    (A) In January
    (B) In February
    (C) In March
    (D) In April

100. What does the business plan to do next quarter?
    (A) Offer a free dyeing event
    (B) Open a new branch
    (C) Use eco-friendly items
    (D) Upgrade a Web site

7회

1.	(C)	21.	(B)	41.	(C)	61.	(C)	81.	(B)
2.	(B)	22.	(A)	42.	(A)	62.	(B)	82.	(D)
3.	(D)	23.	(C)	43.	(C)	63.	(D)	83.	(D)
4.	(A)	24.	(C)	44.	(C)	64.	(B)	84.	(C)
5.	(D)	25.	(B)	45.	(B)	65.	(C)	85.	(B)
6.	(B)	26.	(A)	46.	(C)	66.	(C)	86.	(C)
7.	(B)	27.	(C)	47.	(C)	67.	(A)	87.	(A)
8.	(C)	28.	(A)	48.	(C)	68.	(B)	88.	(B)
9.	(B)	29.	(C)	49.	(C)	69.	(B)	89.	(B)
10.	(C)	30.	(C)	50.	(C)	70.	(C)	90.	(B)
11.	(C)	31.	(B)	51.	(B)	71.	(B)	91.	(C)
12.	(C)	32.	(C)	52.	(C)	72.	(C)	92.	(C)
13.	(A)	33.	(D)	53.	(B)	73.	(A)	93.	(C)
14.	(A)	34.	(C)	54.	(D)	74.	(B)	94.	(D)
15.	(B)	35.	(B)	55.	(C)	75.	(C)	95.	(B)
16.	(B)	36.	(C)	56.	(A)	76.	(A)	96.	(B)
17.	(C)	37.	(D)	57.	(C)	77.	(B)	97.	(D)
18.	(C)	38.	(C)	58.	(A)	78.	(C)	98.	(A)
19.	(B)	39.	(A)	59.	(A)	79.	(D)	99.	(B)
20.	(C)	40.	(B)	60.	(D)	80.	(A)	100.	(A)

Part 1

1. (A) The woman is wearing a scarf.
   (B) The woman is pushing a button on a keypad.
   (C) The woman is handing over a credit card.
   (D) The woman is arranging items on the shelf.

2. (A) The people are dining at an outdoor patio.
   (B) A dish is being passed at a table.
   (C) Water is being poured into a glass.
   (D) Some plates are stacked in a pile.

3. (A) A staircase leads to the kitchen.
   (B) There are some flowerpots hanging from the ceiling.
   (C) A carpet has been rolled up on the floor.
   (D) The sofas are unoccupied.

4. (A) The man is reading the label on an item.
   (B) A cart is being wheeled along the aisle.
   (C) Some merchandise is being loaded onto a cart.
   (D) The man is carrying a can of food to the cashier.

5. (A) The man is looking out of the window.
   (B) The man is turning on the answering machine.
   (C) The man is cleaning the monitor of a laptop.
   (D) The man is doing some work at a desk.

6. (A) None of the tables are vacant.
   (B) The tables are covered with tablecloths.
   (C) A boat is unloading passengers at the dock.
   (D) The restaurant is crowded with dining guests.

Part 2

7. Do we have any extra copies of this document?
   (A) You can place it on my desk.
   (B) Sure, we do.
   (C) Please submit it in duplicate.

8. Who made the restaurant reservation?
   (A) At the entrance.
   (B) They served seafood dishes.
   (C) Mr.Smith was supposed to.

9. What is the problem with the storage?
   (A) Yes, cups and plates.
   (B) We're out of stock.
   (C) They haven't decided when.

10. When should we take a lunch break?
    (A) At the new restaurant across the street.
    (B) It's a quarter to one now.
    (C) After we finish printing all these documents.

11. You'll find an express bus terminal down the street.
    (A) To use a faster delivery service.
    (B) Regular mail is less expensive.
    (C) How far is it to the terminal?

12. Where are the clients from China staying?
    (A) They'll be here tomorrow evening.
    (B) They made a speech in Chinese.
    (C) At the hotel near the company headquarters.

13. How many tables should we set for the banquet?
    (A) I'm not sure how many will come.
    (B) Forty extra chairs.
    (C) There aren't any furniture stores open today.

14. Why did they reschedule the regular meeting?
    (A) No meeting rooms are available.
    (B) On the company Web site.
    (C) Sometime next week.

15. Which smartphone would you like to buy?
    (A) Maybe tomorrow.
    (B) I haven't decided yet.
    (C) He called me to order a blue one.

16. The Vegans' Delight has various vegetarian dishes.
    (A) Some of my coworkers.
    (B) Isn't it expensive?
    (C) Vegetables can be found next to the fruits.

17. She runs a drugstore in our building, doesn't she?
    (A) Yes, she caught a cold.
    (B) Yes, they're running out of stock.
    (C) Yes, on the second floor.

18. Can you tell me how I can install this program?
    (A) The entire program ends at 4:00 P.M.
    (B) From the IT department.
    (C) I can help you after lunch.

19. Will you sign up for the session online or at the site?
    (A) The session is currently offline.
    (B) Probably in person.
    (C) The same lecturer as last month.

20. What is the purpose of the seminar next week?
    (A) Yes, it's postponed to the following week.
    (B) I didn't do it on purpose.
    (C) To discuss the new service.

21. Is there a stationery store nearby?
    (A) You just missed Martin Station.
    (B) There's one across the street.
    (C) It's stationary and not removable.

22. Some parts of this machine seem to be defective.
    (A) Can you tell me which parts should be replaced?
    (B) As soon as the parts are repaired.
    (C) Yes, I'm interested in some part-time work.

23. Can I help with anything?
    (A) It is quite helpful.
    (B) There wasn't anyone but me.
    (C) No, not at the moment.

24. Don't you have to talk to your manager?
    (A) You don't have any.
    (B) So you managed it after all.
    (C) I was just about to call her.

25. Would you like to try it yourself now, or do you need more practice?
    (A) I was just talking to myself.
    (B) I think I'm ready now.
    (C) How'd you like to put it into practice?

26. Who should I forward the e-mail to?
    (A) The assistant manager.
    (B) Via express mail.
    (C) Copy it on both sides.

27. Has Mr. Douglas left for his vacation?
    (A) There are leftovers in the bin.
    (B) It lasted three days.
    (C) Yes, and he'll be back next Tuesday.

28. When can I see the final draft of the article?
    (A) Wednesday evening, at the latest.
    (B) It's about the U. S. government announcement.
    (C) That'll be interesting.

29. We know each other, don't we?
    (A) They're standing next to each other.
    (B) I was going to meet you, too.
    (C) No, I don't think so.

30. Where is Ms.Moore's new apartment?
    (A) In two weeks.
    (B) Apart from her.
    (C) It's in Hillsville.

31. Wasn't Patricia supposed to visit the factory in Michigan?
    (A) I often go to Tokyo.
    (B) I heard her flight was canceled.
    (C) It is one of the most populous cities in Canada.

Part 3

Questions 32-34 refer to the following conversation.

M Hello, I'm calling to check if there are any tickets available for the concert.
W There are several concerts scheduled this month. Do you know the names of the performers or the exact date?
M I don't remember the names. It's a jazz concert on a Friday evening.
W The "Oldies but Goodies" jazz concert is on Friday, October 17th. We have a few seats available at the stage level, which are 115 dollars each, and in the balcony in the back they are 90 dollars each.
M Oh, that's nice. Thank you, and I will call right back after consulting with my friends about the seats.

32. Where most likely does the woman work?
    (A) At a library
    (B) At a stadium
    (C) At a performance hall
    (D) At a music shop

33. What is the purpose of the man's call?
    (A) To ask for a refund
    (B) To cancel a reservation
    (C) To sign up for a class
    (D) To inquire about tickets

34. What will the man probably do next?
    (A) Verify a seating chart
    (B) Check his calendar
    (C) Talk with his friends
    (D) Buy tickets online

Questions 35-37 refer to the following conversation.

M It is a pleasure to meet you, Mr. Anderson. As I let you know last time, our radio channel is running an advertising campaign for local businesses. We would like to feature your company on Monday.
M Thank you for the opportunity, Ms. Taylor. What should we start with?
W Hmm… Would you please summarize the concept behind your business, Good Hands?
M Good Hands started as a home appliance repair shop 7 years ago. Now we mainly service on-site repairs and also cover office supplies and equipment.
W What makes your company different from other similar ones?
M As you know, our competitors hesitate to employ experienced engineers due to the high cost. Instead of a better staff, they tend to rely on newer equipment. But at Good Hands, we believe that skilled manpower is most important in this field.
W Sounds interesting. How do you strengthen the staff expertise?
M We have a great staff training program similar to those at major companies. Many would argue that it is ineffective in small businesses, but we've been running our training system continually since we started the business.

35. Who most likely is the woman?
    (A) A staff trainer in a local company
    (B) A radio producer
    (C) A maintenance engineer
    (D) A TV reporter

36. What items would probably be serviced by Good Hands?
    (A) Toys
    (B) Bicycles
    (C) Photocopiers
    (D) Vehicles

37. According to the man, how does Good Hands differ from its competitors?
    (A) It provides extended guarantees.
    (B) It has a lot of state-of-the-art equipment.
    (C) It provides faster on-site service than its competitors.
    (D) It has very skilled employees.

Questions 38-40 refer to the following conversation.

W Hi, Eric. Can you do me a favor? Will you be in the office on Monday morning? I'm expecting a call from a supplier but I won't be in until after 2 P.M. due to my client meeting.
M Yes, I will be in early on Monday. I have some data to enter onto the computer and was planning to start early. When are you expecting the call?
W They said between 9 and 10 A.M. I will reroute my calls to your phone and let them know that you will be answering. Many thanks, Eric.

38. What does the woman ask the man to do?
    (A) Accept a package
    (B) Attend a morning meeting
    (C) Take a phone call
    (D) Enter some data

39. What information does the man request?
    (A) A time
    (B) A contact number
    (C) An address
    (D) A price

40. What does the woman say she will do?
    (A) Postpone a meeting
    (B) Redirect her phone
    (C) Check her schedule
    (D) Cancel an appointment

Questions 41-43 refer to the following conversation.

M Hello, this is Christopher Brown. I am renting a car while in Oregon for business purposes. But I just found a few scratches on the passenger's door. I hadn't noticed them when I first borrowed it yesterday. So I am worried about whether I might have to pay for the repairs.
W Well, don't worry, Mr. Brown. Our database shows you have insurance coverage, so it will reimburse the expense if needed.
M That's a relief. By the way, do I need to do anything special when I return the car tomorrow?
W There will be some papers for you to fill out at our office. So please give yourself extra time.

41. What type of business does the woman most likely work for?
    (A) A used car dealer
    (B) A repair shop
    (C) A car rental agency
    (D) A paid parking lot

42. What is the man concerned about?
    (A) Being charged for a repair
    (B) Doing some paperwork
    (C) Attending an important meeting
    (D) Driving to Oregon from his company

43. For how long is the man renting the car?
    (A) One day
    (B) Two days
    (C) Three days
    (D) Four days

Questions 44-46 refer to the following conversation.

W Hello, this is Donna Garcia at 16 Wilson Street. I'm calling to inform you that we will be moving out of the house on May 16. My husband has accepted a new job in Atlanta.
M That's great news, Ms. Garcia. However, it is stated in the rental agreement that we need to be informed at least 4 weeks before you vacate the house.
W Yes, I'm aware of that. That means we are liable for the rent until the end of next month.
M Exactly. And I'm hoping to get a new tenant very soon.
W One of my friends is urgently looking for a house. Shall I call her and check if she can move in?
M Yes, please. If she can move in without delay, I guess I can let you be exempted from the excess rent for the 15 days.

44. Why is the woman moving out?
    (A) Her rental agreement has expired.
    (B) She has found a less expensive house.
    (C) Her husband decided to relocate.
    (D) She wants a bigger house.

45. What does the woman offer to do?
    (A) Move out as soon as possible
    (B) Help look for a new tenant
    (C) Contact a moving company
    (D) Pay the rent fee for two months

46. According to the man, why would the woman be willing to help him?
    (A) To find a new house in Atlanta
    (B) To get a new job
    (C) To save the excessive rental fee
    (D) To renovate her house within 4 weeks

Questions 47-49 refer to the following conversation with three speakers.

W1 Many thanks for attending the interview, Edward. I'm Jennifer Davis, and this is Ruth Miller, the floor director.
M   Nice to meet you, Ms. Davis, Ms. Miller. Thank you for the opportunity.
W1 As an assistant art director, you have worked for a number of companies. And some of them are very well known. However, I am a bit confused as to why you want to apply to our theater.
W2 I feel the same as Ms. Davis. Do you understand this is not going to be the same as your previous work?
M   Yes, I do. I have been working as an assistant for many years. And now I feel it is time to move on. I'm eager to manage my own team and expand my area. I'm also very interested in your upcoming performances.
W1 Very well then. This could be a good opportunity for you. But you'll be asked to do a lot of overtime work, since we are seriously understaffed.
W2 In particular, you will be required to work on overnight shoots. Is that okay with you?
M   I don't have an issue with that. I am ready to accept any out-of-hours assignments.

47. What impressed the women about the man?
    (A) His appearance
    (B) His managing skills
    (C) His previous career
    (D) His upcoming performances

48. According to the man, why did he apply to this company?
    (A) He wants to earn more money.
    (B) He is eager to try overnight shoots.
    (C) He wants to lead his own team.
    (D) He wants to work for a bigger company.

49. What does the new job require of the man?
    (A) Excellent presentation skills
    (B) Experience in health matters
    (C) The willingness to work overtime
    (D) Frequent overseas performances

Questions 50-52 refer to the following conversation.

W Have you checked the new company Web site? The IT department has done a great job!
M Yes. It looks fantastic. They finally made the navigation even easier than ever. But when I clicked on the floor guide menu, it took me to a blank page. Did you face the same problem?
W No. I haven't had such problems. Did you try reloading the page? Press the F5 key and it'll be refreshed.
M It didn't work for me. Maybe I'll send an e-mail to Jim.
W Don't forget to attach a screenshot. They usually need that to fix the problem. I am sure they will reply with some positive solutions.

50. What does the man like about the updated Web site?
    (A) The clear images
    (B) The faster response time
    (C) The easier usability
    (D) The detailed floor guide

51. What does the man imply when he says, "It didn't work for me"?
    (A) He did not work yesterday.
    (B) He already tried pressing the F5 key.
    (C) He wants to consult with Jim.
    (D) He had the same issue before the update.

52. What does the woman recommend?
    (A) Installing some new software
    (B) Checking for computer viruses
    (C) Restarting his desktop computer
    (D) Including an image with his report

Questions 53-55 refer to the following conversation.

M Hello, this is Charles Harris from the Margaret Chicken Farm. We have recently hatched a large number of chickens, and I need them to be checked for any diseases, considering the latest outbreak of bird flu.
W Thank you for calling, Mr. Harris. Would you please tell me your management number?
M Um… We don't have a management number, as far as I can remember. I think this is the first time I've called you.
W Oh, that's fine, Mr. Harris. Your wife called us several times last year, and we have your farm on our list. Let me check the schedule. Um… We're able to send our examiners to your farm either on Wednesday or Thursday this week to take blood samples from your chickens. Your farm is near the lake, right?
M Yes, by Loufine Lake. Thursday sounds good. Can I inquire as to the cost, and also, is there any subsidy I can apply for?
W We cannot offer any subsidies directly, but the relevant government department may be able to help you.

53. Where most likely does the man work?
(A) At a laboratory
(B) At a farm
(C) At a fried chicken restaurant
(D) At a government agency

54. What has the man recently done?
(A) Called to confirm the management number
(B) Moved to a new location
(C) Sold a number of eggs
(D) Bred a lot of poultry

55. What does the woman say she is unable to do?
(A) Vaccinate the animals
(B) Offer a discount
(C) Provide financial support
(D) Verify the information of the farm

Questions 56-58 refer to the following conversation.

M Thank you for visiting our Bringham supermarket. How can I help you?
W I ordered some groceries this morning. My name is Karen Williams.
M I was expecting you, Ms. Williams. Your goods are ready for you. Would you prefer to get them from the warehouse yourself, or would you like us to deliver them to you?
W I would like you to deliver them to my house. The frozen items are very heavy. Could someone help me carry them to the third floor?
M Yes, the delivery man will help you carry the items. Which time is the most convenient for you?
W The sooner the better. Here is my address. It's just a ten-minute drive from here. I'll be waiting for the items at my house.
M Alright. I'll tell the delivery man to leave right now.

56. Where does the man most likely work?
(A) At a food store
(B) At a car repair shop
(C) At a cold storage facility
(D) At a delivery service

57. What does the man imply when he says, "I was expecting you"?
(A) He is ready to take the order.
(B) They already know each other.
(C) He knew Ms. Williams would come.
(D) He will deliver the items to Ms. Williams' house himself.

58. What is the woman most likely to do next?
(A) Go home
(B) Provide her telephone number
(C) Pick up the items at the warehouse
(D) Ask for a door-to-door delivery

Questions 59-61 refer to the following conversation.

M Did you see the memo about the company contest? The owner wants suggestions for a theme for the new advertising campaign.
W Yes, I have seen it. I presume the advertising agency hasn't thought of anything suitable. It needs to be attractive to the customers. To be honest, I have to finish these sales figures before the audit, so I don't think I will have time to enter.
M You have a very creative mind and the prize is a trip to France on Eurostar, so perhaps you should find time to come up with something.

59. What is the purpose of the contest?
(A) To create a themed campaign
(B) To reduce expenditure
(C) To increase the customer base
(D) To recruit additional employees

60. Why is the woman unsure about participating?
(A) She is going on vacation.
(B) She will be changing jobs.
(C) She does not have any related experience.
(D) She has a deadline for work.

61. What will the winner receive?
(A) A plaque
(B) A hotel voucher
(C) A trip abroad
(D) A cash bonus

Questions 62-64 refer to the following conversation and map.

M Hello, Betty. I'm wondering if you are still interested in joining our badminton club. We have lost a couple of members recently, so we would like to offer you the opportunity to join.
W I certainly enjoy playing badminton. But as you know, I have moved to a new location, so I would have a long way to drive to your club.
M Yes, I heard you've moved to a new apartment near Stanton High School. But we do have an affiliated gym running some badminton games near your place. I think they have some available spaces, too.
W Really? Where exactly is the gym?
M I'll send you details by e-mail about the club, which meets at the Hillsberry Building. It's just next to the Community Center. Please take a look and call me back.
W I don't know much about the neighborhood. Is it on Alton Street?
M No, it's the new building across from the shopping mall. It's on the same block as the high school.
W I'm confused. I'll have to check your e-mail.

62. What are the speakers mainly talking about?
(A) The woman's new apartment
(B) Joining a sports club
(C) Driving a long distance
(D) A newly arrived student

63. What is the woman concerned about?
(A) The cost of joining a gym
(B) The amount of spare time she has
(C) The location of the new office
(D) The distance she would travel

64. Look at the graphic. Where is the Hillsberry Building?
(A) A
(B) B
(C) C
(D) D

Questions 65-67 refer to the following conversation and checklist.

W Daniel, your photos of the new branches in the newspaper advertisement were so amazing. Can you send those images to me so our web designers can put them on our homepage?
M Sure, Jenny. Just tell me which ones you wish to use.
W I was going to use all of them. In addition, I need some related information on each, such as the names of the manager, phone numbers, and addresses.
M But I'm worried some of them wouldn't look good on your Web site because they were taken at night. Moreover, the Glanstown branch doesn't have a phone number yet, and they haven't decided who will take charge of the McMillan branch.
W I think I can handle the issues with the telephone numbers. But I agree that we should post the pictures taken during the daytime only. Are there any other issues?
M I'm not sure for now. I'll just send you all the images with the information.
W Thank you so much. By the way, the names of the branch managers will be finalized next Monday, right? Then we'd better post all the pictures except for those taken at nighttime.

65. What most likely is the man's job?
(A) Branch manager
(B) Office interior designer
(C) Photographer
(D) Web site developer

66. What does the woman ask the man to help with?
(A) Assigning a manager
(B) Photocopying some images
(C) Getting some photographs
(D) Installing a telephone

67. Look at the graphic. Which site's photograph is not suitable to be posted on the Web site?
(A) Alpha Center branch
(B) Glanstown branch
(C) McMillan branch
(D) Unicorn Building branch

Questions 68-70 refer to the following conversation and floor guide.

W This is Samantha Collins from the Silverstein Employment Agency. I'm calling to confirm that we have received your application for temporary employment, and we will expect you to come into the office to sign the paperwork on Tuesday morning.
M Thank you for calling, Ms. Collins. Shall I come straight up to your office?
W No, let's meet in the administration office downstairs. You will need to bring your qualification certificates and references with you so that we can issue your work permit.
M But I already submitted all the required documents when I met you at the cafeteria last time. Do I need to bring more copies?
W Oh, you are right, Mr. Thompson. Then I'll see you in my office in the counseling department at 1:30 in the afternoon. After a short interview, you'll take part in a 3-hour training program on the third floor.

68. What document will be issued to the man?
(A) An application form
(B) A work permit
(C) A membership card
(D) A recommendation letter

69. Look at the graphic. Where should the man go to meet the woman on Tuesday?
(A) 1st floor
(B) 2nd floor
(C) 3rd floor
(D) 4th floor

70. What does the woman ask the man to do?
(A) Submit an application as soon as possible
(B) Mail extra copies of his certificates
(C) Attend a training session
(D) Give her his autograph

Part 4

Questions 71-73 refer to the following advertisement.

Exo-Spices is one of the leading companies for the food service industry. We recently added quality Indian buffets and various kinds of cold noodles to our menu. With the most competitive prices in the market and the most menu choices, we have a good reputation for superb catering services. And if you are not satisfied with our food or service, we will give you your entire money back! Visit our Web site at www.exospices.ca to see our selection of set menus or create your own by using the "My Taste" option.

71. What type of business is being advertised?
(A) A cold storage facility
(B) A catering firm
(C) A web design service
(D) A cooking institute

72. According to the advertisement, what does Exo Spices guarantee?
(A) Unlimited beverages
(B) Discount vouchers
(C) A full refund
(D) Nutritious food

73. What can listeners do online?
(A) Customize a set menu
(B) Order samples of some food
(C) Leave comments
(D) Track an order

Questions 74-76 refer to the following news report.

This is Eugene Wilson from the City of Eunice with the latest news. The announcement was made this morning that the public swimming pool will be reopened next summer. Local sports minister Martin Floyd announced that since several kinds of harmful substances were found in the ceiling of the pool area 2 months ago, renovation work was forced to a halt. However, thanks to a local environmental organization, they have been cleared off and the work has begun again. The swimming pool is scheduled to receive a new roof, repairs to the pool area, and a new children's pool with waterslides. Employees at local businesses are encouraged to become members of the newly-renovated facility, and a number of incentives will be offered to the residents of Eunice once the pool is reopened in July. They include a weekly prize drawing for 7 free annual memberships.

74. What is being rebuilt in Eunice?
    (A) A shopping mall
    (B) A swimming pool
    (C) A playground
    (D) An environmental center

75. Why was the renovation delayed?
    (A) The location was too remote.
    (B) Local residents objected to the renovation.
    (C) Harmful substances were detected.
    (D) Funding was insufficient.

76. According to the speaker, what will take place in July?
    (A) A weekly prize drawing
    (B) An opening ceremony
    (C) A series of lectures
    (D) A charity event

Questions 77-79 refer to the following announcement.

Just before we start our guitar class, I would like to bring to your attention a big event that is being held here at Jackson Community Center. As you know, we hold a number of music classes here, and we would like to encourage people to try out playing new musical instruments. So if you attend more than two different classes before the end of April, you will be eligible to join one new class free of charge. Pick up a brochure from the office on the first floor with all the details and enroll in more classes. And don't forget to swipe your student card every time you attend a class.

77. What is the purpose of the upcoming event?
    (A) To promote an art class
    (B) To encourage class participation
    (C) To introduce a new lecturer
    (D) To test students' performances

78. What will some students receive?
    (A) Tickets to a musical performance
    (B) Theater discounts
    (C) A complimentary class
    (D) Reduced tuition fees

79. What are the listeners asked to do when entering a class?
    (A) Play the guitar
    (B) Accompany a friend
    (C) Stop by the office
    (D) Apply an ID card

Questions 80-82 refer to the following recorded message.

Thank you for calling the Redwood Trekking Hotline. Due to the unfavorable weather change, we are experiencing more calls than normal. Your call will be answered as soon as one of our representatives is available. To ensure that you are put through to the correct department, please consider the following options. For emergency situations, press number one. For shelter inquiries, press number two. For shuttle service inquiries, press number three. For local traffic information, press number four. For all other inquiries, press the pound sign. You can also check the real-time weather report via the Internet at weather.redwood.com.

80. Why are the callers unable to speak to a representative immediately?
    (A) More people are calling than usual.
    (B) A hotline system is faulty.
    (C) The shuttles are out of service.
    (D) The Internet connection is unavailable.

81. Why would callers press 4 on their phones?
    (A) To check the shuttle schedules
    (B) To get advice on road travel
    (C) To check the weather forecast
    (D) To locate a nearby shelter

82. What does the speaker mention about the Web site?
    (A) It is updated every day.
    (B) It is currently inaccessible.
    (C) You need to log on to check the contents.
    (D) It provides the current weather status.

Questions 83-85 refer to the following talk.

Everyone worked very hard on the sales of the HeatTech Womenswear corner last winter. I'm so happy to announce that everyone in our branch is going to get a bonus for the best sales record. Congratulations, everyone. And now, this meeting has been arranged to inform you of the new product line that we are launching in the spring. On top of our standard collection of suits, shirts, and pants, we are also launching a new collection of knitwear this year. Your job is to present these new products to the clients successfully. However, before I explain the sales strategy, let me show you the knitwear, which is displayed in the showroom.

83. Who most likely are the listeners?
    (A) Fashion designers
    (B) Corporate executives
    (C) Factory workers
    (D) Salespeople

84. What will happen this spring?
    (A) A womenswear collection will be discontinued.
    (B) A new client list will be introduced.
    (C) A new range will be launched.
    (D) A new outlet will be opened.

85. What will the listeners do next?
    (A) Visit their clients
    (B) View sample items
    (C) Report their sales strategies
    (D) Attend a regular meeting

Questions 86-88 refer to the following telephone message.

Hi, this is Carol Foster, head of marketing at Murrey Outdoors. We need your help for a marketing campaign we are launching. We want you to create a montage of pictures based around a vacation theme. Please transpose as many Murrey outdoor wear items and accessories as possible in various locations—such as campsites, ski resorts, and mountains—and make them unique. At the end of the month, we will award the person with the best montage with a holiday discount voucher. Send your entry to design@murrey.com and win money-off vouchers!

86. What type of business does the speaker work for?
 (A) An advertising company
 (B) A photography studio
 (C) A clothing company
 (D) A travel agency

87. What should the listener submit to join the contest?
 (A) A series of photographs
 (B) A sketch
 (C) A video clip
 (D) A travel essay

88. What will the winner receive?
 (A) Cash
 (B) Coupons
 (C) Flight tickets
 (D) Camping equipment

Questions 89-91 refer to the following radio broadcast.

Good evening, and welcome back to Stadium Fever! I am Mike Burns, and I will be with you for the next two hours for today's match. And we have a great prize for some lucky listeners tonight. If you correctly guess the first player to score in the game, we will send twelve winners a pair of tickets to the grand final to be held at Prime Capital Stadium next month. It couldn't be simpler! Just text us your predictions at 050-884-1291. Just make sure you're sending it only one time with one single name! You may send your message now! I will be back after this commercial.

89. Who most likely is the speaker?
 (A) A stadium vendor
 (B) A sports announcer
 (C) A football player
 (D) A match referee

90. What prize is being offered?
 (A) Dinner with an athlete
 (B) Tickets for the final
 (C) A two-week trip
 (D) Autographed football shirts

91. What does the man imply when he says, "It couldn't be simpler"?
 (A) Everyone can send the message free of charge.
 (B) The rules for soccer are not complicated.
 (C) It is easy to join the event.
 (D) All the names of the players need to be memorized.

Questions 92-94 refer to the following announcement.

I wish to inform you all about a change in policy regarding working hours. You recently completed a survey questionnaire on efficient practices in the office, and the consensus is that you would be more productive if you took a shorter lunch break and left earlier in the day. We will try out this suggestion from next week. The lunch break will be halved, but, as most of you indicated, there would be no difficulty in that. On the other hand, you will then be able to leave the office at least 40 minutes earlier than now. This change will enable us to make more efficient use of the time spent in the office. Please note that these adjustments will come into effect following the weekend.

92. What is being announced?
 (A) A meeting schedule
 (B) An increase in salaries
 (C) A new working arrangement
 (D) An overtime project

93. Why is a change being made?
 (A) To attract new employees
 (B) To create to a survey
 (C) To improve working practices
 (D) To reward hard-working employees

94. What does the woman imply when she says, "there would be no difficulty in that"?
 (A) It is impossible to comply with the change.
 (B) The survey was conducted without any trouble.
 (C) The change will cause some confusion.
 (D) A shorter lunch break is not a big deal.

Questions 95-97 refer to the following telephone message and map.

Hello, Ms. Martinez. This is Joseph Rockwood from the Lotus real estate agency. I have located another property on Robinson Road, which looks suitable for you. It's within walking distance to White Pebbles Park, right next to a gas station. It's also close to the train station, and there's a public parking area across the road. I think it is an ideal spot for your new warehouse. But there's one problem. The area is prone to flooding, and, therefore, insurance premiums may be high. I have arranged a meeting with the landlord on Friday morning to check it myself. Since the building is a bit old and in poor condition, I think you can buy it very cheaply. I advise you to sign the contract as soon as possible if it works for you.

95. Why does the speaker recommend the property?
 (A) It is in a flood-prone area.
 (B) The landlord wants to sell it cheap.
 (C) The building is in a good condition.
 (D) There is a subway station nearby.

96. What disadvantage does the speaker mention?
 (A) The deposit is too high.
 (B) The flood risk is high.
 (C) The landlord has another buyer.
 (D) A parking lot is not included.

97. Look at the graphic. Where most likely is the property?
 (A) A
 (B) B
 (C) C
 (D) D

Questions 98-100 refer to the following announcement and schedule.

I would like to inform everyone that the inspectors are going to assess the noise situation of the offices later today. So that employees are no longer affected by the noise coming from the factory site across the street, the office windows are to be double glazed. I ask everyone to take down the blinds and store them in the storeroom on the seventh floor until the work is finished. The replacement will begin on Thursday morning, so you have two days to remove them. And if you have curtains instead of blinds, Mr. Coleman will take them down and wash them tomorrow. Thank you in advance for your cooperation.

98. What problem is the management responding to?
(A) Noise from a factory
(B) A shortage of office supplies
(C) Renovation expenses
(D) Broken windows

99. Look at the graphic. When will Mr. Coleman remove the curtains?
(A) Monday
(B) Tuesday
(C) Wednesday
(D) Thursday

100. What does the speaker encourage listeners to do?
(A) Clear the blinds
(B) Wash the curtains
(C) Change the windows
(D) Work from home

8회

1.	(C)	21.	(C)	41.	(C)	61.	(C)	81.	(C)
2.	(D)	22.	(C)	42.	(B)	62.	(D)	82.	(C)
3.	(B)	23.	(B)	43.	(C)	63.	(C)	83.	(C)
4.	(A)	24.	(B)	44.	(A)	64.	(B)	84.	(C)
5.	(C)	25.	(B)	45.	(C)	65.	(C)	85.	(D)
6.	(A)	26.	(B)	46.	(D)	66.	(A)	86.	(A)
7.	(B)	27.	(B)	47.	(B)	67.	(B)	87.	(B)
8.	(A)	28.	(B)	48.	(B)	68.	(A)	88.	(D)
9.	(A)	29.	(C)	49.	(C)	69.	(B)	89.	(A)
10.	(B)	30.	(C)	50.	(D)	70.	(A)	90.	(D)
11.	(B)	31.	(A)	51.	(A)	71.	(A)	91.	(B)
12.	(A)	32.	(B)	52.	(A)	72.	(D)	92.	(A)
13.	(B)	33.	(D)	53.	(D)	73.	(C)	93.	(D)
14.	(C)	34.	(C)	54.	(C)	74.	(A)	94.	(B)
15.	(C)	35.	(C)	55.	(B)	75.	(D)	95.	(C)
16.	(B)	36.	(A)	56.	(C)	76.	(A)	96.	(B)
17.	(A)	37.	(A)	57.	(B)	77.	(B)	97.	(A)
18.	(C)	38.	(B)	58.	(A)	78.	(C)	98.	(C)
19.	(B)	39.	(A)	59.	(C)	79.	(B)	99.	(C)
20.	(C)	40.	(B)	60.	(A)	80.	(D)	100.	(D)

Part 1

1.
(A) The man has his hand on a bottle.
(B) The shelves are being dusted.
(C) The man is resting his arm on the table.
(D) Some mugs are arranged in a row.

2.
(A) One of the women is cleaning the desk.
(B) The women are wearing long-sleeved shirts.
(C) One of the women is looking out the window.
(D) The women are sitting side by side.

3.
(A) A man is picking up a plastic bag.
(B) Different kinds of goods are displayed.
(C) Leaves are being cleared from the road.
(D) The outdoor market is crowded with people.

4.
(A) The women are preparing some food.
(B) One of the women is chopping some vegetables.
(C) The women are setting the dinner table.
(D) One of the women is tasting some food.

5.
(A) The road passes by a wooded area.
(B) Some pots decorate the entrance to the restaurant.
(C) A wooden structure stands near a lake.
(D) The plants are being watered.

6.
(A) Some people are reading documents.
(B) Some people are placing folders in a cabinet.
(C) One of the men is talking on the phone.
(D) A man is posting a notice on the wall.

Part 2

7. Who left this report on my desk?
(A) In the bottom shelf.
(B) I have no idea.
(C) I'll do it later.

8. When did you learn how to drive a bus?
   (A) Only a month ago.
   (B) I'm not sure which bus I should take.
   (C) Yes, it's a big one.

9. Can you change a 100-dollar bill?
   (A) Sure thing.
   (B) That's too expensive.
   (C) I'd like some small change.

10. My laptop needs to be fixed.
    (A) Fix it to the door.
    (B) What's wrong?
    (C) We inspected them fully.

11. This is the serial number of your desktop, isn't it?
    (A) Actually, Emma wrote it.
    (B) No, it's for the copier.
    (C) Yes, I need your help.

12. Isn't it going to rain this afternoon?
    (A) Yes, you'd better take your umbrella.
    (B) It'll depart at three o'clock.
    (C) No, I'm going to do it tomorrow morning.

13. Can you show me how to install the software?
    (A) The program finishes at nine o'clock.
    (B) I'd be glad to help you.
    (C) He's in the training session now.

14. Should I e-mail this application now, or do you want to revise it again?
    (A) I didn't e-mail it.
    (B) Yes, it was issued without delay.
    (C) Please send it to me.

15. You've met Ms. Harvey before, haven't you?
    (A) Okay, let's meet at lunch.
    (B) I will pick her up at the airport.
    (C) No, not yet.

16. Where can I purchase a train ticket?
    (A) It comes every hour.
    (B) At the automated machine over there.
    (C) Sixteen dollars, please.

17. Wasn't Celia at the cosmetics conference in France last week?
    (A) No, I didn't see her there.
    (B) Yes, she will try out the new products there.
    (C) Where is the main conference room?

18. How many boxes did we order today?
    (A) About five meters tall.
    (B) Can I have one?
    (C) More than eleven.

19. Why did the workshop end so late?
    (A) Some attendees will be late.
    (B) We had a lot to talk about.
    (C) No, the store does not close until ten.

20. Which branch needs more staff members?
    (A) About the job opening.
    (B) Twenty more chairs.
    (C) Most of them.

21. Do you want to go out to see a movie?
    (A) Oh, did you?
    (B) No, I didn't move it.
    (C) Sure, how about seven o'clock?

22. Who's attending the international convention in Paris?
    (A) They've been expanding overseas.
    (B) In the conference center.
    (C) It hasn't been announced yet.

23. What are you intending to bring to Allison's birthday party?
    (A) I bought the same one.
    (B) I'm afraid I can't go.
    (C) She visited me last week.

24. Should I buy the shirts online or at the clothing store?
    (A) The same color.
    (B) Probably at the store.
    (C) It's less expensive.

25. What was the weather like during your business trip?
    (A) I lost my passport.
    (B) It was hot and humid every day.
    (C) Take your coat when you go out.

26. Have you examined the marketing proposal from Benjamin?
    (A) I'm looking forward to meeting them.
    (B) No, it's scheduled to be submitted tomorrow.
    (C) I had my van examined.

27. The flight is an hour late.
    (A) Every thirty minutes.
    (B) That's due to the weather problem.
    (C) No, it will be rescheduled.

28. Would you like some orange for dessert?
    (A) I don't like spicy food.
    (B) Thanks, but I'm full.
    (C) Yes, I can't wait for the main dish.

29. When are you going to review the monthly reports?
    (A) No, he won't.
    (B) Two days ago.
    (C) As soon as I get them.

30. I dry-cleaned all my winter clothes last week.
    (A) Yes, it suits you well.
    (B) Only for regular customers.
    (C) How much did that cost in total?

31. Where do you put the order forms?
    (A) We don't have any.
    (B) It was nearly 10 pages long.
    (C) Don't write on them.

Part 3

Questions 32-34 refer to the following conversation.

W Justin, I found a couple of issues in the economy section in tomorrow's newspaper. We have to replace some tables with the updated ones. I need your assistance along with Kayla and Sam, who are also staying late.
M Sure, I would be glad to do that. Tell me how I can help you.
W Thanks. Please take some time to hear what Sam has to say about it. Meanwhile, I'll order dinner for everyone who will be staying late.

32. What is the woman concerned about?
    (A) A family matter
    (B) A newspaper page
    (C) A travel itinerary
    (D) A group presentation

33. What does the woman ask the man to do?
    (A) Take some pictures
    (B) Revise an article
    (C) Buy some food
    (D) Work overtime

34. What does the woman say she will do?
    (A) Read a proposal
    (B) Mail a package
    (C) Arrange for some food
    (D) Create an advertisement

Questions 35-37 refer to the following conversation.

> M I saw a television commercial with Patrick Spencer, a personal trainer. He said that we could improve a person's posture to make the working environment more comfortable.
>
> W I went to an exercise class held by Mr. Spencer last week that was useful in many ways. For instance, he explained that leaning over a computer causes lower back problems, but a simple set of exercises could help with posture. In addition, he recommended changing the height of the chair.
>
> M I certainly get a lot of pain from constantly working on a computer. How about arranging a lunchtime exercise class?
>
> W That's a good idea. He gave me some DVDs of exercises with step-by-step instructions. I will hand them out to interested staff members.

35. Who is Patrick Spencer?
    (A) A computer engineer
    (B) A DVD seller
    (C) A health trainer
    (D) An ad executive

36. What did Patrick Spencer advise the woman to do?
    (A) Sit up straight in her chair
    (B) Work on her computer
    (C) Lean against a wall
    (D) Upgrade her computer

37. What does the woman offer to do?
    (A) Share some information with her colleagues
    (B) Assist in preparing a demonstration
    (C) Buy the man a computer
    (D) Make a list of interested employees

Questions 38-40 refer to the following conversation.

> W Mr. Yates. Alexa here. Our clients from Starwood want to discuss the paperhanging work for their hotel.
>
> M I heard everything was settled last month. Is there any problem?
>
> W They've approved the color and material already, but now they think the project is too expensive.
>
> M Well, Starwood is one of our biggest customers, so I would like to allay their worries. Maybe if we source cheaper wallpaper for the hotel rooms, we would be able to reduce the overall cost. When is the meeting scheduled?
>
> W Friday morning. We still have some time to come up with some alternatives.
>
> M Excellent. Let's have a meeting with the supplier to see what choices are available.

38. What are the clients worried about?
    (A) The color of the paint
    (B) The cost of the work
    (C) The deadline for the project
    (D) The material of the wallpaper

39. What does the man imply when he says, "I would like to allay their worries"?
    (A) He wants to satisfy the clients.
    (B) He needs more time to finish the project.
    (C) He's going to ask for a budget increase.
    (D) He doesn't want to work for Starwood.

40. What does the man suggest?
    (A) Finding a different hotel
    (B) Consulting with the supplier
    (C) Ignoring the customer's expectations
    (D) Postponing the meeting

Questions 41-43 refer to the following conversation.

> M Hello, Doctor Hopkins. I am Gary Kemp, the chief editor at *Medical Tech Online*. We wish to publish your article on the common cold in our online forum next month.
>
> W That's amazing news. I researched a lot of sources for this article, which was worthwhile and rewarding. But I feel it may be too technical for your Web site.
>
> M I thought the same thing. But I can assist you in simplifying the text. If I send you some easier vocabulary, you can make a start on rewriting the article.

41. What is the conversation mainly about?
    (A) Getting a general checkup
    (B) Designing a book
    (C) Publishing an article
    (D) Giving a talk

42. What are the speakers worried about?
    (A) The length of a text
    (B) The difficulty of an article
    (C) The access to an online forum
    (D) The deadline for publishing

43. What does the man offer to do?
    (A) Participate in the research
    (B) Carry a different article
    (C) Provide a list of words
    (D) Vaccinate the patients

Questions 44-46 refer to the following conversation.

> W Have you noticed how quiet the remodeling work of our office has been?
>
> M Yes, I know. It was even tough to say that there was construction going on.
>
> W I'm very impressed with the workers because they've been so professional and they managed their working schedule so wonderfully that it never overlapped with ours. They even cleaned the workspace every day.
>
> M I agree. I'm going to suggest using the same company in the future.

44. What are the speakers discussing?
    (A) A renovation project
    (B) A job interview
    (C) A road development
    (D) A work schedule

45. What is the woman impressed by?
    (A) The improved environment of the office
    (B) How quickly the job was performed
    (C) The professionalism of the workers
    (D) How little the construction cost

46. What does the man say he will suggest?
    (A) Rescheduling some appointments
    (B) Moving to a new building
    (C) Calling the maintenance office
    (D) Employing the same company again

Questions 47-49 refer to the following conversation.

W   Hello, Glenn. I see you have safely returned from your visit abroad. Did you find any good suppliers for our overseas venture?
M   Yes, I think a firm in Copenhagen is ideal for our company. And there are two other manufacturers in Malmo that make high-quality products. However, Copenhagen is nearer to the harbor and is better placed for transportation.
W   Can you show me the full report when it's finished? Oh, and remember that tomorrow is your last chance to submit your travel expense report. Make sure all of the receipts are sent to the finance department.

47. What was the purpose of the man's trip?
(A) To look at the new factory sites
(B) To source new suppliers
(C) To sell goods abroad
(D) To arrange interviews

48. What does the man say about the company in Copenhagen?
(A) It has many manufacturing plants.
(B) It is favorably located.
(C) It welcomes business from abroad.
(D) It is close to an airport.

49. What does the woman remind the man to do?
(A) Ask for an extended vacation
(B) Report the loss of his luggage
(C) Submit his report
(D) Update his current client details

Questions 50-52 refer to the following conversation.

M   Hi, Ms. Warren. My name is Tim Rhodes, from the human resources department at Morris Shipping Service, calling regarding your application as head receptionist. Following consultation with our interviewers, I am delighted to offer you the job.
W   That is excellent news. However, as I am working now, I must hand in my notice to my current company. What is the start date for the job?
M   Ideally, we want someone to start immediately, but with your experience, we can try to sort a suitable time frame out for you. How soon do you think you could begin?
W   Luckily, I have a capable successor who is to be appointed to my position here. It will take about two weeks to train her properly, so that would be the earliest I can start.

50. What department does the man work in?
(A) Maintenance
(B) Customer service
(C) Reception
(D) Human resources

51. What does the woman ask about?
(A) The start date of a job
(B) The qualifications for a job
(C) The name of the human resources manager
(D) The location of the training session

52. What does the woman say she will probably do?
(A) Hand over her present duties to her colleague
(B) Teach the man how to do his job properly
(C) Move to a new location
(D) Submit a job application

Questions 53-55 refer to the following conversation.

M   I'm moving to the second floor to get started on the painting work in the hallway. Do you know of any other maintenance requests that I've somehow missed?
W   Yes, there is a request I just received. Ms. Stone has informed me that the lights in the meeting room, which is just next to her office, won't turn on.
M   Okay, I will have a look. Do I need to check it before I start painting, or would it be okay if I checked it this afternoon?
W   I think it would be better if you checked it right now because Ms. Stone will be attending a meeting with her clients in there from one o'clock today.

53. Who most likely is the man?
(A) An administrative assistant
(B) A sales representative
(C) An interior designer
(D) A maintenance employee

54. What problem does the woman mention?
(A) A project is not complete.
(B) An office is locked.
(C) Some electric equipment is defective.
(D) Some materials are not available.

55. According to the woman, what is scheduled to take place in the afternoon?
(A) A safety check
(B) A meeting
(C) A job interview
(D) A power outage

Questions 56-58 refer to the following conversation with three speakers.

W   Seth, I am unable to make any telephone calls from the office.
M1   I have the same problem. The message states that the network is unavailable.
M2   I have contacted the telephone company, and the manager explained that the cables have been damaged, which is affecting the communication system on this floor. It won't be fixed until later today.
W   That's no good to me. I have to call two of our clients at lunchtime.
M1   Oh, no. Are there some time-sensitive issues?
W   Yes, I need to explain to them about the urgent changes to be made. But it can't be done in this situation.
M2   Here's a solution. Why don't you try using the phone in the conference room downstairs? As I remember, that allows a three-way call.
W   What a relief! Thank you. I'll go to the conference room to check it right now.

56. What problem is the woman talking about?
(A) She cannot meet her manager today.
(B) She cannot find any problem with her mobile phone.
(C) She cannot contact her clients from the office.
(D) She cannot fix the defective cables.

57. What does the woman imply when she says, "That's no good to me"?
(A) She has to leave early today.
(B) She can't wait for the cables to be repaired.
(C) She will visit the clients in person.
(D) She doesn't want to use a three-way call.

58. What will the woman probably do next?
(A) Check the telephone downstairs
(B) Contact the telephone company again
(C) Make a speech at the conference
(D) List some time-sensitive issues

Questions 59-61 refer to the following conversation.

M   Erin, have you decided to redecorate your office yet?
W   Yes, I have contacted a company called Amberhues. I got a number of estimates from several companies, all within a similar price range. But because the company has been established for over a decade, I decided to use Amberhues.
M   I wondered if you had changed your mind since you have been asked to travel to Miami for work over the next few weeks.
W   Amberhues was very accommodating and has agreed not to start work on the office until I return in July.

59. What type of company is Amberhues?
(A) A travel agency
(B) A moving company
(C) A decorating firm
(D) A hotel

60. Why did the woman choose Amberhues?
(A) It has been in operation for a long time.
(B) It is convenient to her office.
(C) It has a branch in Miami.
(D) It is the most competitively priced.

61. Why will the work start in July?
(A) The company has to give approval.
(B) Furniture cannot be delivered earlier.
(C) The woman will be away until then.
(D) The company is busy with other work.

Questions 62-64 refer to the following conversation and list.

W   James, next Monday is the birthday of our president. Do you think we should arrange a party for him?
M   Let's have a nice dinner together. How about one of his favorite restaurants? Monsoon Lounge, for example. They're offering a 10% discount on their buffet.
W   But that's just for lunchtime. And some of us don't like Thai food. How about the newly opened Japanese restaurant?
M   Hikaru? I doubt he'll enjoy those raw fish. We'd better have some sort of Western food.
W   This isn't easy. Maybe we should take some suggestions.
M   You're right. And we need to book a place that can accommodate 15 people in a separate room.

62. According to the woman, what is the purpose of the event?
(A) To organize an awards ceremony
(B) To taste some exotic food
(C) To open a new business
(D) To celebrate a birthday

63. Look at the graphic. Which place would be most suitable for the event?
(A) Wang's Castle
(B) Beefy Porky
(C) Indiana's
(D) Chili Chili

64. Why does the woman disagree with the man's idea?
(A) The restaurant is not big enough.
(B) They won't be able to get a discount.
(C) The president doesn't like Japanese food.
(D) They have no time to book a room.

Questions 65-67 refer to the following conversation and map.

W   You know what? I've just found the ideal location for your culinary school. It's in the Diana Complex, directly to the north of the city.
M   I've never heard of the Diana Complex. Where is it located?
W   Just across from Tinderbox, where we had dinner together last Wednesday.
M   Hmm… I thought there was a gas station across from the restaurant.
W   No, it's on the other side. It's a five-story building right next to the hotel.
M   I'm not sure which hotel you're talking about. By the way, is it large enough?
W   You would be surprised at the size inside. Can you find some time later today to visit the site with me?
M   Tomorrow afternoon is better, as I am in cooking lessons all day today.

65. What most likely is the man's occupation?
(A) Real estate agent
(B) Building constructor
(C) Cooking teacher
(D) Hotel worker

66. Look at the graphic. Where most likely is the Diana Complex?
(A) A
(B) B
(C) C
(D) D

67. When does the man say he can visit the Diana Complex?
(A) This evening
(B) Later tomorrow
(C) The day after tomorrow
(D) The week after

Questions 68-70 refer to the following conversation and list.

M   Ma'am, your orders are now ready. Is there anything else you need?
W   No, that's all I want. How much do they cost?
M   They're 265 dollars. The speakers are 30 dollars each, since we're offering a 25% discount. Check them on the monitor here.
W   It's strange. I can't find the webcam on the list.
M   Really? You've chosen 6 speakers, 2 keyboards, and a mouse. Oh, I have missed the X-cam 64. It's added onto the list. Now that'll be 340 dollars in total.
W   It's more expensive than I thought. I'll take 2 speakers out of my order. Will you accept a company check? I appear to have forgotten the company credit card.
M   A company check is fine. We need to arrange the shipping schedule. When would be the best time to deliver them to your office?

68. Who most likely is the man?
(A) A storekeeper
(B) A bank teller
(C) A delivery man
(D) A computer repairman

69. What does the woman ask about?
(A) The delivery time
(B) The payment options
(C) The availability of items
(D) A card approval

70. Look at the graphic. Which information on the list has to be changed now?
(A) $180
(B) $50
(C) $35
(D) $75

Part 4

Questions 71-73 refer to the following announcement.

May I have everyone's attention? The new tire-fitting machine is being delivered on Thursday. Without any doubt, this is good news! This state-of-the-art machine can fit tires to cars in half the normal time. In order to ensure that it is installed and is fully functional, we will need to remain in the garage after hours. We are therefore asking as many employees as possible to stay late in order to catch up with any work. If you wish to volunteer, please add your name to the list. As usual, you will be paid overtime rates.

71. What is the announcement mainly about?
(A) A machine installation
(B) A company closure
(C) A safety inspection
(D) A vehicle check

72. What does the man imply when he says, "Without any doubt, this is good news"?
(A) He can fix his car by himself now.
(B) He will gladly do the overtime work.
(C) They have purchased the machine at a low price.
(D) The new machine will help them complete the work in less time.

73. What does the speaker ask the listeners to do?
(A) Attend an opening ceremony
(B) Welcome a new supervisor
(C) Work overtime hours
(D) Review an operations manual

Questions 74-76 refer to the following radio broadcast.

This is The Voice of London on primetime radio. Today, we will be talking to Aiden Elder, Marketing Director of Angel Hearts U.K. This charity specializes in finding employment for homeless youths. Mr. Elder will be talking about the latest figures to be released about the number of homeless on Britain's streets and asking for the public's help for a major new initiative being launched. Angel Hearts is looking for a number of volunteers to mentor young people in the workplace. Keep listening; the interview will follow these commercials.

74. Where does the speaker most likely work?
(A) At a radio station
(B) At an employment agency
(C) At a charity organization
(D) At a publishing house

75. According to the speaker, what will Mr. Elder discuss?
(A) A community building
(B) A fundraising event
(C) A marketing report
(D) A new plan

76. Why are volunteers needed?
(A) To advise young people
(B) To distribute brochures
(C) To conduct interviews
(D) To recruit office workers

Questions 77-79 refer to the following talk.

As chairperson of the local anti-crime society, I welcome you to this meeting. I especially welcome any new members. This is our fifth monthly meeting regarding the safety of our neighborhood. I am delighted to inform you that we have been granted permission to apply for a grant for street lighting in the Willis District, adjacent to the railway track. Our next challenge is to come up with a bid to the grant association to persuade them to give us funding. If you think you can help prepare a bid, please contact Megan Bishop, our treasurer at meganbishop@anticrime.org by November 10.

77. Who is the speaker?
(A) A government officer
(B) A head of a certain society
(C) A police officer
(D) A lighting expert

78. What permission has the group received?
(A) Hosting a fundraising event
(B) Supporting a sports team
(C) Submitting a bid for funding
(D) Sponsoring a lighting company

79. Why should listeners contact Megan Bishop?
(A) To apply to the committee
(B) To help in preparing the bid
(C) To purchase some lighting
(D) To contribute to the newsletter

Questions 80-82 refer to the following excerpt from a meeting.

Today's meeting is about our marketing campaign for the new book launch. This is the third novel in the best-selling series by Jessica Fox, one of the leading authors in the world, and we need to make sure that we market it well. What makes this book so special is that it is a prequel to the previous stories, and therefore, charts the history of the characters and the plot. We have exclusive rights to this book, and I am sure that you will be able to come up with a dynamic and hard-hitting marketing campaign to ensure that the book sells. I am giving each one of you a copy of the novel. Please read it carefully and come up with some original ideas.

80. Who is the intended audience for the talk?
(A) Prospective writers
(B) A proofreading team
(C) A book club
(D) A marketing department

81. According to the speaker, why is the new book unique?
(A) It is being serialized in the newspaper.
(B) It is available in e-book format.
(C) It is the prequel to a series.
(D) It is written in a different language.

82. What will the speaker most likely do next?
(A) Review work assignments
(B) Meet with the editing team
(C) Distribute copies of a book
(D) Work out a budget

Questions 83-85 refer to the following announcement.

Good afternoon. I have a special announcement regarding the promotions we are running, offering customers a 10-minute makeup class. Now I believe you are all proficient in applying makeup. We need to spread the word about this promotion. We have advertised on local radio, and we are offering visitors a free lipstick every day this week. I'm sure this will attract more customers into the salon. But, I am a little worried that we will run out of stock. Can I ask for volunteers to purchase some more stock from the wholesalers on Thursday? Please let me know if you can.

83. What is the announcement mainly about?
(A) A product recall
(B) A store relocation
(C) A store promotion
(D) A remodeling project

84. What were employees recently trained to do?
(A) Design a new promotion
(B) Prepare some cosmetic items
(C) Offer makeovers
(D) Inspect some equipment

85. What is the speaker concerned about?
(A) Finding a new supplier
(B) Having sufficient seating
(C) Lowering operating costs
(D) Providing continuous supplies

Questions 86-88 refer to the following telephone message.

Hello, this is a message from Adam Barnes. Is the Santa Claus costume still available? I noticed it in the window of your clothing store in Lloyd Street. I desperately need one for a party at my children's school. Can you advise me of the measurements as soon as possible? And if it fits, then I can pick it up. My e-mail address is abarnes@tol.net. Thank you.

86. What item is the speaker calling about?
(A) An outfit
(B) A wardrobe
(C) A television
(D) An e-mail account

87. Where has the item been advertised?
(A) In a magazine
(B) In a local shop
(C) On a bus window
(D) On a notice board

88. What does the speaker request?
(A) Some photographs
(B) A delivery date
(C) Pricing information
(D) The size of the item

Questions 89-91 refer to the following telephone message.

Hello, Dr. Lawrence. This is Mason Murray from Darwin Medical Supplies. You recently inquired about our physiotherapy equipment for your clinic. I am visiting your region next week, and I would be more than happy to bring some brochures for you to look at. All of our products come with a three-year warranty, which covers accidental damage and on-site repair. If you are interested, please call me to arrange an appointment at 6551-8918.

89. What does the speaker's company produce?
(A) Medical appliances
(B) Office equipment
(C) Drug supplies
(D) Audio systems

90. What does the speaker want to arrange?
(A) An on-site demonstration
(B) A factory tour
(C) A payment plan
(D) A meeting schedule

91. What does the speaker say about the company's products?
(A) They are highly recommended.
(B) They are covered by a guarantee.
(C) They can be replaced every year.
(D) They are easily transportable.

Questions 92-94 refer to the following recorded message.

Thank you for calling Woodcock Art Center. We have been established in the region for many years, and we hold regular meetings to share our paintings and artistic works with other artists. We are always looking for new people, so if you would like to find out more about us, you can attend our meetings, which are held on the first and third Wednesday of every month. For information on our schedule of artistic events, visit our Web site.

92. What type of organization did the listener call?
(A) An artistic group
(B) A writers' community
(C) A tutoring program
(D) A sporting club

93. What does the woman imply when she says, "we are always looking for new people"?
(A) To inform the listener that they are newly opened
(B) To find a new place to hold an exhibition
(C) To reschedule the next event
(D) To invite more members to the meeting

94. According to the speaker, what is available on the organization's Web site?
(A) A display of artwork
(B) A calendar of events
(C) An application form
(D) A date for the next meeting

Questions 95-97 refer to the following excerpt from a meeting and graph.

I see everyone here now, so let's start the meeting. You may already know that our sales declined severely last quarter, and the conditions did not improve this month. As indicated in this graph, the sales of refrigerators, which definitely were our best seller, have been dropping over the past six months. To make matters worse, the sales of televisions seem to pass their peak in November and have started to decrease. On the other hand, the computer line, which was a nuisance to us last quarter, is up slightly, but it still didn't meet our expectations. The company is launching a new laptop in February, when the computer sales usually show an explosive increase. So today, we are here to come up with marketing plans to boost the sales of the new item, for this is a good chance to reverse the situation.

95. What does the speaker want to discuss in this meeting?
(A) Moving up the release date of the new item
(B) Criticizing the sales department for the poor performance
(C) Making a successful marketing plan
(D) Deciding which products should be discontinued

96. Look at the graphic. Which line indicates the sales results of the computers?
(A) A
(B) B
(C) C
(D) D

97. What does the speaker say about the new item?
(A) It will be released in February.
(B) It won't meet the customers' expectations.
(C) It is the best-seller as usual.
(D) It only took 6 months to be developed.

Questions 98-100 refer to the following announcement and table.

Good morning, everyone. This is Zoe Miller in human resources. I'd like everyone to remember that today is the first day of the lunchtime speaker series, which was designed to give us a good opportunity to learn about all the running projects in the company. We have three sessions this week, and the first speaker will be Leah Bennett, who represents the research department. I regret notifying you that Mr. Hunt is now at the Chicago branch to take care of an urgent matter. So, those who are interested in the recent changes in the marketing department, please expect his speech on Thursday. To make the session more interactive and informative, he has asked all attendees to send any questions about the new marketing projects. Please send your questions to his assistant, Julia Watson, by the end of today.

98. What will happen later today?
(A) Mr. Hunt will leave for Chicago.
(B) The current marketing plans will be changed.
(C) A speech will be given by Ms. Bennett.
(D) A seminar will be postponed to the following week.

99. Look at the graphic. Which information needs to be changed?
(A) Room 407
(B) Leah Bennett
(C) Wed.
(D) Refreshments provided

100. According to the speaker, why would the listeners contact Julia Watson?
(A) To report an urgent matter
(B) To notify her of their availability
(C) To reschedule a session
(D) To make inquiries to Mr. Hunt

9회

1.	(B)	21.	(B)	41.	(A)	61.	(A)	81.	(D)
2.	(B)	22.	(B)	42.	(B)	62.	(A)	82.	(B)
3.	(A)	23.	(C)	43.	(D)	63.	(A)	83.	(C)
4.	(C)	24.	(A)	44.	(C)	64.	(A)	84.	(D)
5.	(B)	25.	(A)	45.	(D)	65.	(D)	85.	(C)
6.	(C)	26.	(A)	46.	(B)	66.	(C)	86.	(B)
7.	(B)	27.	(C)	47.	(D)	67.	(D)	87.	(D)
8.	(B)	28.	(A)	48.	(B)	68.	(A)	88.	(C)
9.	(A)	29.	(B)	49.	(C)	69.	(C)	89.	(C)
10.	(A)	30.	(A)	50.	(D)	70.	(C)	90.	(B)
11.	(C)	31.	(A)	51.	(D)	71.	(D)	91.	(A)
12.	(C)	32.	(A)	52.	(A)	72.	(A)	92.	(B)
13.	(C)	33.	(B)	53.	(A)	73.	(D)	93.	(D)
14.	(B)	34.	(A)	54.	(A)	74.	(B)	94.	(D)
15.	(B)	35.	(B)	55.	(A)	75.	(B)	95.	(B)
16.	(C)	36.	(C)	56.	(B)	76.	(B)	96.	(D)
17.	(B)	37.	(D)	57.	(D)	77.	(D)	97.	(C)
18.	(A)	38.	(A)	58.	(A)	78.	(D)	98.	(A)
19.	(B)	39.	(A)	59.	(C)	79.	(C)	99.	(D)
20.	(B)	40.	(D)	60.	(B)	80.	(C)	100.	(A)

Part 1

1. (A) The woman is looking at the white board.
(B) The woman is standing next to an office machine.
(C) The woman is folding a piece of paper.
(D) The woman is placing a notebook on the shelf.

2. (A) The woman is doing the dishes.
(B) The man is fastening the woman's apron.
(C) The woman is preparing some food for the man.
(D) The man is cooking something on a grill.

3. (A) Heavy machinery has been brought in to dig the ground.
(B) Some people are strolling along the road.
(C) The vehicles are parked in a line on the ground.
(D) The workers are fixing a defective machine.

4. (A) The man is posing for a photo.
(B) The man is painting a fence rail.
(C) Paintings have been hung on the fence.
(D) Benches are positioned under the paintings.

5. (A) Glass doors lead out to a garden.
(B) A conversation is taking place near a doorway.
(C) People are gathered for a meeting.
(D) The office is separated by a wooden partition.

6. (A) Curtains are flapping in the wind.
(B) Cushions are being removed from the sofas.
(C) Chairs have been positioned around the table.
(D) A light fixture is being installed in the room.

Part 2

7. I see that you have a teaching qualification.
(A) Sure, I'll look through it.
(B) Yes, from Caroline University.
(C) Are they qualified teachers?

8. Would you like a mug or a disposable cup to drink from?
(A) On the label.
(B) I prefer a mug.
(C) Some coffee with milk.

9. Who closes the main entrance to the firm?
   (A) The security staff.
   (B) Enter the code.
   (C) It is closed all day.

10. How will you get to the theater?
    (A) I'll take a bus.
    (B) I haven't got it yet.
    (C) I'm on stage.

11. Where did Sean go on holiday?
    (A) He left yesterday.
    (B) Yes, he did.
    (C) To Japan.

12. Did you talk to Ms. Collins when you were transferred to our headquarters?
    (A) No, not yet. I'm eager to see her.
    (B) No, just through Friday.
    (C) We haven't talked about it yet.

13. I heard Blake got the Employee of the Year at the awards ceremony.
    (A) A celebration for new employees.
    (B) No, early this week.
    (C) I'm glad to hear that.

14. Who does this jacket belong to?
    (A) About 50 dollars.
    (B) It's Chase's.
    (C) It's too short.

15. You've been to that seminar, haven't you?
    (A) On the semiconductor.
    (B) Which one?
    (C) Let me introduce myself.

16. Where did Mr. Brown work before joining us?
    (A) Much larger than I expected.
    (B) Yes, Ms. Adams employed him.
    (C) At a marketing agency in Canada.

17. Didn't Maya already sign the lease contract?
    (A) To rent a two-bedroom apartment.
    (B) No, she'll do it tomorrow.
    (C) The sign on the corner.

18. When can I expect to receive my travel expenses?
    (A) In two days.
    (B) In the office.
    (C) It's not that expensive.

19. My review article will be issued in tomorrow's newspaper.
    (A) A new editor will be employed.
    (B) I'll certainly look out for it.
    (C) You've run out of paper.

20. Will you come to our company banquet on Saturday?
    (A) They always provide excellent service.
    (B) I have plans that day.
    (C) It was really interesting.

21. When will my dress suit be ready?
    (A) I already met him.
    (B) In another hour.
    (C) On Jeremiah Street.

22. Does the utility bill include maintenance costs?
    (A) He led the public utilities.
    (B) No, it doesn't.
    (C) It's priceless.

23. Why did the seminar start so early?
    (A) Mr. Rogers will be in late today.
    (B) No, the shop is closed at seven.
    (C) We had a lot to discuss.

24. Isn't Sam out of the office this week?
    (A) Actually, his trip was rescheduled.
    (B) It's close to the office building.
    (C) More samples will arrive tomorrow.

25. Which parking area is for our customers?
    (A) The one that is on the corner.
    (B) It's twenty-five dollars a day.
    (C) Into the cabinet.

26. What department do you work in?
    (A) Research and development.
    (B) It stopped working.
    (C) There's a part missing.

27. Patrick's been working hard recently, hasn't he?
    (A) I would rather work on it later.
    (B) Actually, I thought it was simple.
    (C) Yes, he certainly has.

28. How do I know when the machine has finished washing the dishes?
    (A) You will hear a beeping sound.
    (B) Put them on top of the shelf.
    (C) Yes, I have finished working on it.

29. Why don't we leave for the theater right after dinner?
    (A) It leaves at noon.
    (B) That might be too late.
    (C) No, we can have dinner instead.

30. Will you be stopping by the post office or the bank?
    (A) Both actually.
    (B) Around eleven.
    (C) Yes, they're in the corner.

31. What time does the gallery open on Monday?
    (A) Actually, it's closed on Mondays.
    (B) There is a lot of artwork.
    (C) On Melissa Street.

Part 3

Questions 32-34 refer to the following conversation.

W: I would like to discuss the campaign for exhibiting at the trade show in April. Have you checked the rates for exhibiting at the venue yet?

M: I spoke with the event manager last week. The rates have increased dramatically since last year. Unfortunately, our budget does not allow us to take the same-sized display stand as last time.

W: We can save money by having a smaller stand. Last time, our display involved thirty products. We can reduce that number to twenty.

32. What type of event are the speakers planning to attend?
    (A) A trade exhibition
    (B) A sports event
    (C) A budget committee
    (D) An office opening

33. What problem does the man mention?
    (A) A venue is fully booked.
    (B) The cost has increased.
    (C) A company has gone bankrupt.
    (D) An exhibition has been canceled.

34. What does the woman recommend?
    (A) Reducing the size of the display
    (B) Contacting other venues
    (C) Promoting the event on television
    (D) Asking for a discount

Questions 35-37 refer to the following conversation.

W This is the manager of the Sunrise Hotel here. I have received a brochure about your marble floor tiles, and I would like to see some samples, if possible.
M I can send you a selection of what we have on offer if you would like to specify the color range you are interested in.
W Yes, please, that would be great. I also need someone who would be able to fit the tiles onto our floors. Do you offer that service?

35. What kind of product is the woman inquiring about?
(A) Computer software
(B) Flooring materials
(C) Lab equipment
(D) Hotel pieces

36. What does the man offer to do?
(A) Stop by the hotel
(B) Send the woman an order form
(C) Provide some samples
(D) Consult a flooring expert

37. What does the woman request?
(A) An instruction manual
(B) A use of a product
(C) An online tutorial
(D) A tile specialist

Questions 38-40 refer to the following conversation.

M Look at the line. The check-in area for the airline is full of people, and there is only one person at the check-in counter. It will take us ages to check our baggage.
W Yes, and we have less than 40 minutes before our flight. Why don't we use the express check-in service over there? It may be quicker.
M Good plan. But what if we have to pay extra? I only have traveler's checks on me. I wonder if they accept other forms of payments.
W I doubt it. But don't worry about it. I have a company credit card we can use.

38. What problem is mentioned about the airport?
(A) The check-in line is too long.
(B) The baggage area is blocked.
(C) An airplane has been delayed.
(D) An employee has not arrived.

39. What does the man ask the woman about?
(A) Payment options
(B) Business hours
(C) Round-trip airfares
(D) Beverage choices

40. What does the woman say she will do?
(A) Find another airline
(B) Lend the man some money
(C) Contact her office
(D) Use a credit card

Questions 41-43 refer to the following conversation.

W I see you have a new vacuum cleaner. Which brand is it? I need to buy one, but I have no idea which one is best.
M It's the Hurricane Power. Although it costs a little more than other models, I chose it because it seemed to perform better than the others.
W The Hurricane Power has received a lot of comments on the online forum. A lot of people complained about the accessories that come with it. Apparently, they can be quite difficult to attach.
M Yes, I heard that, but I haven't found that to be a problem. Why don't you visit the Elan Store? I got my cleaner from there, and they have a large selection.

41. What does the woman want to do?
(A) Purchase a product
(B) Read a product review
(C) Complain about a device
(D) Return an item

42. What did the woman read about the Hurricane Power?
(A) It is inexpensive.
(B) It is complicated to use.
(C) It is unreliable.
(D) It is the most popular model.

43. What does the man suggest the woman do?
(A) Post messages on a forum
(B) Browse online
(C) Contact a sales assistant
(D) Visit a specific store

Questions 44-46 refer to the following conversation.

M Good morning, Ms. Ross. I am Jeffrey from B&P Books. The diaries you ordered from our best-seller list are now ready. I can have them delivered on Friday afternoon.
W That would be great. I may be a little late, but please just put them through the mailbox.
M Unfortunately, it is against policy not to get a signature when delivering our merchandise. Perhaps Saturday would be better?
W Leave it with my son. I believe my son will be at his home on Friday, and he can sign for the items instead. Let me call him immediately, and I'll let you know if it's possible to deliver to his house then.

44. What type of business does the man work for?
(A) A food supply company
(B) A post office
(C) A bookstore
(D) A courier service

45. What policy does the man mention?
(A) Delivered goods must be put in the mailbox.
(B) The invoice must be issued on delivery.
(C) Damaged items must be returned to the supplier.
(D) A signature must be provided.

46. What does the woman want to check?
(A) Her shipping receipt
(B) Her son's availability
(C) Her order form
(D) Her tracking number

Questions 47-49 refer to the following conversation.

W   Mark, according to the present need, I have to make some changes in my schedule, as the regional director wants me to visit the newly purchased production facility, where I have to stay one more day. So I won't be able to return on Thursday.
M   Okay. I guess it won't be a problem. I will change your flight and hotel reservations. A rescheduled taxi will take you to the airport.
W   Actually, I'm thinking it would be better for me to rent a car near here. The facility is over 100 miles from the airport, and it would be easier and cost less to get there if I have my own vehicle.
M   That makes sense. I'll make all the necessary changes and get back to you.

47. What was the woman asked to do?
    (A) Drive a coworker to the airport
    (B) Prepare a presentation
    (C) Hire additional workers
    (D) Visit a production facility

48. What does the man imply when he says, "That makes sense"?
    (A) He will pick the woman up at the airport.
    (B) He thinks renting a car is a good idea.
    (C) He knows taking a taxi costs less.
    (D) He can send a taxi for the woman.

49. What does the woman decide to do?
    (A) Leave a meeting early
    (B) Get back to a branch manager
    (C) Use another form of transportation
    (D) Make extra copies of a report

Questions 50-52 refer to the following conversation.

W   Hi, I am calling to check on an insurance claim for my laptop. I misplaced it on a visit to Hawaii in June, and I still haven't received a check.
M   I'm sorry about that. When did you put the claim in?
W   I will have to check the exact date in my diary. But I am sure it was about four weeks ago.
M   Okay. Usually, it takes longer for us to pay claims for items lost abroad. There is a lot of paperwork to be examined. Let me take your claim number, and I will contact you tomorrow.

50. What does the woman want to discuss with the man?
    (A) A refund policy
    (B) A travel itinerary
    (C) A checklist sheet
    (D) An insurance claim

51. When does the woman say she submitted the paperwork?
    (A) In June
    (B) Yesterday
    (C) Last week
    (D) Last month

52. According to the man, what may have caused the delay?
    (A) Regular procedure
    (B) Computer errors
    (C) Lost paperwork
    (D) Foreign policy

Questions 53-55 refer to the following conversation.

W   When can we expect our foreign clients? We could entertain them on Friday evening. What do you think of the Cebuana Lounge? I went there last week, and they served exquisite food.
M   I understand that it is excellent, but we need to check what is available on the menu. It's possible for some of them to dislike Filipino dishes.
W   They also serve Spanish dishes as well as a selection of seafood and pasta, but why don't we check the full menu online? It will be quicker to use my smartphone for the Internet.

53. Who does the woman want to take to the Cebuana Lounge?
    (A) Clients
    (B) The management team
    (C) Family members
    (D) Colleagues

54. What does the man want to know about the restaurant?
    (A) Its menu
    (B) Its opening hours
    (C) Its prices
    (D) Its location

55. What does the woman suggest?
    (A) Using her mobile phone
    (B) Booking a table
    (C) Making a phone call
    (D) Checking room availability

Questions 56-58 refer to the following conversation with three speakers.

W   Mike, Henry, the director told me to inform you to discard unwanted items in accordance with the updated recycling guidelines.
M1 Okay, that's nice. I had heard that we are going to have new guidelines.
M2 Then, we need to recycle all the documents from now on, right?
W   Except for financial documents. Those are considered confidential materials. You should store them in the green bin at the corner of the hall.
M1 Where should we put the others?
W   Other documents, cardboard, and magazines can go in the regular recycling bins. Is it clear, Mike?
M2 Yes. Thanks for the information. Now that I have a clear idea about what to do, I can throw out all the unwanted papers now without worrying about it.

56. What is the woman mainly notifying the men of?
    (A) Financial confidentiality
    (B) Recycling guidelines
    (C) Client information
    (D) Presentation schedules

57. What are the men advised to do with confidential documents?
    (A) Keep them in their desk
    (B) Give them to the director
    (C) File them in a locked cabinet
    (D) Keep them in a special container

58. What does Mike imply when he says, "Thanks for the information"?
    (A) He's glad to be informed about the change.
    (B) He's not asked to comply with the regulations.
    (C) He's going to update all the financial documents.
    (D) He's allowed to store all the documents in a cabinet.

Questions 59-61 refer to the following conversation.

M Excuse me. Do you have this sweater in a different color? I'm looking for blue, but I can only find it in black.
W My apologies, sir. Black is the only color we have left. It is now part of the clearance sale, and we are not ordering any more of these items.
M That's a shame. I like the style of this sweater. There's nothing else like it in other shops.
W You could try looking at our online store, then. We may have some left in the color that you want and if so, you will still only be charged the sale price.

59. What is the man interested in purchasing?
(A) A coat
(B) A hat
(C) A sweater
(D) A scarf

60. What is the problem?
(A) A product is faulty.
(B) An item is unavailable in a certain color on site.
(C) Some merchandise has been misplaced.
(D) Some clothes are too expensive.

61. What does the woman suggest the man do?
(A) Check on the store's Web site
(B) Go to a different store
(C) Return within a week
(D) Choose another color

Questions 62-64 refer to the following conversation and report.

M Good morning, Jasmine. It's Aiden George from the accounts department. I want to make an appointment to discuss your expense claim. Can you come down between 10 and 11 A.M.?
W I heard that I only need to submit the expense report. What did I miss?
M You've missed one of the receipts. Let's see, that's the largest amount on the report.
W That's not good. I'm afraid I'm going out to visit a client now. I can make it in the afternoon, though.
M I will be in a meeting all afternoon. Let me check to see if my colleague Brandon is free then. I will call him now and get back to you.

62. What does the woman have to do in the morning?
(A) Meet with a customer
(B) Fill out an expense form
(C) Use her computer
(D) Organize a training session

63. Look at the graphic. Which item didn't the woman attach a receipt for?
(A) Round-trip ticket
(B) Hotel bills
(C) Car rental
(D) Meals

64. What does the man say he will do?
(A) Contact a colleague
(B) Create a database
(C) Reschedule his meeting
(D) Meet the woman in the afternoon

Questions 65-67 refer to the following conversation and table.

W Hi, this is the first time I've visited the art gallery. I heard that "Body Worlds" is now on display here.
M Indeed, the exhibition has been attracting a lot of attention. The only drawback is that currently there are too many people visiting this specific event, even though the tickets are expensive.
W No wonder. It's not common to see such a great exhibit in this town. I've always looked forward to it.
M In that case, can I book you in for the next available guided tour? It starts at 7 P.M.
W Is there any additional charge?
M No, it's free but must be booked in advance.
W That's perfect. I can be here then. In the meantime, I will look around the other halls.

65. What problem does the man mention?
(A) A piece of art is missing.
(B) A staff member is unavailable.
(C) Some displays are faulty.
(D) An exhibition is crowded.

66. Look at the graphic. Where is the exhibition the woman wants to see being held?
(A) Event Hall A
(B) Event Hall B
(C) Event Hall C
(D) Event Hall D

67. What will the woman do next?
(A) Stay with the man
(B) Get a free ticket at the box office
(C) Come back tomorrow
(D) Go and see another exhibit

Questions 68-70 refer to the following conversation and price list.

M Good morning, my name is Austin Phillips. I'm calling about the sports classes you advertised in the local paper.
W Hello, Mr. Phillips. The gym is right next to the Graham Complex, and we currently have boxing and yoga classes available.
M I'm interested in boxing classes. What time does the earliest class start?
W We have one at 6 A.M. if that suits your schedule. It's on Tuesdays and Thursdays.
M 6 A.M. is convenient for me. The Graham Complex is not that far from my office. How much is the tuition fee?
W It's $60 per month. If you pay for three months in advance, we give you a 10 percent discount.
M Okay, I'll do that. However, I don't have a decent pair of boxing shoes. Do you sell them or rent them out?
W No, we don't, but there's a sports shop on the first floor. And if you tell them you're our member, they take $10 off the regular price.
M I'll stop by in the evening and pay for three months, and get those shoes, too.

68. What is the man calling about?
(A) Taking sports lessons
(B) Moving into the Graham Complex
(C) Returning a pair of boxing gloves
(D) Leaving his office earlier than usual

69. Look at the graphic. How much is the man going to pay for the equipment he needs?
(A) $44
(B) $64
(C) $152
(D) $162

70. What is suggested about the gym?
(A) It closes at 6 P.M.
(B) It's on the first floor.
(C) It's near the Graham Complex.
(D) It is far from Mr. Phillips's office.

Part 4

Questions 71-73 refer to the following announcement.

Welcome to all members of staff. Thank you for attending this event, which is celebrating the promotion of Charles Bailey to the general manager of IT. Charles has spent over 15 years with the company, beginning as a technician in the factory before working his way up the ladder to specialize in the computerization of this manufacturing company. Now he will be able to spend more time in the office rather than the factory floor. I would like to congratulate Charles for the dedication and loyalty that he has shown to this company and present him with a special gift that marks 15 years of service. Charles, please join me to accept this gift.

71. What special event is being held?
(A) A retirement event
(B) A training session
(C) A grand opening ceremony
(D) A promotion party

72. What is Charles Bailey's profession?
(A) Computer specialist
(B) Office manager
(C) Mechanic
(D) Factory operative

73. What will most likely happen next?
(A) Some refreshments will be offered.
(B) An interview will be conducted.
(C) A seminar will take place.
(D) A gift will be presented.

Questions 74-76 refer to the following telephone message.

Good morning! I am calling to make an appointment with Dr. Stevenson. I was released from Kenwood Hospital last week, but I am still not well enough to return to work. Kenwood Hospital is too far from my house, so I want to consult Dr. Stevenson about what kinds of painkillers are more suitable for me. I'm out to buy something soon, so I would like to make an appointment to see the doctor this afternoon if that is possible. Please call me back at 765-4803. Thank you.

74. What kind of business is the speaker calling?
(A) A holiday resort
(B) A medical clinic
(C) An employment agency
(D) A pharmaceutical company

75. What does the speaker ask about?
(A) Vaccination requirements
(B) Better medication
(C) A medicine price
(D) A return to work

76. When does the speaker say she will be available?
(A) This morning
(B) This afternoon
(C) Tomorrow morning
(D) Tomorrow afternoon

Questions 77-79 refer to the following instructions.

This week, every member of the front-of-shop sales team has to attend a demonstration on operating the new electronic cash register. The session will take place on Thursday, October 11, during the lunch break. This also applies to the temporary staff. I am also handing out a leaflet on the new cash register, which I want you to familiarize yourselves with before Thursday. This will explain how the new equipment works and how it is directly connected to the order department. You will see how it works in detail at the demonstration.

77. What will happen on October 11?
(A) Lunchtime will be extended.
(B) Paychecks will be distributed.
(C) A leaflet will be sent out.
(D) A demonstration will take place.

78. What does the woman imply when she says, "This also applies to the temporary staff"?
(A) They are not included in a lunchtime session.
(B) They are required to fill out a form.
(C) They will receive less pay.
(D) They must be in attendance.

79. What are listeners asked to read?
(A) A customer questionnaire
(B) A health and safety document
(C) An instruction flyer
(D) Dismissal procedures

Questions 80-82 refer to the following introduction.

Welcome, everyone, to our annual awards ceremony at the Guild of Master Practitioners. This year, we have been concentrating on the theme of sustainable development without damage to the environment, and tonight, those who have effected a change in the workplace using sustainable methods will be awarded. All of the nominations and categories can be found in the booklets you will find on your seats. And *Good Energy Magazine* has kindly sponsored tonight's event.

80. What will happen at the event?
(A) A sustainable program will be reviewed.
(B) A magazine will be introduced.
(C) Awards will be presented.
(D) New legislation will be announced.

81. What can listeners find on their seats?
(A) Information about past projects
(B) Results of a questionnaire
(C) A membership form
(D) A list of nominations

82. What is mentioned about *Good Energy Magazine*?
(A) It is a leading magazine in the environment.
(B) It is supporting the event.
(C) It is recruiting new practitioners.
(D) It is found on the seats.

Questions 83-85 refer to the following excerpt from a talk.

One more thing before you leave. Can you ensure that all items are properly stored away when you lock up? This mainly concerns the factory staff. I have posted a Health and Safety brochure on the noticeboard that explains how to safely store chemicals and preservatives. It also details correct handling techniques for these hazardous substances when using the items in the automobile painting shop. If the items are properly stored in the correct place, we can begin work much more efficiently in the mornings.

83. Who is the speaker most likely addressing?
    (A) Safety inspectors
    (B) Interior designers
    (C) Factory workers
    (D) Laundry staff

84. What is the main topic of the talk?
    (A) Car painting
    (B) Appliance repairs
    (C) Factory inspections
    (D) Safety procedures

85. Where will listeners find the guidelines?
    (A) Near the chemicals
    (B) In the preservatives
    (C) On a bulletin board
    (D) In front of the paint shop

Questions 86-88 refer to the following recorded message.

Thank you for contacting the Doris Fitness Center. We are located in the Tintroy Building near the Danao subway station, a block away from the city hall. We offer a range of sports classes, such as Aerobics, Yoga, Table Tennis, and Squash. We are currently offering a new Tae-Bo class, with two experienced trainers from Korea. We are open every weekday between 6 A.M. and 9 P.M. If you wish to sign up for the new class, please press one now.

86. Where is the fitness center located?
    (A) In the vicinity of Danao City
    (B) Near a subway station
    (C) Right next to the city hall
    (D) In front of the community center

87. What class is newly offered?
    (A) Aerobics
    (B) Yoga
    (C) Squash
    (D) Tae-Bo

88. Why would listeners press one?
    (A) To cancel a class
    (B) To arrange a tutorial
    (C) To enroll in a class
    (D) To get directions

Questions 89-91 refer to the following excerpt from a meeting.

Lastly, I have good news for everyone. We began this current quarter aiming to increase the market share of our Shiny Clean range in the eastern region by 10 percent. I am delighted to announce that this has been achieved. Due to a larger client base, we are expanding operations and opening a new branch in Wilmington. The store needs experienced staff, and we would like to hire those who are currently working here at headquarters. If you are interested in relocating to Wilmington, please let me know as soon as possible. The final date for receiving applications is in three weeks' time, on June 15, and the following week, we will be shortlisting candidates.

89. What has Shiny Clean accomplished over the quarter?
    (A) It launched a new range of products.
    (B) It relocated to Wilmington.
    (C) It increased its share in a specific market.
    (D) It recruited more employees.

90. Who is encouraged to apply for the new position in Wilmington?
    (A) Employees with several years' experience
    (B) Current staff willing to relocate
    (C) Sales managers with an interest in cleaning products
    (D) Those with experience in managing stores

91. What does the man imply when he says, "I have good news for everyone"?
    (A) He's pleased to let everyone know about their success.
    (B) He's willing to move to the headquarters.
    (C) He's glad to have more staff in the new branch.
    (D) He's happy to have a lot of candidates.

Questions 92-94 refer to the following advertisement.

Come and join Aerial Helicopters on a journey across the city of Cairo. This exciting tour encompasses the sites along the Nile, covering the ancient monuments and the mighty structures as dusk begins to fall on them. We are the only aerial tour in the city that operates at sunset. Our tour guides will take you on an audio journey, explaining the history of the city's rise from a Middle Eastern village to the center of trade and commerce. The helicopter tour leaves from Cairo Airport and lasts 50 minutes. In order to comply with health and safety regulations, we ask you to arrive 30 minutes prior to the stated departure times.

92. What kind of service is being advertised?
    (A) Online reservations
    (B) Aerial tours
    (C) Vehicle rental
    (D) Boat rides

93. According to the speaker, what is special about the service?
    (A) It is exclusively a daytime trip.
    (B) It is a brand-new service.
    (C) It takes off once a week.
    (D) It takes place at dusk.

94. What are listeners asked to do?
    (A) Provide a health certificate
    (B) Carry identification
    (C) Reserve a place
    (D) Arrive early

Questions 95-97 refer to the following telephone message and contact list.

Good afternoon. This is Harold Scott, and I am the manager of the George Fisher Restaurant. I have received a leaflet from your business and would like some details. We have recently been unhappy with our current supplier, so I would be very interested in your organic flour if you can guarantee daily deliveries to us. My telephone number is 567-0271. Can you call me back, as I would like to get some samples?

95. Who is the speaker?
(A) A delivery man
(B) A restaurant manager
(C) A grocer
(D) A millworker

96. What does the speaker intend to do?
(A) Offer an online service
(B) Alter a menu
(C) Deliver to local bakeries
(D) Change his supplier

97. Look at the graphic. Which store is the man most likely calling?
(A) Miller's Joy
(B) Herbalist's Delight
(C) Mrs. Millers'
(D) Harmony

Questions 98-100 refer to the following telephone message and schedule.

Hello, this is Walter James calling for Professor Bonnie Holt. I am a presenter on YSBC TV and I am doing a research for a feature on adult obesity. I saw your lecture on "Eating Habits of Adults" live yesterday, and I would like to talk to you about your views on eliminating fats from the diet. I understand that as a university lecturer and a regular newspaper columnist you are very busy, but I would like to come and see you. I'm visiting your university the day after tomorrow. We would very much like to feature your opinions and research within the broadcast.

98. According to the speaker, what has Professor Holt recently done?
(A) Delivered a lecture
(B) Organized a seminar
(C) Participated in a university debate
(D) Published an article

99. Look at the graphic. When does Mr. James say he wants to meet Professor Holt?
(A) Tuesday
(B) Wednesday
(C) Thursday
(D) Friday

100. What does the speaker ask Professor Holt to do?
(A) Contribute to a TV program
(B) Undertake a newspaper interview
(C) Review some books
(D) Take a university lecture

10회

1.	(B)	21.	(A)	41.	(C)	61.	(D)	81.	(D)
2.	(D)	22.	(B)	42.	(C)	62.	(A)	82.	(D)
3.	(A)	23.	(C)	43.	(A)	63.	(B)	83.	(B)
4.	(C)	24.	(B)	44.	(D)	64.	(C)	84.	(D)
5.	(A)	25.	(C)	45.	(C)	65.	(D)	85.	(C)
6.	(D)	26.	(A)	46.	(A)	66.	(B)	86.	(D)
7.	(A)	27.	(C)	47.	(B)	67.	(D)	87.	(A)
8.	(B)	28.	(A)	48.	(C)	68.	(A)	88.	(C)
9.	(C)	29.	(C)	49.	(B)	69.	(B)	89.	(A)
10.	(C)	30.	(B)	50.	(C)	70.	(C)	90.	(B)
11.	(A)	31.	(C)	51.	(A)	71.	(A)	91.	(C)
12.	(B)	32.	(C)	52.	(D)	72.	(D)	92.	(B)
13.	(B)	33.	(B)	53.	(D)	73.	(A)	93.	(C)
14.	(A)	34.	(A)	54.	(B)	74.	(D)	94.	(A)
15.	(A)	35.	(C)	55.	(B)	75.	(B)	95.	(C)
16.	(B)	36.	(D)	56.	(C)	76.	(C)	96.	(C)
17.	(A)	37.	(B)	57.	(D)	77.	(B)	97.	(C)
18.	(B)	38.	(D)	58.	(A)	78.	(D)	98.	(B)
19.	(B)	39.	(A)	59.	(A)	79.	(C)	99.	(C)
20.	(C)	40.	(A)	60.	(C)	80.	(A)	100.	(D)

Part 1

1.
(A) He's serving food in a restaurant.
(B) He's cooking meat on a grill.
(C) He's pouring water into a container.
(D) He's holding a mixing bowl.

2.
(A) Some people are looking for their bags.
(B) Some people are staring at their notebooks.
(C) Some people are standing next to the chairs.
(D) Some people are waiting on the subway platform.

3.
(A) Clothes are hanging on some racks.
(B) Clothes are being carried upstairs.
(C) A customer is trying on a dress.
(D) Clothes are being stacked neatly on the shelves.

4.
(A) A man is reaching over his chair.
(B) A man is opening a book.
(C) A man is writing something down.
(D) A man is turning on a lamp.

5.
(A) A woman is admiring a painting.
(B) A woman is hanging up a picture.
(C) A woman is leaning against a wall.
(D) A floor is being mopped.

6.
(A) A roof is being repaired.
(B) People are sweeping the floor.
(C) Lights are being turned on.
(D) Columns line a walkway.

Part 2

7. When did Kelly clean out the living room?
(A) After we left.
(B) She lived there.
(C) She cleaned the supply room.

8. Where is your new house located?
(A) Two hours from now.
(B) It's next to the post office.
(C) I don't think he's late in the morning.

9. How much did sales revenue increase this year?
   (A) Yes, it is now on sale.
   (B) By year's end.
   (C) By 20%.

10. Would you have more dessert?
    (A) No, he didn't.
    (B) At the restaurant.
    (C) Yes, that would be great!

11. Who informed the employees of the schedule changes?
    (A) The human resources department.
    (B) A lot of changes.
    (C) With their colleagues.

12. Which dates do you want to reserve a restaurant table for?
    (A) I placed an order for a table.
    (B) From the 14th to the 15th, please.
    (C) It's downstairs.

13. The dinner comes with free side dishes, doesn't it?
    (A) He wants to come with me.
    (B) That's right.
    (C) It's excellent and tasty.

14. Aren't we waiting for the same bus?
    (A) No, mine departs earlier.
    (B) The food truck is at the corner of the street.
    (C) You can wait for some of these.

15. Do you know which dish the customer ordered?
    (A) The pasta on the blue plate.
    (B) I'd prefer pizza.
    (C) In the dining room.

16. Do you have the shirts in stock?
    (A) Under 10 dollars.
    (B) They are all sold out.
    (C) You wear the red shirts.

17. Please let us know when you finish using the copy machine.
    (A) Sure, I'll be done in a minute.
    (B) For the new supply room.
    (C) No, it isn't working now.

18. Should we provide a free dinner at the conference or just cold beverages?
    (A) He provided me with a gift.
    (B) It would be great to serve some food.
    (C) At 9 in the morning.

19. What was Tim from the R&D department asked to submit this Monday?
    (A) Right, I'll ask him to do it.
    (B) The report on last month's test results.
    (C) Late on Monday evening.

20. Serena took a test, didn't she?
    (A) I failed the test.
    (B) After the result came out.
    (C) I'll ask her.

21. How did a new delivery man enter the building?
    (A) The security team let him in.
    (B) The building was opened last month.
    (C) It was not delivered on time.

22. Where should I hang the accounting certificate?
    (A) This Wednesday.
    (B) Maybe behind the desk on the wall?
    (C) For a gift certificate.

23. We had better let Kimberley find the location.
    (A) At the post office.
    (B) Please get on the bus.
    (C) But Karen knows this area better than anyone.

24. How do you know if the food is safe?
    (A) Food and beverage, I think.
    (B) Check the date marked on the container.
    (C) At the store.

25. Why was Mr. Anthony out of town?
    (A) The town held a festival last year.
    (B) They will be there within an hour.
    (C) He went on a business trip.

26. Would you like to stay here or go to a hotel?
    (A) I don't want to walk anymore.
    (B) The hotel is all booked up.
    (C) Yes, I do.

27. I can't reach the top shelf.
    (A) Maybe it's next to the restroom.
    (B) No, you don't need a top score.
    (C) You can use the ladder from a warehouse.

28. Can we delay our dinner until next Tuesday?
    (A) The restaurant will charge a cancellation fee.
    (B) For a dinner reservation.
    (C) Yes, it was an excellent dinner.

29. How soon will I receive the results of the request?
    (A) Yes, I left home earlier than usual.
    (B) Your proposal will be accepted.
    (C) We'll call you next Thursday.

30. Are you ready to end the test, or do you still need some more time?
    (A) We will arrive at the classroom.
    (B) Our class doesn't finish until 6.
    (C) Is Mr. Button moving to Australia?

31. The hotel cannot accommodate any more tourists.
    (A) Just a few kilometers from the city hall.
    (B) Yes, we'll book a reservation for a restaurant tomorrow.
    (C) I will call other hotels to see if they are available.

Part 3

Questions 32-34 refer to the following conversation.

W Mr. Dickerson, this is Jane Roberts from Mulberry Publishing. I am calling to let you know that we'd like to publish some recipes from your blog.
M That's fantastic. I've been a big fan of your company for a long time. You have published some great cookbooks. So it would be a great opportunity for me, and I think my recipes would be a good fit.
W We do believe they would be suitable for publication. Actually, I'd like you to visit our company to discuss details about your book. So please let me know when you are available.

32. What did the man write about?
    (A) His favorite pets
    (B) Visiting famous museums
    (C) How to make various dishes
    (D) Writing stories on a blog

33. Why is the man delighted?
    (A) He was given a prize for his writings.
    (B) His work will be published.
    (C) His articles earned favorable reviews.
    (D) He was promoted to editor in a publishing company.

34. Why does the woman want to meet with the man?
    (A) To talk about a future project
    (B) To reschedule an appointment
    (C) To receive some samples
    (D) To organize an exhibition

Questions 35-37 refer to the following conversation.

W   I think your pharmacy received a prescription for some medicine from my doctor nearly 30 minutes ago. I'm wondering if the order is ready for me. My name is Joshua Jane.
M   Let me check on that. Yes, we got the order. But I'm sorry, it's not ready yet. Monday is the busiest day for our pharmacy, so we're getting behind with our work. If you wait ten more minutes, it will be ready.
W   All right. I will spend some time shopping at a nearby store and come back in a little while to pick up my prescription.

35. What are the speakers discussing?
    (A) A shopping list
    (B) A tourist attraction
    (C) A doctor's prescription
    (D) A canceled appointment

36. Why is the man behind schedule?
    (A) A staff member is out sick.
    (B) A doctor didn't write him a prescription.
    (C) He went out for lunch.
    (D) A pharmacy has been busy.

37. What does the woman say she will do?
    (A) Visit the doctor's office
    (B) Go to a nearby store
    (C) Make a phone call
    (D) Make an appointment

Questions 38-40 refer to the following conversation.

M   Hello, this is Timothy Adams from AIF Electronics. Our records indicate that you've purchased a product in our store before, so we'd like to inform you of our special promotion this week. We will give you a 15 percent discount coupon for newly-released TVs through your online account.
W   Unfortunately, I just bought a TV, but I am planning to buy another air conditioner soon.
M   Umm… If you'd like, I can send you a text message about any future promotions.

38. Why is the man calling?
    (A) To schedule a meeting
    (B) To complain about a product
    (C) To check a delivery schedule
    (D) To advertise a special promotion

39. What types of products does the man's company sell?
    (A) Home appliances
    (B) Computers
    (C) Office supplies
    (D) Furniture

40. What does the man offer to do for the woman?
    (A) Send a message
    (B) Refund her in full
    (C) Offer free delivery
    (D) Call her office

Questions 41-43 refer to the following conversation.

M   Hello, this is Jonathan Edwards in room 1213. The air conditioner in this room isn't working properly. Although the unit turns on, the air isn't cold.
W   I'm sorry, sir. Sadly, none of our repairmen is available right now. Instead, I can change your room, and I'll upgrade you to an executive suite free of charge. Would that be okay?
M   Great. But would you send someone to move my luggage to the new room immediately? Because I don't have time to do it myself. I have to go to a client meeting right away.

41. What is the man's complaint?
    (A) His room is dirty.
    (B) His reservation was canceled.
    (C) His air conditioner is broken.
    (D) His room is too small.

42. What does the woman offer to the man?
    (A) A free meal
    (B) A free shuttle bus to the airport
    (C) A room upgrade
    (D) A gift certificate

43. What does the man request?
    (A) Help with his luggage
    (B) A room change
    (C) Free Internet service
    (D) A discount coupon

Questions 44-46 refer to the following conversation.

W   Thank you for calling Boston Clinic. This is Carey speaking. How can I help you?
M   Hi, my name is Michael Kane. I am scheduled to go on a trip to Africa next month, so I need to get vaccinated. Is it possible to make an appointment?
W   Unfortunately, we are fully booked this week, Mr. Kane, but we have several openings available next week. Does 11 A.M. work for you on Tuesday?
M   Sorry, that's not going to work.
W   Okay. Then, what about 3 P.M. on Wednesday? Can you make it?
M   That works for me. Thank you. I'll see you then.

44. Where does the woman work?
    (A) At a travel agency
    (B) At a department store
    (C) At a national museum
    (D) At a health clinic

45. What does the man say he will be doing next month?
    (A) Participating in a conference
    (B) Making a presentation
    (C) Traveling overseas
    (D) Writing a novel

46. What does the man imply when he says, "that's not going to work"?
    (A) He needs a different appointment.
    (B) He does not work on that day.
    (C) He prefers to work on schedule.
    (D) He will go abroad.

Questions 47-49 refer to the following conversation.

M Hi, Monica. How are you?
W Fine. I've been waiting to talk to you. I'm saving up my money to buy a house. I've heard that you bought one recently.
M Right, and I'm thrilled. It was really tough for me to cut down on expenses and save up for it. I was able to do it thanks to an online money-saving program.
W And it helped?
M Absolutely. If you want to try it, I recommend money-saving.com.
W Hmm… How much does it cost? It might not be a good idea to spend money to save money.
M Well, they are now offering a one-month free trial. It would be a good opportunity for you to see if you like it. And it's only $50 a year.
W I'll take a look at it. Thank you.

47. Why does the woman want to save money?
(A) To replace a computer
(B) To purchase a house
(C) To go on vacation
(D) To buy a car

48. What does the man recommend?
(A) Applying for a loan
(B) Selling a house
(C) Using an online program
(D) Cutting down on expenses

49. What is the woman concerned about?
(A) Web site reliability
(B) Service costs
(C) Scheduling conflicts
(D) A program's expiration date

Questions 50-52 refer to the following conversation.

M Hi, Ms. Fox? It's Gabriel Silva. Have you looked at the final version of the design for your online advertisement?
W Yes, I thought the design matches what I wanted. I particularly like the way you modified the logo of my store.
M I'm pleased that you like it. Before we finalize this project, what about making the logo a little bigger?
W Yes! It's a good idea! I think an ad with a larger logo enables people to recognize the store's name better.

50. Who most likely is the woman?
(A) A graphic designer
(B) An advertising agent
(C) A store owner
(D) A writer

51. What is the woman pleased about?
(A) A final draft of an advertisement
(B) Recent online reviews
(C) A store location
(D) Contact information

52. What does the man offer to do?
(A) Install a computer program
(B) Confirm service request
(C) Print an advertisement
(D) Enlarge an image

Questions 53-55 refer to the following conversation.

M Amie, why are you still at your office? Aren't you participating in the company charity event today?
W I took part in the event last year, but this time around I should take care of some delays regarding some of our translation service last month.
M Oh, that's too bad. What happened?
W Some customers complained about receiving their translations too late. And I'm really concerned, as I'm not sure how to handle this issue to resolve their inconvenience.
M I understand. I'm pretty sure you'll do all right. Actually, I've done this same thing before. I need to volunteer at the charity event now, but I'll discuss this at the next staff meeting tomorrow to find the best ways to make up for the customers' inconvenience.

53. What does the woman imply when she says, "I'm really concerned"?
(A) She is able to do volunteer work.
(B) She is proud of attending the event.
(C) She is indifferent about the matter.
(D) She is worried about the complaints.

54. What is the woman concerned about?
(A) Making a presentation
(B) Responding to client complaints
(C) Translating a different language
(D) Doing multiple tasks at the same time

55. What does the man say he will do tomorrow?
(A) Submit some paperwork
(B) Bring a problem up at a meeting
(C) Prepare the event
(D) Conduct a customer survey

Questions 56-58 refer to the following conversation with three speakers.

W1 Thank you for coming for an interview on such short notice, Mr. McCain. I'm Amber Hayek, manager of the human resources department here at ABF Books.
W2 And I'm Kate Stone. I am in charge of the Children's Books division.
M   Good to see you.
W2 We've looked your résumé and career history, and you seem to be eligible for the director of the design team. However, we're concerned that you might not want the position, as it requires some overtime work. We have a new series due out in November.
M   I understand that. That's no problem.
W1 Okay, so let's take a look at some of your work. I heard that you brought a portfolio. Can you show us?
M   Sure, just a minute.

56. Where do the interviewers most likely work?
(A) At a bookstore
(B) At a kindergarten
(C) At a publisher
(D) At a broadcasting company

57. What job requirement do the speakers discuss?
(A) Possessing the proper license
(B) Owning some film equipment
(C) Having related experience
(D) Being able to work extra hours

58. What does the man agree to do next?
(A) Show some previous work
(B) Conduct a survey
(C) Watch a presentation
(D) Meet a president

Questions 59-61 refer to the following conversation.

W   Okay, Lemar. Here's our problem. For the past three months, the number of customers visiting our restaurant has decreased by 15 percent compared to last year. So, we need to do something to attract more customers. I'd like to hear your opinions, as you're the head chef of our restaurant.
M   Well, how about offering a discount for Friday and the weekend? I'll create healthy and appealing menus that are not too expensive.
W   Okay, that's a good idea! Let's get started. I want you to prepare samples before putting them on the menu.

59. What problem does the woman mention?
(A) Business is unusually slow.
(B) A restaurant received several complaints.
(C) A restaurant is short-staffed.
(D) The rent has been gone up.

60. What does the man suggest?
(A) Offering an outdoor event
(B) Moving into a different location
(C) Lowering prices
(D) Acquiring popular restaurants

61. What does the woman ask the man to do?
(A) Hire a manager
(B) Train employees
(C) Get ready for the holiday season
(D) Prepare some food samples

Questions 62-64 refer to the following conversation.

M   Linsey, I want to talk about my presentation for the medical science conference.
W   I'm so sorry; it slipped my mind.
M   That's okay. I heard that you've been busy doing pioneering research into the new medicine for liver cancer.
W   Yeah. The results are impressive. We'll be able to create the medication within two years.
M   That's fantastic! So, can I show you some slides right now? They are related to your research.
W   Great.
M   All right. Would you please check if all the researchers' names are included on the final page of the slides?
W   Okay. Let me see… um… Wait! Didn't Martial participate in this project?
M   Oh, you're right! Thanks for the help.

62. What industry do the speakers most likely work in?
(A) Pharmaceutical
(B) Finance
(C) Construction
(D) Entertainment

63. What does the woman say will happen within two years?
(A) Some research will receive a prize.
(B) A new product will be introduced.
(C) A company will hire more employees.
(D) Another conference will be held.

64. What does the woman imply when she says, "Didn't Martial participate in this project"?
(A) Some results are not promising.
(B) A project will be finished soon.
(C) A slide is missing some information.
(D) The man must attend the conference.

Questions 65-67 refer to the following conversation and building directory.

W   Hi, I had an appointment to see the doctor at 11 A.M. I was a bit late because parking was tricky in this building, and I couldn't find where I should pay for parking.
M   As a matter of fact, parking fees are free for visitors in this building, and we will validate the tickets you received when you entered the building.
W   That's great. This is the first time I'm visiting Dr. Lauren. Her name is not listed on the building directory, though. Please tell me where I should go.
M   Dr. Lauren just moved in just three days ago, so we didn't have much time to change it. We will ask the building manager to list her name as soon as possible. She's in Suite 114.

65. What is the purpose of the woman's visit?
(A) To deliver a package
(B) To have a client meeting
(C) To go to the pharmacy
(D) To have a medical appointment

66. What does the man say about parking?
(A) It is available on the street near the building.
(B) It is free for visitors with a validated parking ticket.
(C) It is for tenants in the building.
(D) It has a time limit.

67. Look at the graphic. Which office name has to be updated on the building directory?
(A) Prudential Finance
(B) York Foods
(C) UK Express
(D) Morris International

Questions 68-70 refer to the following conversation and invoice.

W   Will that be all, sir? Just the new computer, a computer bag, and a case?
M   I'd like to ask you one last question before I buy the laptop. Do I have to pay for this all at once? I want to buy this on an installment plan, if possible.
W   Yes, you can. I can set that up for you. For this week only, we are offering an interest-free installment plan for up to 12 months.
M   Okay, that's great! Umm… I've changed my mind, though. I don't think I really need the extended warranty. It already comes with a two-year warranty. Could you remove that from my invoice?
W   Yes. No problem.

68. Who most likely is the woman?
(A) A salesperson
(B) An engineer
(C) A bank clerk
(D) A computer programmer

69. What does the man ask about?
(A) A contract renewal
(B) A payment method
(C) Computer accessories
(D) The price of a computer

70. Look at the graphic. Which amount will be removed from the invoice?
(A) $50
(B) $80
(C) $200
(D) $1500

Part 4

Questions 71-73 refer to the following information.

Welcome back to The Interviews on AKSP Radio Station. Today's guest is Dr. Kasper Dooling, professor of business administration at the University of Copenhagen and author of the recently-released best seller *How to Use Your Time Wisely*. Today, Dr. Dooling will share his insights into the best ways to manage your valuable time. From now on, he will be asked questions from listeners over the phone. Please call us here at 555-0198 if you have any questions for Dr. Dooling.

71. Where does the speaker work?
(A) At a radio station
(B) At a bookstore
(C) At a university
(D) At a consulting firm

72. What will Dr. Dooling be discussing?
(A) Career management
(B) Publishing books
(C) Communication skills
(D) Time management

73. What does the speaker encourage listeners to do?
(A) Call in with questions
(B) Register in advance
(D) Save money
(D) Buy more books

Questions 74-76 refer to the following telephone message.

Hi, Ms. Ederson, it's Wagner. I'm still waiting for the airline to find my suitcase, which has our new microwave oven in it. Given the circumstances, I think that they bring me nothing before my presentation on Monday. And if so, without a prototype, the presentation won't make a deep impression on the audience. At this point, therefore, I think the best option is for you to bring another prototype here in person. I know it's a difficult job, but I think there's no other way.

74. What is the man waiting for?
(A) His passport to be issued
(B) His airline ticket to be purchased
(C) His colleagues to arrive
(D) His luggage to be returned

75. What is scheduled for Monday?
(A) A meeting
(B) A product presentation
(C) A doctor's appointment
(D) A press conference

76. Why does the man say, "I know it's a difficult job"?
(A) To advise the listener to finish the job quickly
(B) To warn that the job is unnecessary
(C) To apologize for an inconvenience
(D) To remind the listener of its risks

Questions 77-79 refer to the following excerpt from a meeting.

As you know, we are now installing fingerprint reader devices at the entrance to enhance the security of the building. Employees will have to scan their enrolled finger on the fingerprint reader whenever they enter the building, starting next Tuesday. So, please make sure that all employees register their fingerprints by the end of this week. It won't take long to register, but this registration process will have to be finished before the new system is introduced on Tuesday.

77. What is the talk mainly about?
(A) A wage system
(B) Security enhancements
(C) Head office relocation
(D) A training schedule

78. According to the speaker, what will happen on Tuesday?
(A) Additional staff will be employed.
(B) An inspection will be carried out.
(C) Office supplies will be purchased.
(D) New procedures will take effect.

79. What must employees do this week?
(A) Use a different entrance
(B) Update a company's accounts
(C) Register their fingerprints
(D) Apply for the program

Questions 80-82 refer to the following excerpt from a meeting.

As you already know, employees are using our coffee makers in the staff lounge all day long. As they are old models, we're thinking about changing these coffee machines. So tomorrow, three providers will be offering different coffee machines in the lobby. You can taste free cups of coffee from these devices. What we want to do is just gathering some feedback. It will help us know which one you prefer. Plus, the feedback form only takes around 5 minutes to complete, and you can leave the forms with Belotti in the maintenance department.

80. What does the speaker say the company is considering?
(A) Buying a new product
(B) Changing the lunch time
(C) Starting a new business
(D) Extending business hours

81. What can listeners receive for free tomorrow?
(A) A laptop
(B) A T-shirt with a company logo
(C) Stationery
(D) Beverages

82. Why should listeners visit Belotti's office?
(A) To pick up an employee ID card
(B) To sign up for an employee program
(C) To donate money
(D) To submit a form

Questions 83-85 refer to the following announcement.

Attention, employees in the production line. As you know, the operation of the conveyor belt is temporarily suspended. The staff from the maintenance department said that belt repairs will take approximately six hours. The production line will resume after the completion of its repairs. Meanwhile, all production line employees will be assigned to special duties. Assembly managers will call you to offer more details about schedule changes for tomorrow's work.

83. Where most likely is this announcement being made?
(A) At a customer service center
(B) At a factory
(C) At a department store
(D) At an auto repair shop

84. What problem does the speaker mention?
(A) Some supplies are sold out.
(B) A manager is sick.
(C) Inclement weather is expected.
(D) Some equipment is not working.

85. What will employees be informed about by assembly managers?
(A) Test results
(B) Safety regulations
(C) Work schedule changes
(D) Hygiene inspection

Questions 86-88 refer to the following news report.

Good morning. This is Prime News on Channel 11. According to a recent study released by *UPG Food Magazine*, the best healthy food is home-made meals. Those who participated in the survey were asked about their eating habits and the results revealed that people eating food cooked at home tended to consume more fruits and vegetables compared to people eating food at restaurants. Dr. Jessie Watson, who led the study, said that individuals have to make their own meals to control what they eat better. You can check a full list of questions participants answered on the *UPG Food Magazine* Web site.

86. What is the news report about?
(A) A celebrity's recipe book
(B) A new seafood restaurant
(C) Tips for selecting vegetables
(D) Healthy eating habits

87. What does Dr. Watson recommend that people do?
(A) Prepare meals at home
(B) Buy special equipment
(C) Enroll in a cooking class
(D) Download recipes online

88. According to the speaker, what can listeners do on a Web site?
(A) Make a reservation
(B) Place an order
(C) Read some survey questions
(D) Sign up for a subscription

Questions 89-91 refer to the following excerpt from a meeting.

Before we start the staff meeting, I have an announcement to make. I've just found out that our president, Jessica Stewart, will make a visit to our office next Monday. As you already know, the renovation project was just finished, and it was designed to enhance the working environment in branch offices as well as at the headquarters. The president is making visits to all our offices, and we're next. Now, as this is not a formal visit, extensive preparations are not necessary. However, there will be a luncheon for her. Please come and give her a warm welcome and let me know your availability by Thursday.

89. Why is the president coming for a visit?
(A) A project has been completed.
(B) A facility has been moved.
(C) A manager will retire.
(D) A sales record has been accomplished.

90. Why does the speaker say, "this is not a formal visit"?
(A) To settle a dispute
(B) To reassure employees
(C) To apologize for problems
(D) To check a procedure

91. What event have the listeners been invited to?
(A) A retirement party
(B) An opening ceremony
(C) A welcome reception
(D) A dinner party

Questions 92-94 refer to the following information and floor plan.

And that completes the tour of the oil painting collections. If you want to learn more about the exhibition, you can find a museum guidebook in our gift shop. I hope you stop by and purchase the book. That's because it is highly recommended by renowned artists and critics. Now that we finished the tour, please continue exploring the artworks on your own. For your convenience, a map of the museum is ready at the entrance. And you don't want to miss the opportunity to see Chagall's work in our modern art gallery, which is located next to the museum entrance.

92. What did the listeners see on the tour?
(A) Sculptures
(B) Paintings
(C) Photographs
(D) Pottery

93. What does the guide recommend listeners do to learn more about the exhibition?
(A) Visit a Web site
(B) Attend a program
(C) Buy a book
(D) Watch a related movie

94. Look at the graphic. In which room is the exhibition on the works of Chagall?
(A) Gallery 1
(B) Gallery 2
(C) Gallery 3
(D) Gallery 4

Questions 95-97 refer to the following announcement and map.

Attention, Delta Controls employees. As announced last Friday, there will be a street parade this afternoon. And because of this, the streets in the area will be closed to traffic this afternoon, from two o'clock. It will end by five, so you don't need to worry about your commute home. However, those who have parked their cars in the basement, please keep in mind that you cannot take your cars out during the event. In particular, if you have an off-site duty, please move your car into the paid parking area right next to Mayfair Park now. The parking fee will be covered by the company.

95. Why is the announcement being made?
    (A) To inform listeners about a change in working hours
    (B) To encourage employees to take part in the parade
    (C) To notify listeners of the unavailability of a parking space
    (D) To check the off-site duties for today

96. According to the speaker, what is going to happen in the area today?
    (A) Delta Controls will be closed.
    (B) There will be a big parade all day long.
    (C) Vehicles will be regulated for about 3 hours.
    (D) The streets will get jammed with cars during rush hour.

97. Look at the graphic. Which parking area was recommended by the speaker?
    (A) A
    (B) B
    (C) C
    (D) D

Questions 98-100 refer to the following excerpt from a meeting and graph.

Good afternoon, I'd like to start by reviewing the number of new subscribers at Leisure Trends Magazine. As you can see, we attracted the most subscribers last month. The same thing has happened every year, and this August was not an exception. On the other hand, the special feature articles in our 5th anniversary edition didn't seem to be very successful compared to our expectations. The figures show the discount event in June worked even better, but we should not jump to conclusions. The marketing team is planning a survey next month to analyze the exact factors. I hope this can explain why the special edition showed the worst result in the past four months.

98. Where most likely does the speaker work?
    (A) At an advertising company
    (B) At a magazine publisher
    (C) At a leisure supplies manufacturer
    (D) At a market research institute

99. Look at the graphic. When did the company have its 5th anniversary?
    (A) In May
    (B) In June
    (C) In July
    (D) In August

100. According to the speaker, what does the business plan to do next month?
    (A) Offer a promotional event
    (B) Launch a new product
    (C) Get new advertisers
    (D) Conduct a survey

books.english.co.kr

ANSWER SHEET

실전 모의고사 2

LISTENING (PART I ~ IV)

실전 모의고사 1

LISTENING (PART I ~ IV)

books.english.co.kr

ANSWER SHEET

실전 모의고사 4

LISTENING (PART I ~ IV)

ANSWER SHEET

실전 모의고사 3

LISTENING (PART I ~ IV)

books.english.co.kr

books.english.co.kr

ANSWER SHEET

실전 모의고사 8
LISTENING (PART I~IV)

(Answer sheet grid for questions 1-100)

ANSWER SHEET

실전 모의고사 7
LISTENING (PART I~IV)

(Answer sheet grid for questions 1-100)

books.english.co.kr

ANSWER SHEET

수험번호							No.
성명	한글						
	영자						

실전 모의고사 9

LISTENING (PART I ~ IV)

NO.	ANSWER				NO.	ANSWER				NO.	ANSWER				NO.	ANSWER				NO.	ANSWER			
	A	B	C	D		A	B	C	D		A	B	C	D		A	B	C	D		A	B	C	D
1	Ⓐ	Ⓑ	Ⓒ	Ⓓ	21	Ⓐ	Ⓑ	Ⓒ		41	Ⓐ	Ⓑ	Ⓒ	Ⓓ	61	Ⓐ	Ⓑ	Ⓒ	Ⓓ	81	Ⓐ	Ⓑ	Ⓒ	Ⓓ
2	Ⓐ	Ⓑ	Ⓒ	Ⓓ	22	Ⓐ	Ⓑ	Ⓒ		42	Ⓐ	Ⓑ	Ⓒ	Ⓓ	62	Ⓐ	Ⓑ	Ⓒ	Ⓓ	82	Ⓐ	Ⓑ	Ⓒ	Ⓓ
3	Ⓐ	Ⓑ	Ⓒ	Ⓓ	23	Ⓐ	Ⓑ	Ⓒ		43	Ⓐ	Ⓑ	Ⓒ	Ⓓ	63	Ⓐ	Ⓑ	Ⓒ	Ⓓ	83	Ⓐ	Ⓑ	Ⓒ	Ⓓ
4	Ⓐ	Ⓑ	Ⓒ	Ⓓ	24	Ⓐ	Ⓑ	Ⓒ		44	Ⓐ	Ⓑ	Ⓒ	Ⓓ	64	Ⓐ	Ⓑ	Ⓒ	Ⓓ	84	Ⓐ	Ⓑ	Ⓒ	Ⓓ
5	Ⓐ	Ⓑ	Ⓒ	Ⓓ	25	Ⓐ	Ⓑ	Ⓒ		45	Ⓐ	Ⓑ	Ⓒ	Ⓓ	65	Ⓐ	Ⓑ	Ⓒ	Ⓓ	85	Ⓐ	Ⓑ	Ⓒ	Ⓓ
6	Ⓐ	Ⓑ	Ⓒ	Ⓓ	26	Ⓐ	Ⓑ	Ⓒ		46	Ⓐ	Ⓑ	Ⓒ	Ⓓ	66	Ⓐ	Ⓑ	Ⓒ	Ⓓ	86	Ⓐ	Ⓑ	Ⓒ	Ⓓ
7	Ⓐ	Ⓑ	Ⓒ		27	Ⓐ	Ⓑ	Ⓒ		47	Ⓐ	Ⓑ	Ⓒ	Ⓓ	67	Ⓐ	Ⓑ	Ⓒ	Ⓓ	87	Ⓐ	Ⓑ	Ⓒ	Ⓓ
8	Ⓐ	Ⓑ	Ⓒ		28	Ⓐ	Ⓑ	Ⓒ		48	Ⓐ	Ⓑ	Ⓒ	Ⓓ	68	Ⓐ	Ⓑ	Ⓒ	Ⓓ	88	Ⓐ	Ⓑ	Ⓒ	Ⓓ
9	Ⓐ	Ⓑ	Ⓒ		29	Ⓐ	Ⓑ	Ⓒ		49	Ⓐ	Ⓑ	Ⓒ	Ⓓ	69	Ⓐ	Ⓑ	Ⓒ	Ⓓ	89	Ⓐ	Ⓑ	Ⓒ	Ⓓ
10	Ⓐ	Ⓑ	Ⓒ		30	Ⓐ	Ⓑ	Ⓒ		50	Ⓐ	Ⓑ	Ⓒ	Ⓓ	70	Ⓐ	Ⓑ	Ⓒ	Ⓓ	90	Ⓐ	Ⓑ	Ⓒ	Ⓓ
11	Ⓐ	Ⓑ	Ⓒ		31	Ⓐ	Ⓑ	Ⓒ		51	Ⓐ	Ⓑ	Ⓒ	Ⓓ	71	Ⓐ	Ⓑ	Ⓒ	Ⓓ	91	Ⓐ	Ⓑ	Ⓒ	Ⓓ
12	Ⓐ	Ⓑ	Ⓒ		32	Ⓐ	Ⓑ	Ⓒ	Ⓓ	52	Ⓐ	Ⓑ	Ⓒ	Ⓓ	72	Ⓐ	Ⓑ	Ⓒ	Ⓓ	92	Ⓐ	Ⓑ	Ⓒ	Ⓓ
13	Ⓐ	Ⓑ	Ⓒ		33	Ⓐ	Ⓑ	Ⓒ	Ⓓ	53	Ⓐ	Ⓑ	Ⓒ	Ⓓ	73	Ⓐ	Ⓑ	Ⓒ	Ⓓ	93	Ⓐ	Ⓑ	Ⓒ	Ⓓ
14	Ⓐ	Ⓑ	Ⓒ		34	Ⓐ	Ⓑ	Ⓒ	Ⓓ	54	Ⓐ	Ⓑ	Ⓒ	Ⓓ	74	Ⓐ	Ⓑ	Ⓒ	Ⓓ	94	Ⓐ	Ⓑ	Ⓒ	Ⓓ
15	Ⓐ	Ⓑ	Ⓒ		35	Ⓐ	Ⓑ	Ⓒ	Ⓓ	55	Ⓐ	Ⓑ	Ⓒ	Ⓓ	75	Ⓐ	Ⓑ	Ⓒ	Ⓓ	95	Ⓐ	Ⓑ	Ⓒ	Ⓓ
16	Ⓐ	Ⓑ	Ⓒ		36	Ⓐ	Ⓑ	Ⓒ	Ⓓ	56	Ⓐ	Ⓑ	Ⓒ	Ⓓ	76	Ⓐ	Ⓑ	Ⓒ	Ⓓ	96	Ⓐ	Ⓑ	Ⓒ	Ⓓ
17	Ⓐ	Ⓑ	Ⓒ		37	Ⓐ	Ⓑ	Ⓒ	Ⓓ	57	Ⓐ	Ⓑ	Ⓒ	Ⓓ	77	Ⓐ	Ⓑ	Ⓒ	Ⓓ	97	Ⓐ	Ⓑ	Ⓒ	Ⓓ
18	Ⓐ	Ⓑ	Ⓒ		38	Ⓐ	Ⓑ	Ⓒ	Ⓓ	58	Ⓐ	Ⓑ	Ⓒ	Ⓓ	78	Ⓐ	Ⓑ	Ⓒ	Ⓓ	98	Ⓐ	Ⓑ	Ⓒ	Ⓓ
19	Ⓐ	Ⓑ	Ⓒ		39	Ⓐ	Ⓑ	Ⓒ	Ⓓ	59	Ⓐ	Ⓑ	Ⓒ	Ⓓ	79	Ⓐ	Ⓑ	Ⓒ	Ⓓ	99	Ⓐ	Ⓑ	Ⓒ	Ⓓ
20	Ⓐ	Ⓑ	Ⓒ		40	Ⓐ	Ⓑ	Ⓒ	Ⓓ	60	Ⓐ	Ⓑ	Ⓒ	Ⓓ	80	Ⓐ	Ⓑ	Ⓒ	Ⓓ	100	Ⓐ	Ⓑ	Ⓒ	Ⓓ

ANSWER SHEET

수험번호							No.
성명	한글						
	영자						

실전 모의고사 10

LISTENING (PART I ~ IV)

NO.	ANSWER				NO.	ANSWER				NO.	ANSWER				NO.	ANSWER				NO.	ANSWER			
	A	B	C	D		A	B	C	D		A	B	C	D		A	B	C	D		A	B	C	D
1	Ⓐ	Ⓑ	Ⓒ	Ⓓ	21	Ⓐ	Ⓑ	Ⓒ		41	Ⓐ	Ⓑ	Ⓒ	Ⓓ	61	Ⓐ	Ⓑ	Ⓒ	Ⓓ	81	Ⓐ	Ⓑ	Ⓒ	Ⓓ
2	Ⓐ	Ⓑ	Ⓒ	Ⓓ	22	Ⓐ	Ⓑ	Ⓒ		42	Ⓐ	Ⓑ	Ⓒ	Ⓓ	62	Ⓐ	Ⓑ	Ⓒ	Ⓓ	82	Ⓐ	Ⓑ	Ⓒ	Ⓓ
3	Ⓐ	Ⓑ	Ⓒ	Ⓓ	23	Ⓐ	Ⓑ	Ⓒ		43	Ⓐ	Ⓑ	Ⓒ	Ⓓ	63	Ⓐ	Ⓑ	Ⓒ	Ⓓ	83	Ⓐ	Ⓑ	Ⓒ	Ⓓ
4	Ⓐ	Ⓑ	Ⓒ	Ⓓ	24	Ⓐ	Ⓑ	Ⓒ		44	Ⓐ	Ⓑ	Ⓒ	Ⓓ	64	Ⓐ	Ⓑ	Ⓒ	Ⓓ	84	Ⓐ	Ⓑ	Ⓒ	Ⓓ
5	Ⓐ	Ⓑ	Ⓒ	Ⓓ	25	Ⓐ	Ⓑ	Ⓒ		45	Ⓐ	Ⓑ	Ⓒ	Ⓓ	65	Ⓐ	Ⓑ	Ⓒ	Ⓓ	85	Ⓐ	Ⓑ	Ⓒ	Ⓓ
6	Ⓐ	Ⓑ	Ⓒ	Ⓓ	26	Ⓐ	Ⓑ	Ⓒ		46	Ⓐ	Ⓑ	Ⓒ	Ⓓ	66	Ⓐ	Ⓑ	Ⓒ	Ⓓ	86	Ⓐ	Ⓑ	Ⓒ	Ⓓ
7	Ⓐ	Ⓑ	Ⓒ		27	Ⓐ	Ⓑ	Ⓒ		47	Ⓐ	Ⓑ	Ⓒ	Ⓓ	67	Ⓐ	Ⓑ	Ⓒ	Ⓓ	87	Ⓐ	Ⓑ	Ⓒ	Ⓓ
8	Ⓐ	Ⓑ	Ⓒ		28	Ⓐ	Ⓑ	Ⓒ		48	Ⓐ	Ⓑ	Ⓒ	Ⓓ	68	Ⓐ	Ⓑ	Ⓒ	Ⓓ	88	Ⓐ	Ⓑ	Ⓒ	Ⓓ
9	Ⓐ	Ⓑ	Ⓒ		29	Ⓐ	Ⓑ	Ⓒ		49	Ⓐ	Ⓑ	Ⓒ	Ⓓ	69	Ⓐ	Ⓑ	Ⓒ	Ⓓ	89	Ⓐ	Ⓑ	Ⓒ	Ⓓ
10	Ⓐ	Ⓑ	Ⓒ		30	Ⓐ	Ⓑ	Ⓒ		50	Ⓐ	Ⓑ	Ⓒ	Ⓓ	70	Ⓐ	Ⓑ	Ⓒ	Ⓓ	90	Ⓐ	Ⓑ	Ⓒ	Ⓓ
11	Ⓐ	Ⓑ	Ⓒ		31	Ⓐ	Ⓑ	Ⓒ		51	Ⓐ	Ⓑ	Ⓒ	Ⓓ	71	Ⓐ	Ⓑ	Ⓒ	Ⓓ	91	Ⓐ	Ⓑ	Ⓒ	Ⓓ
12	Ⓐ	Ⓑ	Ⓒ		32	Ⓐ	Ⓑ	Ⓒ	Ⓓ	52	Ⓐ	Ⓑ	Ⓒ	Ⓓ	72	Ⓐ	Ⓑ	Ⓒ	Ⓓ	92	Ⓐ	Ⓑ	Ⓒ	Ⓓ
13	Ⓐ	Ⓑ	Ⓒ		33	Ⓐ	Ⓑ	Ⓒ	Ⓓ	53	Ⓐ	Ⓑ	Ⓒ	Ⓓ	73	Ⓐ	Ⓑ	Ⓒ	Ⓓ	93	Ⓐ	Ⓑ	Ⓒ	Ⓓ
14	Ⓐ	Ⓑ	Ⓒ		34	Ⓐ	Ⓑ	Ⓒ	Ⓓ	54	Ⓐ	Ⓑ	Ⓒ	Ⓓ	74	Ⓐ	Ⓑ	Ⓒ	Ⓓ	94	Ⓐ	Ⓑ	Ⓒ	Ⓓ
15	Ⓐ	Ⓑ	Ⓒ		35	Ⓐ	Ⓑ	Ⓒ	Ⓓ	55	Ⓐ	Ⓑ	Ⓒ	Ⓓ	75	Ⓐ	Ⓑ	Ⓒ	Ⓓ	95	Ⓐ	Ⓑ	Ⓒ	Ⓓ
16	Ⓐ	Ⓑ	Ⓒ		36	Ⓐ	Ⓑ	Ⓒ	Ⓓ	56	Ⓐ	Ⓑ	Ⓒ	Ⓓ	76	Ⓐ	Ⓑ	Ⓒ	Ⓓ	96	Ⓐ	Ⓑ	Ⓒ	Ⓓ
17	Ⓐ	Ⓑ	Ⓒ		37	Ⓐ	Ⓑ	Ⓒ	Ⓓ	57	Ⓐ	Ⓑ	Ⓒ	Ⓓ	77	Ⓐ	Ⓑ	Ⓒ	Ⓓ	97	Ⓐ	Ⓑ	Ⓒ	Ⓓ
18	Ⓐ	Ⓑ	Ⓒ		38	Ⓐ	Ⓑ	Ⓒ	Ⓓ	58	Ⓐ	Ⓑ	Ⓒ	Ⓓ	78	Ⓐ	Ⓑ	Ⓒ	Ⓓ	98	Ⓐ	Ⓑ	Ⓒ	Ⓓ
19	Ⓐ	Ⓑ	Ⓒ		39	Ⓐ	Ⓑ	Ⓒ	Ⓓ	59	Ⓐ	Ⓑ	Ⓒ	Ⓓ	79	Ⓐ	Ⓑ	Ⓒ	Ⓓ	99	Ⓐ	Ⓑ	Ⓒ	Ⓓ
20	Ⓐ	Ⓑ	Ⓒ		40	Ⓐ	Ⓑ	Ⓒ	Ⓓ	60	Ⓐ	Ⓑ	Ⓒ	Ⓓ	80	Ⓐ	Ⓑ	Ⓒ	Ⓓ	100	Ⓐ	Ⓑ	Ⓒ	Ⓓ

점수환산표

LISTENING 맞은 갯수	LISTENING 환산 점수	READING 맞은 갯수	READING 환산 점수
96-100	480~495	96-100	460~495
91-95	435~490	91-95	410~475
86-90	395~450	86-90	380~430
81-85	355~415	81-85	355~400
76-80	325~375	76-80	325~375
71-75	295~340	71-75	295~345
66-70	265~315	66-70	265~315
61-65	240~285	61-65	235~285
56-60	215~260	56-60	205~255
51-55	190~235	51-55	175~225
46-50	160~210	46-50	150~195
41-45	135~180	41-45	120~170
36-40	110~155	36-40	100~140
31-35	85~130	31-35	75~120
26-30	70~105	26-30	55~100
21-25	50~90	21-25	40~80
16-20	35~70	16-20	30~65
11-15	20~55	11-15	20~50
6-10	15~40	6-10	15~35
1-5	5~20	1-5	5~20
0	5	0	5